# JOURNAL FOR THE STUDY OF THE OLD TESTAMENT
## SUPPLEMENT SERIES
# 104

Editors
David J A Clines
Philip R Davies

JSOT Press
Sheffield

# PSALM STRUCTURES

## A Study of Psalms with Refrains

Paul R. Raabe

Journal for the Study of the Old Testament
Supplement Series 104

To my parents

Bernard O. Raabe and Evelyn L. Raabe

*pîhem yĕdabbēr ḥokmôt*
*wĕhāgût libbām tĕbûnôt*

(adapted from Psalm 49.4)

Copyright © 1990 Sheffield Academic Press

Published by JSOT Press
JSOT Press is an imprint of
Sheffield Academic Press Ltd
The University of Sheffield
343 Fulwood Road
Sheffield S10 3BP
England


Printed on acid-free paper in Great Britain
by Billing & Sons Ltd
Worcester


British Library Cataloguing in Publication Data

Raabe, Paul
    Psalm structures.
    1. Bible. O.T. Psalms—Critical studies
    I. Title    II. Series
    223.206

    ISSN 0309-0787
    ISBN 1-85075-262-1

# CONTENTS

## ACKNOWLEDGMENTS

At the conclusion of a project such as this, it is my happy privilege to acknowledge the contributions of others to the work. Dr David Noel Freedman has been most helpful and generous with his time throughout the project. Many of his contributions are noted in the text, but his unseen influence extends throughout. His learned, extensive, and rapid responses to materials submitted to him are legendary among his doctoral students and Anchor Bible contributors, and I benefited from these all along the way.

Dr Charles R. Krahmalkov and Dr Gernot L. Windfuhr of the Department of Near Eastern Studies and Dr H.D. Cameron of the Department of Classical Studies have been encouraging and supportive during the project and have been most gracious to serve as readers. Dr Krahmalkov especially has contributed heavily to my formation as a student of Northwest Semitic Languages.

I would also like to thank my present institution, Concordia Seminary of St Louis, Missouri, for providing me library services and monetary support. All of my colleagues here have been encouraging and supportive, but thanks are especially due to Horace D. Hummel, Andrew H. Bartelt, and Paul L. Schrieber. I am also deeply grateful to Greg Seltz and Robert Clancy for typing the manuscript, and to Professor David Clines of Sheffield who gave a close editorial scrutiny to the proofs of the book.

This work, a slightly revised version of my dissertation, is dedicated to my parents who from early on led me to know the God of the psalmists and who have always been model parents.

*Note*

The system of text referencing used in this study is that described in *The Chicago Manual of Style* and currently used in such journals as *Biblical Archaeologist* and the *Bulletin of the American Schools of Oriental Research*. The abbreviation of biblical books and transliteration of Hebrew follow the standard schemes in the above journals and the *Journal of Biblical Literature*.

Chapter 1

## CONTEMPORARY APPROACHES
## AND METHODOLOGICAL CONSIDERATIONS

### 1.0 *Introduction*

The psalms of the Hebrew Bible have fascinated readers for centuries. They have served as the basis for Jewish and Christian liturgies and hymns. They have been prayed by the faithful throughout the centuries. In academic circles dozens of learned articles and books dealing with the Psalter are written every year.

Yet in spite of all this attention, or maybe because of it, there are numerous heated debates surrounding the Psalter. All scholars recognize the psalms as poetry. A few, however, question whether there is much of a difference between Hebrew poetry and prose. Do these Hebrew poems exhibit 'meter'? If so, how is that 'meter' to be defined? What constitutes 'parallelism'? Does a psalm have larger blocks of material above the verse level, such as 'strophes' and 'stanzas'? If so, is there a correspondence between such units in terms of size? What criteria indicate the breaks between them? What is the relationship between structure and content? The questions could be multiplied. All these issues are vital to the basic question: How does one 'read' a psalm?

The purpose of this work is not to resolve all these debates. Such an undertaking would result in a ten-volume set of commentaries on 150 psalms. Rather, its purpose is to identify and describe the basic 'building blocks' of a psalm. Its primary focus is on the larger units that constitute a psalm, strophes and stanzas. For this purpose we have selected seven psalms—six poems in all, as Pss. 42–43 comprise one poem— whose stanzas are clearly demarcated by the presence of refrains. This corpus consists of Pss. 42–43, 46, 49, 56, 57, and 59. Sections 3.4, 3.5, and 3.6 also include data from four other psalms with refrains—Pss. 39, 67, 80, and 99. The reason for this choice is that each of these psalms has a clear stanzaic structure. Only by beginning with psalms whose structures are easily recognized can one develop the resources and expectations necessary for studying the structures of other psalms. In other words, one needs to move from the known to the unknown. The failure to follow this procedure is precisely the weakness of many contemporary studies of psalm structures.

To our knowledge, only one study has previously examined these 'refrain-psalms' as a group, that of Segal (1935). However, his approach of radical emendation, eliminating and adding lines, and repositioning verses calls for a re-examination of this corpus.

This work consists of three chapters. Chapter 1 identifies the important issues that we will address. It also surveys some of the contemporary approaches to these issues and explains the methodology followed here. Chapter 2 presents the texts, a translation, translation notes, a description of the 'building block' structures, a survey and evaluation of various scholarly views, comments regarding the psalms's *Leitwörter*, and an examination of the relationship between the psalm's structure and content. Chapter 3 collates the data from Chapter 2 and on that basis makes conclusions regarding each of the 'building blocks' that constitute these psalms. We do not maintain that every psalm has all of these 'building blocks'— refrains, for example, obviously do not always occur—but we do believe that this corpus of seven psalms, 88 masoretic verses, and 247 cola is representative. Hopefully this study will contribute toward a clearer understanding of a psalm's 'building blocks' and therefore a more sensitive 'reading' of a psalm.

## 1.1 *Text and Translation*

The text that is followed is the Masoretic Text as printed in BHS. Contemporary scholars generally eschew radical emendations and revisions such as those of older scholars, and rightfully so in our opinion. Systematic deletion and rearrangement of lines, as practiced by Briggs (1906; 1907) and Segal (1935) for example, are simply not convincing. Nor is it in vogue any longer to emend *metri causa*. Following Freedman we assume 'generally the integrity and accuracy of the received Hebrew text (MT), i.e. that the poems are unified compositions and that the text has been transmitted faithfully...' (1976b: 86). The striking infrequency of so-called 'prose particles' in the poems of our corpus indicates at least that these poems have not been 'prosaicized' (see Appendix I), and we feel justified in assuming that there has been no other kind of significant editorial alteration.

This assumption, however, does not eliminate the need for textual criticism; it does not lead to a sort of 'Masoretic Text fundamentalism'. There are, of course, places where scribal errors have occurred. For example, we follow most scholars in believing that a refrain was accidentally omitted in Ps. 46 (see discussion under Ps. 46.4). The initial word of Ps. 49.12—קרבם —is a case of metathesis from קברם. There are other examples as well. But in general the MT seems to be in good shape.

We have also included a translation and translation notes for each psalm. It is our firm conviction that the 'building blocks' and structures of these psalms can only be ascertained in conjunction with thorough exegesis.

## 1.2 *Terminology*

The terminology employed here is traditional. These terms are not necessarily the best. Some of them can be misleading— our 'verses' do not always correspond to the MT 'verses'; our 'strophes' should not be confused with the strophe of classical Greek poetry. We use these terms simply for the sake of communication; they are the terms that most scholars employ. The following defines these terms proceeding from the smallest unit to the largest. These are the basic 'building blocks' which constitute each of the psalms studied here.

| | |
|---|---|
| Colon | a unit of text, usually a clause, with two, three or four stresses; others designate it 'hemistich', 'stich', 'stichos', 'line', 'verset'. |

| | |
|---|---|
| Verse | sometimes a single colon (= monocolon) but usually a combination of two cola (= bicolon) or three cola (= tricolon) that are connected by semantics, grammar, and/or phonology; others designate it 'stich', 'tichos', 'line'. |
| Strophe | sometimes a bicolon or tricolon but usually a combination of two or more verses that exhibits a semantic and/or syntactic unity; also designated 'batch'. |
| Stanza | a major subdivision of a poem which comprises one or more strophes; in our corpus a stanza is the block of material preceding and/or following each refrain; also designated 'stave', 'canticle'. |
| Refrain | a verse that is repeated at regular intervals in a poem. |
| Section | a stanza-plus-refrain. |

Finally, a discussion dealing with the term 'poetry' is perhaps necessary. We freely use the term 'poem' and that presupposes, of course, the belief that these seven psalms consist of 'poetry' and not 'prose'. Almost all scholars would agree. However, recently Kugel (1981) has attacked the notion of a basic difference between poetry and prose in the Bible. Kugel questions the distinction on the basis of three major arguments (1981: 59-95). First, not all 'poetic lines' exhibit parallelism and parallelism occurs in 'prose' passages as well. Second, 'there is no word for "poetry" in Biblical Hebrew' (p. 69). Third, biblical 'poems' do not exhibit 'meter'. Instead of a basic distinction between 'prose' and 'poetry', Kugel prefers to speak of a *continuum* between sporadically parallelistic passages (normally labelled 'prose') and consistently paralleled clauses (normally labelled 'poetry')—in other words, a continuum between unheightened speech and heightened speech. Christensen agrees and even goes further in levelling out the difference. He calls the books of Jonah and Deuteronomy, for example, 'narrative poems', and even attempts to scan them (1983; 1985b).

As to the first of Kugel's arguments, we agree with Berlin's response (1985: 4-17). It is certainly true that parallelisms are also found in 'prose' sections and not all 'poetic' verses have parallelism. Kugel's insistence on this point is commendable. But this only proves that 'parallelism is not in and of itself a mark of poetry... it is a common feature of all language' (p. 4). 'It is not parallelism per se, but the predominance of parallelism, combined with terseness, which marks poetic expression of the Bible' (p. 5). Parallelism, with concomitant terseness, is the constitutive or constructive device of poetry 'while nonpoetry, though it contains parallelism, does not structure its message on a systematic use of parallelism' (p. 16).

To Kugel's second point, it is true that no biblical Hebrew term for 'poetry' exists. But neither is there a biblical Hebrew term for Kugel's 'line' (= bicolon) nor for the 'A and B' clauses which comprise that line (as Kugel acknowledges on pp. 2-3). In fact, if we limited ourselves to a biblical vocabulary, we would not be able to say much of anything about Hebrew style. Certainly the Israelites perceived a difference between Judges 4 and Judges 5, for example, which was more than the fact that the latter was sung while the former was not.

With respect to Kugel's third point, the psalms in our corpus are not totally *irregular* in verse-length or rhythm. While they do not exhibit a strict 'meter' in the usual definition, they do manifest an overall regularity that can be described (see 1.4; 3.2).

Finally, one should note the significant difference in the frequency of the so-called 'prose particles' between sections normally considered prose and those normally considered poetry (Andersen–Freedman 1980: 60-66; Andersen–Forbes 1983; Freedman 1987). The very low frequency of 'prose particles' in the psalms that are studied here confirms that our corpus, at least, is poetry (see Appendix I).

## 1.3 *Versification*

There is recent scholarly disagreement over the nature of the poetic 'line'. For a historical review of the debate before 1975, mostly among European scholars, see van der Lugt 1980: 121-71. Some designate the colon as the 'line' (Geller 1979; O'Connor 1980; Berlin 1985). Others designate the bicolon or tricolon as the 'line' (Collins 1978; Kugel 1981; Alter 1985;

Pardee 1981; 1988). Yet they all agree that both colon and bicolon/tricolon are fundamental to Hebrew poetry. Because of this terminological disagreement, a disagreement which we do not intend to resolve, this study avoids the term 'line' and instead speaks of 'colon' and 'verse'

Clearly the colon is the basic unit. The acrostics of Pss. 111–12 begin each colon with a successive letter of the alphabet. The colon can be described as a passage of poetic discourse which obeys certain syntactic constraints (O'Connor 1980) or as a clause consisting of two to four stressed words (Hrushovski 1971).

Equally clear is the fact that rarely does a colon stand alone. We found only two monocola (Ps. 56.2a and Ps. 57.2a) in our corpus of 247 cola. (On monocola, see Watson 1984: 168-174. Cola almost always come in sets of two or three, i.e. bicola or tricola. The alphabetic acrostics of Psalms 25, 34, 119, 145; Prov. 31.10-31; and Lamentations 3 indicate this. There is a minor pause between cola and a major pause at the end of each bicolon/tricolon (Kugel 1981). Usually there is at least one aspect of grammar, semantics, and/or phonology which binds the cola together.

Recently a considerable amount of progress has been achieved and a growing consensus is developing toward identifying those linguistic features which hold cola together in a bicolon or tricolon. The aspects being studied are those of grammar, semantics, and phonology. The Lowthian categories of 'synonymous', 'antithetic', and 'synthetic' parallelism have been discarded as simplistic and imprecise.

Grammatical parallelism has been examined by Collins (1978), Geller (1979), O'Connor (1980), Greenstein (1982), and Berlin (1985). Collins finds four basic line Types (i.e. types of bicola):

    I.    The line contains one Basic Sentence.
    II.   The line contains two Basic Sentences which match with all of the same constituents (subject, object, verb, verb modifier) in each sentence.
   III.  The line contains two Basic Sentences which match, but with one or more of the constituents ellipsed in the second colon.
   IV.  The line contains two different Basic Sentences.

O'Connor's trope of 'matching' which includes verb gapping
(= ellipsis) is basically similar to Collins' Line-Types II and III.
His trope of 'syntactic dependency' generally corresponds to
Collins' Line-Type I. That the two cola of Line-Types I, II, and
III are connected or 'parallel' is obvious. However, Collins'
Line-Type IV creates difficulties. Yet the cola of this bicolon,
which on the surface do not appear to be grammatically
parallel, are often shown to be grammatically parallel on a
deeper level by Geller, Greenstein, and Berlin. By 'reconstruct-
ing' the one basic sentence underlying the two cola, Geller can
equate on a deeper level constituents which do not correspond
on the surface level. Greenstein designates grammatically
parallel two cola which have the same deep structure. Berlin
observes not only syntactic correspondence between cola but
also morphological correspondence between the words in each
half.

Greenstein believes that parallelism is only grammatical
parallelism, but Geller, Berlin, and O'Connor also include lexical features. They argue that split 'word-pairs'—where one
word occurs in the A-colon and its lexically related partner
occurs in the B-colon—serve to create the impression of parallel cola. Also, repetition cements the two cola together. Berlin
argues further that one can frequently observe a semantic
relationship between the meanings of the cola as a whole.

Finally, Berlin includes the phonologic aspect in parallelism.
She discusses both 'sound pairs' and the phonological equivalence of cola. A sound pair is 'the repetition in parallel words or
lines of the same or similar consonants in any order within
close proximity' (p. 104). Sound pairs need not be related lexically or semantically. The phonological equivalence on the
colon level occurs when there is a great amount of sound
repetition between the cola. Sometimes there is colon-initial
alliteration or colon-final rhyme.

According to Berlin, all three aspects—grammatical, lexical-semantic, and phonological—create the feeling of
'connectedness' between the contiguous cola. Yet, the reader
perceives both equivalences *and contrasts* between them. Even
the cola that Lowth would label 'synonymously parallel'
involve contrasts, and the cola that he would label 'antitheti-
cally parallel' or 'synthetically parallel' involve similarity. It is

this contrast within equivalence created by the three linguistic aspects that is at the heart of parallelism. Or in the words of Kugel,

> To the extent that B identifies itself as A's 'mere parallel', it asserts A = B; while to the extent that it differentiates itself from A in meaning and morphology, it asserts A + B to be a *single statement*. B becomes A's complement or completion (1981: 16).

Not only do grammatical, lexical-semantic, and phonological aspects connect the cola of a bicolon or tricolon, they also form the basis upon which one can ascertain the colonic divisions in the first place. 'Parallelism', that is grammatical (both morphological and syntactic), lexical, semantic, and/or phonological correspondence, is the major clue to the 'lineation' or 'stichometry' of a verse.

Usually such correspondence between the two or three contiguous cola is readily apparent, producing scholarly agreement as to a verse's lineation—usually, but not always. For example, BHS divides Exod. 15.1b-18, the Song of the Sea, into 70 cola; Freedman (1974) finds 76 cola; Stuart (1976; 79-91) finds 64 cola; and O'Connor (1980: 178-85) finds 53 cola. Problems in lineation often occur when one encounters two contiguous short clauses or even sentences. Should they be treated as a bicolon of short cola or as one long colon? One is often uncertain where precisely to make the break between two cola which together form one sentence, as in Collins' Line-Type I.

Because of the uncertainty involved, we include a defense of our versification for every psalm studied (2.1.4.1), something that too few psalm studies do. This defense does not exhaustively treat every grammatical, lexical, semantic, and phonological link between the cola of the verse. For the present work, after all, does not claim to be a thorough discussion of the nature of parallelism. But we feel it is necessary to make some remarks regarding every verse. (For a thorough discussion of some of the latest linguistic approaches to parallelism, see Pardee 1988.)

Usually our colonic divisions conform to the 'syntactic constraints' which, O'Connor argues, determine the shape of the 'line', i.e. colon (1980). The overall constraints are that every line has 0–3 clause predicators (finite verbs, infinitives and participles acting as predicators, zero-predicators of verbless clauses, vocatives and focus markers), 1–4 constituents (verbs or nominal phrases, along with dependent particles), and 2–5 units (individual verbs or nomina). They are complemented by the nominal phrase constraints—no nominal phrases of more than 4 units in a line and no more than one predicator and two constituents in a line with a 4-unit nominal phrase, and the clause predicator constraints—lines with three clause predicators contain nothing else and in lines with two clause predicators only one predicator has dependent nominal phrases.

However, not all of O'Connor's constraints coincide with the line shapes found in the alphabetic acrostics. The lines of Ps. 119.31b, 36b, and 46b each have only one 'unit' though they have 4–5 syllables and 2 stresses. Some lines have two clause predicators where each predicator has a dependent nominal phrase. In Ps. 34.7a both predicators have dependent nominal phrases. The parallel in v. 18a indicates that one cannot split v. 7a into two lines. The same phenomenon occurs in Ps. 119.145a and again the parallel construction in v. 146a prohibits a split into two. Another clear example is found in Lam. 4.18c. Kugel (1981: 318) draws attention to Judg. 5.12b as a case where a line has three predicators but four constituents, i.e. three finite verbs plus object. These three constraints are also broken occasionally in our corpus, at least, according to our lineation. Ps. 43.3d has only one 'unit'. Pss. 46.7a-b, 10b, 11b; 59.7a, 14a, and 15a all have 'lines' in which each of the two predicators has dependent nominal phrases. And Ps. 46.11a does not conform to the last constraint.

The masoretic 'verses' in our corpus range from two to six cola. Since the turn of the century scholars have generally recognized that poetic 'verses' do not always coincide with the masoretic 'verse' divisions. (For the history of research regarding this issue, see van der Lugt 1980: 121-64.) For example, Psalms 111 and 112 have 10 masoretic verses each and Psalm 37 has 40 masoretic verses, even though each clearly has 22 divisions because of its alphabetic acrostic structure. For the sake of simplicity, we prefer to reduce all masoretic verses to one of three types—monocola, bicola, or

tricola. Larger groupings are usually treated as 'strophes'
Thus, a MT tetracolon is parsed as two bicola, a MT pentacolon
as one bicolon plus one tricolon, and a MT hexacolon as three
bicola or two tricola.

## 1.4 *Stress and Syllable Counts*

Most scholars in the past accepted the Ley–Sievers–Budde
system of accentual meter. (For surveys of the history of
research, see Hillers 1972: xxx-xxxvii; Stuart 1976: 1-10;
Kugel 1981: 287-304; for critiques, see O'Connor 1980: 29-54
and Kugel 1981.) Recently however, scholarly debate regarding meter has been heated. Does 'meter' exist or not? Those
who answer affirmatively include Kosmala (1964; 1966),
Kuryłowicz (1972; 1975), Margalit (1975), Stuart (1976),
Cooper (1976), Christensen (1983; 1984; 1985a; 1985b) and
Watson (1984). Those who deny its existence include
O'Connor (1980), Kugel (1981) and Pardee (1981).

In the former group there are various systems for analyzing
meter. Kosmala and Margalit study 'word-meter'. (For a critique of the latter, see Pardee 1981.) Kuryłowicz developed a
system of 'syntactic-accentual meter' which is followed by
Watson, Cooper and Christensen. (For a critique, see Longman 1982). Stuart proposes a system of 'syllabic-meter'. (For
critiques, see Pardee 1981 and Longman 1982.)

Those in the latter group generally recognize that phonological or 'rhythmic' regularities may be seen in places. Pardee
(1978; 1981; 1988) speaks of an 'approximate comparability of
length of line' (= bicolon). O'Connor explains this regularity as
a result of his 'syntactic constraints'. Certain colonic lengths
are favored 'because certain syntactic structures are favored
and these tend to have mean lengths' (1980: 152). Kugel
explains this regularity as the result of the 'seconding' structure or binary form of these verses together with their tendency toward 'terseness'.

There is nothing objectionable in the observations of the latter group as far as they go. But part of the goal of this book is to
describe more precisely the lengths of cola and bicola. What
are the average lengths, the most favored lengths, the least
favored lengths, and the range of diversity? Is there any

overall or dominant pattern in a given psalm? To simply say that cola and bicola tend to be 'terse' does not tell us much. In Psalms 42–43 for example, the A-colon usually exhibits a '3-stress terseness' and the B-colon a '2-stress terseness', whereas in Psalm 49 both A- and B-cola usually exhibit a '3-stress terseness'. There are different types of 'terseness' and they can be described.

If we limit ourselves to recording only O'Connor's 'line-types' based on syntax, much of this regularity will not be recognized. Pardee has recently analyzed Proverbs 2, a clearly lineated poem of 22 bicola, according to O'Connor's system. The 'line' (= colon) configurations are as follows:

| | | | | |
|---|---|---|---|---|
| 0 clause / | 2 constituents / | 2 units | = | 1 line |
| 0 clause / | 2 constituents / | 3 units | = | 1 line |
| 1 clause / | 2 constituents / | 2 units | = | 10 lines |
| 1 clause / | 2 constituents / | 3 units | = | 15 lines |
| 1 clause / | 3 constituents / | 3 units | = | 16 lines |
| 2 clauses / | 3 constituents / | 3 units | = | 1 line |

Can one deduce from this syntactic variety that Proverbs 2 is really quite regular and that there is a general comparability in the length of its cola and bicola? O'Connor's system produces 33 cola with 3 'units' each and 11 cola with 2 'units' each. The reader might conclude that it contains a mix of balanced 3+3-stressed bicola and unbalanced 3+2-stressed bicola. But according to our stress count, 15 of the 22 bicola have 3+3 stresses and only 2 have 3+2 stresses. The others include one 2+2 bicolon and four bicola with 7 stresses each. (Our stress count does not correspond to Pardee's 'word count' [p. 71] because he counts monosyllabic particles while we do not. But even his 'word count' does not reflect a mixture of 3-stress and 2-stress cola. He finds 28 cola with 3 words and only 3 cola with 2 words.) Margalit's system shows even more regularity with eighteen 3+3 bicola (p. 71). Pardee's syllable counts confirm that Proverbs 2 is very regular, based on a 3+3 stress pattern. Forty of the forty-four cola are 7–10 syllables long, and thirty of them have 8–9 syllables. Eighteen of the 22 bicola have 15–18 syllables. By observing syntax alone, one misses this regularity.

Our intention is not to resolve the issue of 'meter'. Much of the dispute seems to be centered around the definition of the term. Pardee (1981) has argued, convincingly in our opinion, that biblical Hebrew poetry (and Ugaritic poetry for that matter) does not have 'meter' in the usual sense of the term. Rhythmic impulses are not organized into preconceived patterns which are *consistent* and *predictable*. Therefore, this work studiously avoids using the term 'meter'. However, simply to assert that there is no meter and to leave it at that would be misleading. The psalms in our corpus exhibit an overall regularity and dominant lengths yet with a considerable degree of internal variation and freedom. It is precisely the combination of both features which should be studied rather than insisting on one to the exclusion of the other (Freedman 1986; 1987). The results are presented in sections 2.1.4.2 and 3.2.

Freedman has recently advocated combining syllable counts with stress counts and integrating the two (1986). This procedure will be followed here. Others count consonants (Loretz), morae (Christensen), words (Pardee) or word-units (Margalit). One could even count 'vocables', i.e. consonants plus vowels (Freedman 1974). We do not dispute the legitimacy of these other methods. We opt for counting syllables and stresses simply because we find it the most efficient; it is not too crude nor does it provide more data than necessary. It should be noted that Freedman, who has practiced the syllable-counting method of descriptive analysis for years, does not claim that the ancient poets counted syllables nor does he believe in 'syllabic meter' *à la* Stuart (1976). Rather, this procedure claims merely to describe the existing phenomena. By counting stresses one can determine the overall and dominant stress patterns of a psalm. By counting syllables one can determine the precise size not only of cola and verses but also of larger units such as stanzas. Syllabic length serves as a necessary check given the uncertainties involved in determining stresses and verses.

With respect to counting stresses, we follow generally accepted procedures. Each nomen and verb (O'Connor's 'unit') generally receives one stress. Particles and prepositions we treat as 'anceps'; they may or may not bear a stress. There are two guidelines involved. First, monosyllabic words usually do not have a stress while polysyllabic words usually do. When there are two monosyllabic particles in a colon, we generally treat it as a single stress. Second, when there is doubt we count in the direction of the norm. If the overall pattern is 3″3, for example, then if there is doubt whether a particular colon is 2 or 3, or 3 or 4, we would opt for 3. Also, the colon's syllable length can help decide. We do not emend *metri causa*, nor do we count secondary stresses although they probably existed. (On the problem, see Gray 1915.)

Given the uncertainties involved in determining stresses, the syllable count serves as an important check. With respect to counting syllables, we generally follow the Tiberian vocalization of the MT but with certain minor modifications which attempt to reflect more accurately the pronunciation of Classical Hebrew. Thus, we treat segolates as monosyllabic and we do not count secondary vowels with laryngeals (unless they substitute for vocal shewas) or furtive *patah*. It must, however, be stressed that these minor modifications do not significantly affect the data. The same patterns would emerge were one simply to follow the masoretic vocalization.

## 1.5 *Strophes and Stanzas*

The primary focus of this study concerns units larger than the verse. It is clear from some of the alphabetic acrostic poems that the ancient poets worked with units larger than the bicolon or tricolon. Psalm 37 and Lamentations 4 have 22 strophes, each of which usually has 4 cola. Chapters 1–3 of Lamentations have 22 strophes, each of which usually has 6 cola. Psalm 119 has 22 units, which we consider stanzas, with 16 cola in each. Most scholars acknowledge the existence of these larger units today, although in the past some have doubted it.

### 1.5.1 *Survey of Approaches*
Here we will briefly survey some of the more significant views of past and present scholars who affirm the existence of units larger than the verse. (For more extensive surveys of the history of research, see Kraft 1938; Wahl 1977; van der Lugt

1980. For examples from Neo-Punic poetry, see Krahmalkov 1975. Regarding Ugaritic poetry, see de Moor 1978b; 1980, and Korpel–de Moor 1986, who affirm their existence, but Pardee 1978 is skeptical.)

Although there were precursors, Köster (1831) is generally regarded as the pioneer of the study of strophes. He argued that a parallelism of verses comparable to that between cola exists in Hebrew poetry. However, he denied the necessity of uniformity in length among a poem's strophes. He defined the strophe as simply a union of several verses.

Müller (1898) elaborated a complex theory in which the strophes of a poem were marked by *responsio, concatenatio,* and *inclusio. Responsio* is the correspondence between the verses in successive strophes; the first verse in strophe A parallels the first verse in strophe B, and so on. *Concatenatio* is the binding of successive strophes by parallelism between the last verse of strophe A and the first verse of strophe B. *Inclusio* designates a correspondence between the first and last verses of a strophe. He tried to force all poems into this responsion system.

Briggs (1906; 1907) insisted on uniformity in meter and length among the strophes of a psalm, at least for most psalms. In order to achieve such regularity, he often resorted to radical surgery of the text. He followed Köster in believing that groups of verses are arranged on the same principles of parallelism as are cola within a verse. Thus strophe B parallels strophe A in some way.

Möller (1932) did not insist that all of a poem's strophes must be the same size, but he did expect them to be arranged in an identical or chiastic pattern. Strophes A, B, and C should correspond to the next set—either A, B, and C or C, B, and A. Mixed structures are also possible in which the first two sets have an identical pattern and the next two sets have a chiastic pattern. The corresponding strophes must be identical in length.

Kraft (1938) insists that the strophes of a psalm must exhibit some regularity, if not uniformity, in length. He concludes that most strophes are either couplets (two bicola/tricola) or triplets (three bicola/tricola). These two types are not mixed; normally a poem has only couplets or triplets. He found that stanzas, i.e. two or more strophes, occur infrequently. At most, sixteen of his corpus of forty-one psalms have stanzas. Kraft, like Briggs, finds regularity and uniformity by emending the text and deleting cola.

None of the approaches surveyed so far is very convincing. Briggs and Kraft found strophes of identical size in a psalm but they had to emend the text in order to achieve this. Actually our view is similar to Köster's in that the strophes in our corpus often vary in size (see 3.3.1). The approaches of Müller and Möller end up forcing a psalm's strophes into a Procrustean bed. In our corpus one occasionally sees such a pattern. For example, Psalm 46 exhibits a sort of *concatenatio*. But often the only basis upon which one could say that two strophes are parallel is that they repeat the same word.

Recently, several different approaches have been advocated that deserve comment. Scholars such as Alden (1974; 1976; 1978), Auffret (1977; 1981; 1982) and Girard (1984) generally look for alternating or chiastic arrangements of strophes on the basis of repeated words. Alden, for example, sees a chiastic structure in Psalm 59 (1976: 193):

| vv. 2-3 | A. | Prayer to be set on high |
| vv. 4-9 | B. | Complaint against the wicked |
| v. 10 | C. | Testimony of trust in God |
| v. 11 | C. | Testimony of trust in God |
| vv. 12-15 | B. | Curses on the wicked |
| vv. 17-18 | A. | Praise to God, the high tower |

The only connection between the A-sections is the root *śgb*. Yet vv. 2-3 comprise a petition and vv. 17-18 comprise a vow of praise. Why label the refrain of v. 10 as C but its partner—the refrain of v. 18—as A? Or consider Girard's analysis of Psalms 42–43 (1984: 338-51). He proposes that the poem consists of two overlapping panels: 42.2-11 and 42.6–43.5. Each panel is shaped chiastically:

| 42.2-4 | A | 42.6 | C |
| 42.5 | B | 42.7-9 | D |
| 42.6 | C | 42.10-11 | E |
| 42.7-8 | B | 43.1 | F |
| 42.9-11 | A | 43.2 | E |
| | | 43.3-4 | D |
| | | 43.5 | C |

Again, the structure is based on repeated words or word-pairs. When a word in one verse is repeated in another verse, those two verses are said to be parallel. Yet how does 42.2 relate to 42.9-11 or 42.10 to 42.2-4 on the left panel? How is 42.11 parallel to 43.2 on the right panel? He considers 42.12 to be a later interpolation because, as he admits, it does not fit into his diptychic structure (p. 348). Very often the charting of repeated words is helpful and a positive contribution. But to force psalms into chiastic or alternating strophic structures solely on this basis is not very convincing.

O'Connor (1980) argues that larger units such as 'batches' and 'staves' (= strophes and stanzas) are demarcated primarily by shifts in line (= colon) 'type' or in the amount of 'troping' (see 1.3). For example, when 'class IV' lines occur (lines with 3 clause predicators or 4 constituents or 5 units), that signals a break. A break can also be signaled when an 'untroped' line is preceded or followed by 'troped' lines.

O'Connor's desire for objectivity is commendable. However, we do not believe that his methodology produces very convincing results. For example, he finds three staves in Habakkuk 3: vv. 2-8, 9-16, and 17-19. This contradicts the obvious breaks between v. 2 and v. 3, between v. 7 and v. 8, and between v. 15 and v. 16. As Hiebert (1986: 59-80) has recently shown, the Psalm of Habakkuk has an introduction (v. 2) and a conclusion (vv. 16-19) which frame two stanzas (vv. 3-7, 8-15). The deity is addressed in second person in the introduction, third person in the first stanza, back to second person in the second stanza, and back to third person in the conclusion. Also, each stanza has inclusion—place names in vv. 3 and 7 and a reference to the 'sea' in vv. 8 and 15. Nor are all of O'Connor's batch divisions persuasive; he unites vv. 2-3b and vv. 7-8. In his treatment of Genesis 49 and Deuteronomy 33 he splits the Judah oracle in the former by beginning a new batch (and stave!) with v. 10, and he splits the Levi oracle in the latter by beginning a new batch with v. 9d.

The root of our doubts regarding his method lies in the fact that he ignores many literary devices in his structural analysis, devices such as shifts in address, shifts in person of verbs or verbal moods, and inclusion. His approach does not correlate structure with content.

Another problem is that a rare 'line' form does not always indicate a break. For example, in the clearly structured poem of Psalms 42–43, there are only three occurrences of a 'class IV line', each of which has four constituents (vv. 2b, 4a, 9a). One would expect these to indicate major breaks. While v. 2b is at the beginning of the poem and therefore the first stanza, vv. 4a and 9a are both stanza-internal. Earlier we expressed disagreement with some of his 'syntactic constraints' (see 1.3). For these reasons, his method will not be followed here. (For a similar critique, see Hiebert 1986: 163-64.)

Finally, van der Lugt has recently proposed a unique approach based on his study of the psalms (1980). He presents a full analysis of 57 psalms and also includes a section containing his strophic and stanzaic divisions for the other psalms as well. His methodology consists of studying three features: content, formal structure, and length. To determine length he counts bicola/tricola. He employs two criteria for marking formal structure: key-words and word-repetition. The first criterion consists in collecting words and grammatical forms which mark a turning-point in the psalms. One group of key-words marks the beginning of a strophe. In this group we find vocatives, imperatives, first and second person pronouns, emphasizing particles, and others. Another group marks the end of strophes, such as *selāh*, expressions of time, third person pronouns, and some particles. He does admit that the location of many key-words contradicts his strophic divisions. He lists these as *contra-indicaties*. The second criterion he uses is word-repetition beyond the bicolon. The repetition of words serves to unify a section.

After dividing each psalm into strophes, usually two to three bicola long, he groups the strophes into stanzas. It is on this level, the level of stanzas, that he finds structural patterns and regularity. Two main structural patterns emerge: poems with stanzas of equal length (e.g. 4 bicola/4 bicola) and poems with a symmetrical sequence of stanzas (e.g. 2 bicola/4 bicola/2 bicola). A stanza may consist of strophes equally long (e.g. 2 bicola.2 bicola/2 bicola.2 bicola = stanza-pattern 4/4) or strophes of unequal length (e.g. 1 bicolon.3 bicola/2 bicola.2 bicola = stanza-pattern 4/4).

It is commendable that van der Lugt does not insist on uniformity of strophic length. We also agree that studying a
psalm's use of key-words and repetition is important. However, in our opinion he relies too heavily on these key-words
and forms as indicators of a psalm's breaks. Frequently his
stanza breaks do not correspond to the psalm's refrain-struc-
ture because of this. For example, in Psalm 49 he makes
stanza breaks between v. 11 and v. 12 and between v. 15 and
v. 16. He begins a stanza with v. 12 because of the presence of
the key-phrase דור ודור and another stanza with v. 16 because
of the particle אך (pp. 521, 511). Yet clearly the break lies with
v. 13 because it is the refrain. In Psalm 56 he begins one stanza
with v. 4 because of the presence of the pronoun אני and
another stanza with v. 9 because of the pronoun אתה (p. 513).
Again, this disregards the refrains of v. 5 and vv. 11-12. The
basic problem is that his method and criteria are not based on
a set of clearly structured psalms. At any rate, our corpus of
psalms permits one to evaluate his approach objectively.

### 1.5.2 *The Issues*
Our present corpus of psalms with clearly demarcated stanzas provides an objective basis upon which to answer some
crucial questions regarding units larger than the verse.
    First, is there a distinction between a strophe and a stanza?
Again, we define a 'strophe' as a unit of one or more verses
(usually two to four) that exhibit a unity of structure and content. This is an extended use of the term and should not be
confused with the technical usage of denoting the initial division of a Greek choral interlude in classical Greek drama (cf.
Preminger 1974: 811). We define a 'stanza' as 'a major subdivision of a poem—which comprises one or more strophes'
(Watson 1984: 161; cf. Häublein 1978: 1-17). Some scholars
tend to recognize only the strophe level (Briggs 1906; 1907;
Kraus 1978) or at least rarely find larger units (Kraft 1938).
Others frequently find both strophes and stanzas (Wahl 1977;
van der Lugt 1980; Watson 1984; O'Connor designates them
'batches' and 'staves', 1980; Korpel–de Moor designates them
'strophes' and 'canticles', 1986).
    Second, which criteria are the most helpful in determining
the divisions of larger units? The stanzas, of course, are iso-

lated by the refrains. What other devices also contribute toward unifying and demarcating these stanzas? Of the possible devices such as inclusion, repetition, initial vocatives or imperatives, which occur most frequently? Which criteria should one use to determine strophic divisions? Weiser (1962), Kraus (1978), and Gerstenberger (1988) base their divisions on form-critical criteria. Briggs (1906; 1907), Segal (1935), and Kraft (1938) often emend so that the strophes of a psalm are identical in size. Alden (1974; 1976; 1978), Auffret (1977; 1981; 1982), and Girard (1984) base their divisions on repeated words and look for chiastic or alternating strophic structures. Van der Lugt (1980) puts a great deal of emphasis on key words or forms which he believes introduce or conclude a strophe, such as vocatives, imperatives, pronouns, and particles.

The criteria we prefer for determining strophic divisions are basically those of Wahl (1977). They include many of the above plus some others. They are: the reference to the deity— usually second or third person; repetition (verbatim repetition and root repetition); word pairs; inclusion; syntax; congeries of similar verbal moods such as imperatives/jussives or 'indicatives' (perfects and imperfects); initial question, imperative/jussive, vocative, pronoun, interjection, or particle; and alternating parallelism. Of these plus the ones above, which occur most frequently and which occur least often?

Third, what are the sizes of strophes and stanzas? Do the strophes of a psalm tend to be identical in length (Briggs 1906; 1907; Segal 1935; Kraft 1938) or do they vary in size (van der Lugt 1980)? Are the stanzas in a psalm identical in length? If not, do they at least exhibit some measure of symmetry in their sizes (van der Lugt 1980)?

Fourth, what is the best way to determine strophe and stanza size? Some count cola (Müller 1898; Briggs 1906; 1907; O'Connor 1980; Watson 1984). Others count verses, i.e. bicola and tricola (Kraft 1938; van der Lugt 1980). Möller (1932) counted masoretic verses.

Fifth, what are the types of stanzaic structures which one can expect? How many stanzas occur in a short or long psalm? (Our corpus, including those of Appendix II, has psalms which range from 15-66 cola.) What types of stanzaic arrangements—for example, one half-stanza followed by two full stanzas—can one find?

Sixth, how do refrains 'work' in a psalm? Are they stanza-internal (usually, Kissane 1953; Weiser 1962; Kraus 1978; van der Lugt 1980) or stanza-external, i.e. structurally distinguished from the surrounding material (usually, Briggs 1906; 1907; Segal 1935; Beaucamp 1976; Wahl 1977)? If they are external to a stanza, do they introduce the following material or conclude the preceding material, i.e. are they section-initial or section-final? Are the refrains of a psalm identical in spelling and wording or do they vary? If they vary, how much variation is permissible? What can these facts tell one about audience participation?

Finally, what is the relationship between structure and content? How does a psalm's stanzaic structure relate to the elements of its form-critical *Gattung*? (For introductions to form-critical research on the psalms, see Sabourin 1974; Kraus 1978, I: 36-68; Westermann 1981; Gerstenberger 1988.) How does recognizing a psalm's stanzaic structure contribute toward a more sensitive 'reading' of a psalm?

These are the crucial questions which form the focus of this study and in their answers lies its primary contribution. Yet, the answers can be found only by a thorough analysis of the texts. To that we now turn.

# Chapter 2

## THE TEXTS

### 2.1 *Psalms 42–43*

#### 2.1.1 *Text*

| | Text | Syllables | | Total | Stresses |
|---|---|---|---|---|---|
| 42.1 | למנצח משכיל לבני־קרח | | | | |
| 2a. | כאיל תערג על־אפיקי־מים | 3+2 +1+3+1 | = | 10 | 4 |
| b. | כן נפשי תערג אליך אלהים | 1+2+2+3+3 | = | 11 | 4 |
| 3a | צמאה נפשי לאלהים | 3+2+3 | = | 8 | 3 |
| b. | לאל חי | 2+1 | = | 3 | 2 |
| c. | מתי אבוא | 2+2 | = | 4 | 2 |
| d. | [ואראה] פני אלהים | 3+2+3 | = | 8 | 3 |
| 4a. | היתה־לי דמעתי לחם | 3+1+3+1 | = | 8 | 3 |
| b. | יומם ולילה | 2+3 | = | 5 | 2 |
| c. | באמר אלי כל־היום | 3+2+1+2 | = | 8 | 3 |
| d. | איה אלהיך | 2+4 | = | 6 | 2 |
| 5a. | אלה אזכרה | 2+3 | = | 5 | 2 |
| b. | ואשפכה עלי נפשי | 4+2+2 | = | 8 | 3 |
| c. | כי אעבר בסך | 1+2+2 | = | 5 | 2 |
| d. | אדם עד־בית אלהים | 3+1+1+3 | = | 8 | 3 |
| e. | בקול־רנה ותודה | 2+2+3 | = | 7 | 3 |
| f. | המן חוגג | 2+2 | = | 4 | 2 |
| 6a. | מה־תשתוחחי נפשי | 1+4+2 | = | 7 | 3 |
| b. | ותהמי עלי | 3+2 | = | 5 | 2 |
| c. | הוחילי לאלהים | 3+3 | = | 6 | 2 |
| d. | כי־עוד אודנו | 1+1+3 | = | 5 | 2 |
| e. | ישעות פני ואלהי | 3+2+3 | = | 8 | 3 |
| 7a. | עלי נפשי תשתוחח | 2+2+3 | = | 7 | 3 |
| b. | על־כן אזכרך | 1+1+3 | = | 5 | 2 |
| c. | מארץ ירדן וחרמונים | 2+2+4 | = | 8 | 3 |
| d. | מהר מצער | 2+2 | = | 4 | 2 |
| 8a. | תהום־אל־תהום קורא | 2+1+2+2 | = | 7 | 3 |
| b. | לקול צנוריך | 2+4 | = | 6 | 2 |
| c. | כל־משבריך וגליך | 1+4+4 | = | 9 | 3 |

| | | | | | |
|---|---|---|---|---|---|
| d. | עלי עברו | 2+3 | = | 5 | 2 |
| 9a. | יומם יצוה יהוה חסדו | 2+3+2+2 | = | 9 | 4 |
| b. | ובלילה שירה עמי | 4+2+2 | = | 8 | 3 |
| c. | תפלה לאל חיי | 3+2+2 | = | 7 | 3 |
| 10a. | אומרה לאל סלעי | 3+2+2 | = | 7 | 3 |
| b. | למה שכחתני | 2+4 | = | 6 | 2 |
| c. | למה־קדר אלך | 2+2+2 | = | 6 | 3 |
| d. | בלחץ אויב | 2+2 | = | 4 | 2 |
| 11a. | ברצח בעצמותי | 2+4 | = | 6 | 2 |
| b. | חרפוני צוררי | 4+3 | = | 7 | 2 |
| c. | באמרם אלי כל־היום | 3+2+1+2 | = | 8 | 3 |
| d. | איה אלהיך | 2+4 | = | 6 | 2 |
| 12a. | מה־תשתוחחי נפשי | 1+4+2 | = | 7 | 3 |
| b. | ומה־תהמי עלי | 2+2+2 | = | 6 | 2 |
| c. | הוחילי לאלהים | 3+3 | = | 6 | 2 |
| d. | כי־עוד אודנו | 1+1+3 | = | 5 | 2 |
| e. | ישׁעת פני ואלהי | 3+2+3 | = | 8 | 3 |
| 43.1 | שפטני אלהים | 3+3 | = | 6 | 2 |
| b. | וריבה ריבי | 3+2 | = | 5 | 2 |
| c. | מגוי לא־חסיד | 2+1+2 | = | 5 | 2 |
| d. | מאיש־מרמה ועולה תפלטני | 2+2+3+5 | = | 12 | 4 |
| 2a. | כי־אתה אלהי מעוזי | 1+2+3+3 | = | 9 | 3 |
| b. | למה זנחתני | 2+4 | = | 6 | 2 |
| c. | למה־קדר אתהלך | 2+2+3 | = | 7 | 3 |
| d. | בלחץ אויב | 2+2 | = | 4 | 2 |
| 3a. | שלח־אורך ואמתך | 2+3+5 | = | 10 | 3 |
| b. | המה ינחוני | 2+3 | = | 5 | 2 |
| c. | יביאוני אל־הר־קדשך | 4+1+1+3 | = | 9 | 3 |
| d. | ואל־משכנותיך | 2+5 | = | 7 | 2 |
| 4a. | ואבואה אל־מזבח אלהים | 4+1+2+3 | = | 10 | 3 |
| b. | אל־אל שמחת גילי | 1+1+2+2 | = | 6 | 3 |
| c. | ואורך בכנור | 4+3 | = | 7 | 2 |
| d. | אלהים אלהי | 3+3 | = | 6 | 2 |
| 5a. | מה־תשתוחחי נפשי | 1+4+2 | = | 7 | 3 |
| b. | ומה־תהמי עלי | 2+2+2 | = | 6 | 2 |
| c. | הוחילי לאלהים | 3+3 | = | 6 | 2 |
| d. | כי־עוד אודנו | 1+1+3 | = | 5 | 2 |
| e. | ישׁעת פני ואלהי | 3+2+3 | = | 8 | 3 |
| TOTALS | | 66 cola | | 442 | 168 |

### 2.1.2 *Translation*

42.1   For the musical director. A Maskil. Of the sons of Korah.

  2a.   As a stag that pants for streams of water,
   b.   so does my soul pant for you, O God.

  3a.   My soul thirsts for God,
   b.   for the living God.
   c.   When will I go
   d.   and see the face of God?

### MINOR REFRAIN A

  4a.   *My tears have become my food*
   b.   *day and night,*
   c.   *when one says to me all day long:*
   d.   *'Where is your God?'*

  5a.   The following things I remember
   b.   as I pour out my soul within me:
   c.   how I used to traverse with the throng,
   d.   (how) I used to walk with them to the house of God,
   e.   with the sound of shouting and thanksgiving,
   f.   with the crowd keeping festival.

### MAJOR REFRAIN

  6a.   *Why are you cast down, O my soul,*
   b.   *and so groan within me?*
   c.   *Wait for God,*
   d.   *for again I will praise him,*
   e.   *the salvation of my countenance and my God.*

  7a.   Within me my soul is cast down
   b.   because I remember you,
   c.   from the land of Jordan and the Hermon range,
   d.   from Mount Mizar.

  8a.   Deep roars to deep
   b.   at the thunder of your shafts.
   c.   All your breakers and your rollers
   d.   have swept over me.

  9a.   By day Yahweh used to commission his steadfast love,
   b.   and by night my song of him was with me,
   c.   my prayer to my living God.

## MINOR REFRAIN B

10a. *I say to El my rock:*
   b. *'Why have you forgotten me?*
   c. *Why in dark mourning do I walk*
   d. *because of the oppression of the enemy?'*

## MINOR REFRAIN A′

11a. *As with a breaking in my bones*
   b. *my foes taunt me,*
   c. *when they say to me all day long:*
   d. *'Where is your God?'*

## MAJOR REFRAIN

12a. *Why are you cast down, O my soul*
   b. *and why do you groan within me?*
   c. *Wait for God*
   d. *for again I will praise him,*
   e. *the salvation of my countenance and my God.*

43.1a. Judge me, O God,
    b. and defend my cause.
    c. From an impious nation,
    d. from deceitful and perverse men, deliver me.

## MINOR REFRAIN B′

2a. *For you are my Fortress-God.*
  b. *Why have you rejected me?*
  c. *Why in dark mourning do I walk about*
  d. *because of the oppression of the enemy?*

3a. Send your light and truth;
  b. let them lead me.
  c. Let them bring me to your holy mountain,
  d. and to your dwelling.

4a. Then I will go to the altar of God,
  b. to El with my exceeding joy.
  c. Then I will praise you with a lyre,
  d. O God my God.

## MAJOR REFRAIN

5a. *Why are you cast down, O my soul,*
 b. *and why do you groan within me?*
 c. *Wait for God,*
 d. *for again I will praise him,*
 e. *the salvation of my countenance and my God.*

### 2.1.3 *Translation notes*

42.2a. כאיל תערג—'as a stag that pants'
איל, like other names of animals, is epicene (GKC 122b-f). The feminine verb is used here to prepare for the following נפשי תערג. Or one might consider that the ה of כאילה was lost by haplography. The phrase is a relative clause (GKC 155g).

42.3d. ואראה—'and see'
The MT points the verb as a niphal, 'appear (before) the face of God', which probably reflects later orthodoxy's dogma that no one can see God (Kraus 1978: 472). (On 'seeing God' in the OT, see Fretheim 1984.) Read the qal, *wĕ'er'eh*.

42.5a. אזכרה ואשפכה—'I remember as I pour out'
The cohortatives are used to express self-encouragement and inward deliberation (GKC 108 b). Cf. 42.10a.

42.5b. עלי נפשי—'my soul within me'
Dahood (1965a: 257) understands the suffix of עלי as third person singular, 'before him'. In light of the usage of this phrase throughout the psalm (42.6, 7, 12; 43.5), it is preferable to understand it the same way here, 'within me' or 'before me'. Cf. Jon. 2.8; Ps. 131.2; 142.4; 143.4; Lam. 3.20.

42.5c. בסך—'with the throng'
*sāk* is a *hapax*. Since it seems to be a collateral form of *sōk*, 'thicket', it is understood here figuratively ('throng') and as the antecedent of the suffix of אדדם with המון in apposition. Deriving it from *sākak*, 'to screen', Dahood (1965a: 257; cf. Tsevat 1955: 83) suggests that it might mean 'the barrier' which separates the temple enclosure from the court of the Gentiles. In that case it would be a parallel to בית אלהים, and המון would be a post-positive antecedent of the suffix of אדדם.

42.5d. אדדם—'I used to walk'
אדדם is parsed as hithpael of דדה plus suffix, 'move slowly' (BDB). On Dahood's derivation from Ugaritic *ndd*, see Craigie 1983: 324.

42.7b. עַל־כֵּן אֶזְכָּרְךָ—'because I remember you'
עַל־כֵּן is understood as 'because' rather than the usual 'therefore'. (So also Dahood 1965a: 258 and Kruse 1960: 337.) 'Because' the poet remembers Yahweh from a distant land, his soul is cast down. Cf. 42.5a-b.

42.7c-d. מֵאֶרֶץ יַרְדֵּן וְחֶרְמוֹנִים—'from the land of Jordan and the Hermon range'
מֵהַר מִצְעָר—'from Mount Mizar'
We follow most commentators in understanding these expressions in the following way. The poet was located at Mt Mizar, a peak whose precise location is unknown, but which was apparently in the Hermon range at the source of the Jordan. (On its location, see Smith 1932: 477.) The geographic references move from the general to the specific local- ity, 'from the land of Jordan, the Hermon range, from Mt Mizar'. Far away from Mt Zion, the 'center of the earth', the poet felt he was in the realm of the dead (cf. Pss. 61.3-5; 65.8-9; on this common ancient near eastern motif, see Keel 1978: 38f.). He expresses this belief with the tra- ditional imagery of the waters of chaos (42.8; cf. Pss. 69.2-3, 15-16; 88.8, 17-18; Keel 1978: 73-75). Possibly the waters in the area around the sources of the Jordan inspired his imagery of the chaotic primeval ocean (Kraus 1978: 476).

Dahood (1965a: 258-59) reinterprets the phrase: 'From the land of descent and of nets, from the mountains at the rim'. He takes אֶרֶץ יַרְדֵּן as a poetic name for the nether world. However, nowhere in Hebrew and Ugaritic is *yardēn* a name of the underworld. He understands *ḥermônîm* as a by-form of *ḥērem*, 'net'. Although this is possible, it is preferable to understand it as 'the Hermon range' in light of the proper name יַרְדֵּן and the following הַר מִצְעָר. Finally, Dahood reads MT מֵהַר מִצְעָר as צֵעָר מֵהַר־ם and interprets צֵעָר as a metathesis of Ugaritic *ġṣr*. The Ugaritic basis of the proposal is doubtful (Craigie 1983: 324).

Kruse (1960) translates: 'I think of thee more than of the whole land of the Jordan and all Hermons, thou tiny mountain!' He understands the first *mēm* (מֵאֶרֶץ) as a comparative *min*, attaches the *mēm* of מֵהַר to the Syriac variant *ḥrmwn*, and takes the words הַר מִצְעָר as vocative. The poet is therefore addressing Mt Zion, 'the tiny mountain'. Kruse interprets the suffixes of 42.8 as also referring to Mt Zion. Against this view is the fact that nowhere else in the poem is Mt Zion in the second person. Also, the phrase in 42.8c-d occurs in Jon. 2.4 where the suffixes have Yahweh as their antecedent.

Goulder (1982: 23-27) interprets the geographical references in light of his Danite hypothesis, believing the psalms of the sons of Korah to be part of an extended feast of Tabernacles liturgy at Tel Dan). The poet wants to go and worship God in the land of the Jordan and the Her- mon range. He vows, 'I will remember you (O God)... from the little hill', which is Tel Dan. The waters of 42.8 are not a metaphor for the waters of death but are the life-giving waters at Tel Dan. עלי עברו (42.8d) should not be translated 'they have passed over me' but rather 'they pass by/beside me'. Space does not permit us to enter into a thorough discussion of Goulder's thesis. However, two points will be made. First, the sanctuary to which the poet longs to go is clearly Mt Zion. The phrases הר־קדשך, 'your holy mountain' (43.3), and בית אלהים, 'the house of God' (42.5), consistently refer to Mt Zion in the Psalter. Second, the waters in 42.8 are metaphorically the 'waters of death' as the parallel in Jon. 2.4 indicates (see above).

### 42.8b. צנוריך—'your shafts'

The meaning of *ṣinnôr* is unknown. It occurs only here and in 2 Sam. 5.8 where it is also unclear. Based on the related word *ṣantĕrôt*, 'oil pipes', it apparently means a pipe of some kind. It could refer to the waterfalls at the source of the Jordan near Paneas (LXX: τῶν καταρρακτῶν σου) or to the thunderbolts with which God strikes the sea (Sukenik 1928: 126; Dahood 1965a: 259).

### 42.9. יצוה—'used to commission'

יצוה is interpreted here as the poet's reflection on Yahweh's past merciful dealings with the psalmist, following אזכרך in 42.7b (so also Auffret 1981: 111; Ridderbos 1976: 16-17). The prefixing verbs of 42.5 also refer to the past. On the meaning of *ṣiwwâ*, 'to commission', see Dahood 1965a: 259.

### 42.9b. שירה—'my song of him'

The suffix is objective in the light of the following colon (cf. Ps. 137.4; 1 Chron. 16.42; 2 Chron. 7.6; 29.27). Yahweh's חסד was toward the psalmist and the psalmist used to respond with a song of/to Yahweh. The antecedent of the suffix could also be חסד, 'my song praising it' (Tournay 1972: 39-43).

### 42.9c. לאל חיי—'to my living God'

On the syntax, see Weingreen 1954; cf. 42.3b, 10a; 43.2a.

### 42.11a. ברצח בעצמותי—'as with a breaking in my bones'.

On this translation see Waldman, 1974: 548-49.

### 43.4b. שמחת גילי—'with my exceeding joy'

Usually שמחה and גילי form a hendiadys (Isa. 16.10; Jer. 48.33; Joel 1.16; 2.23; Ps. 45.16; Hab. 1.15) but here they form a construct chain. In light of the word pair שמחה... גיל, Dahood's suggestion (1965a: 262), 'the joy of my life', which understands גילי as related to a verb גיל, 'to live', is less likely. There is no need to emend the text to *'āgîlâ* (contra Kraus 1978: 472 and Craigie 1983: 328). The *beth* of בכור is ellipsed from שמחה. Compare the similar phrase in 42.5e.

### 2.1.4 *Structure*

2.1.4.1 *Versification.* The poem is based on a 'non-alphabetic' acrostic structure with 66 cola (= 22 × 3; see Freedman: 1986). There are 31 verses according to our versification (16 verses according to MT) which include 27 bicola and 4 tricola. Three of the 4 tricola are located in the major refrains and the other is located approximately in the middle of the poem (42.9—29 cola preceding and 34 cola following.)

| | |
|---|---|
| 42.2 | Bicolon—the two cola are joined by syntax (כן...כ) and repetition (תערג), and they alliterate (כן...כ). |
| 42.3a-b | Bicolon—Colon B (לאל חי) is an extension of its parallel לאלהים in A. |
| 42.3c-d | Bicolon—A and B form a sentence. The two first person singular prefixing verbs are in sequence: 'When will *I go/* and *see* (read *wĕ'er'eh* for MT *wĕ'ērā'eh.* |
| 42.4a-b | Bicolon—B is a temporal clause dependent on A. |
| 42.4c-d | Bicolon—D forms the quote introduced by C. אלי in C and אלהיך in D form a sound pair. |
| 42.5a-b | Bicolon—Each colon contains a cohortative (אזכרה, ואשפכה). |
| 42.5c-d | Bicolon—The two first person prefixing verbs are parallel (אעבר...אדדם). The antecedent of the suffix of אדדם in B is בסך in A. |
| 42.5e-f | Bicolon. |
| 42.6a-b | Bicolon—The two verbs are parallel (... תשתוחחי והמי). Because the syllable count is 12, we count מה as one stress, producing a stress pattern of 3'2. This pattern dominates the poem (see below). |
| 42.6c-e | Tricolon—The antecedent of the suffix of אודנו in B is אלהים in A. Colon C is in apposition to the suffix of אודנו. אלהים and אלהי connect cola A and C. Read *wĕ'lōhāy* as in 42.12e and 43.5e. |
| 42.7a-b | Bicolon—על-כן in B begins the causal clause (see under Notes) following the main clause in A. (Cf. the similar bicolon in 42.5a-b.) Repetition of the preposition על in initial position joins both cola. |
| 42.7c-d | Bicolon—The preposition *min* begins both cola. 'Mt Mizar' in B is apparently located in the 'Hermon range' mentioned in A (see under Notes). |
| 42.8a-b | Bicolon—The two cola are joined by syntax to form a sentence. |

| 42.8c-d | Bicolon—The two cola are joined by syntax to form a sentence. Because the syllable count is 14 we count כל as accented for a regular stress count of 3'2. |
|---|---|
| 42.9a-c | Tricolon—The word pair יומם...לילה joins A and B (cf. 42.4b). The word pair שיר...תפלה joins cola B and C with עמי ellipsed in the latter. |
| 42.10a-b | Bicolon—A introduces the quote which follows. B is the first question of the quote. |
| 42.10c-d | Bicolon—D is a prepositional phrase syntactically joined to C. |
| 42.11a-b | Bicolon—A is a prepositional phrase dependent on B, the main clause. They both have final rhyme (*ay*). |
| 42.11c-d | Bicolon—The temporal clause in C introduces the direct quote of D (cf. 42.4). |
| 42.12a-b | Bicolon—Verse 12 is the same as 42.6 except that the interrogative מה is repeated in B. We take the stress count to be the same as 42.6a-b (3'2) in spite of the extra מה. |
| 42.12c-e | Tricolon—Same as 42.6c-e. |
| 43.1a-b | Bicolon—Both cola begin with an imperative. אלהים is gapped from the second colon. |
| 43.1c-d | Bicolon—The preposition *min* begins each colon, and גוי in A and איש in B form a word pair. |
| 43.2a-b | Bicolon—Both A and B rhyme with *î*. They also address God in the second person. |
| 43.2c-d | Bicolon—B is a prepositional phrase dependent on A. |
| 43.3a-b | Bicolon—This bicolon is an abba chiasm: imperative + two nouns // pronoun whose antecedent is the two nouns + jussive. |
| 43.3c-d | Bicolon—The phrase אל-הר-קדשך in A parallels the phrase אל-משכנותיך in B. |
| 43.4a-b | Bicolon—The preposition אל is repeated and אלנים...אל form a word pair. |
| 43.4c-d | Bicolon—אלהים אלהי in B are vocatives in apposition to the suffix of ואורך in A. |
| 43.5a-b | Bicolon—The same as 42.12a-b. |
| 43.5c-e | Tricolon—The same as 42.6c-e and 42.12c-e. |

## 2.1.4.2 *Stress and Syllable Counts*

| Verse | Syllables | | Totals | Stresses | | Totals |
|---|---|---|---|---|---|---|
| 42.2 | 10 + 11 | = | 21 | 4 + 4 | = | 8 |

| | | | | | | |
|---|---|---|---|---|---|---|
| 3a-b | 8 + 3 | = | 11 | 3 + 2 | = | 5 |
| 3c-d | 4 + 8 | = | 12 | 2 + 3 | = | 5 |
| 4a-b | 8 + 5 | = | 13 | 3 + 2 | = | 5 |
| 4c-d | 8 + 6 | = | 14 | 3 + 2 | = | 5 |
| 5a-b | 5 + 8 | = | 13 | 2 + 3 | = | 5 |
| 5c-d | 5 + 8 | = | 13 | 2 + 3 | = | 5 |
| 5e-f | 7 + 4 | = | 11 | 3 + 2 | = | 5 |
| 6a-b | 7 + 5 | = | 12 | 3 + 2 | = | 5 |
| 6c-e | 6 + 5 + 8 | = | 19 | 2 + 2 + 3 | = | 7 |
| 7a-b | 7 + 5 | = | 12 | 3 + 2 | = | 5 |
| 7c-d | 8 + 4 | = | 12 | 3 + 2 | = | 5 |
| 8a-b | 7 + 6 | = | 13 | 3 + 2 | = | 5 |
| 8c-d | 9 + 5 | = | 14 | 3 + 2 | = | 5 |
| 9 | 9 + 8 + 7 | = | 24 | 4 + 3 + 3 | = | 10 |
| 10a-b | 7 + 6 | = | 13 | 3 + 2 | = | 5 |
| 10c-d | 6 + 4 | = | 10 | 3 + 2 | = | 5 |
| 11a-b | 6 + 7 | = | 13 | 2 + 2 | = | 4 |
| 11c-d | 8 + 6 | = | 14 | 3 + 2 | = | 5 |
| 12a-b | 7 + 6 | = | 13 | 3 + 2 | = | 5 |
| 12c-e | 6 + 5 + 8 | = | 19 | 2 + 2 + 3 | = | 7 |
| 43.1a-b | 6 + 5 | = | 11 | 2 + 2 | = | 4 |
| 1c-d | 5 + 12 | = | 17 | 2 + 4 | = | 6 |
| 2a-b | 9 + 6 | = | 15 | 3 + 2 | = | 5 |
| 2c-d | 7 + 4 | = | 11 | 3 + 2 | = | 5 |
| 3a-b | 10 + 5 | = | 15 | 3 + 2 | = | 5 |
| 3c-d | 9 + 7 | = | 16 | 3 + 2 | = | 5 |
| 4a-b | 10 + 6 | = | 16 | 3 + 3 | = | 6 |
| 4c-d | 7 + 6 | = | 13 | 2 + 2 | = | 4 |
| 5a-b | 7 + 6 | = | 13 | 3 + 2 | = | 5 |
| 5c-e | 6 + 5 + 8 | = | 19 | 2 + 2 + 3 | = | 7 |
| TOTALS | 31 verses/66 cola | | 442 | | | 168 |

### Distribution of Stresses

| Cola | Bicola | Tricola |
|---|---|---|
| 2' - 34 | 2'2 - 3 | 2'2'3 - 3 |
| 3' - 28 | 2'3 - 3 | 4'3'3 - 1 |
| 4' - 4 | 3'2 - 18 | |
| | 3'3 - 1 | |
| | 2'4 - 1 | |
| | 4'4 - 1 | |

The dominant stress pattern is 3'2. Of the poem's 27 bicola, 18 exhibit this pattern and 3 exhibit its inverse, 2'3. Of the poem's tricola, 3 exhibit its inverse, 2′2′3. Thus 24 of the 31 verses (77%) are based on this pattern.

That this poem is based on a 3′2 stresss pattern is confirmed by the distribution of 2-stress and 3-stress cola and the total number of stresses. The 2-stress cola and 3-stress cola are distributed fairly evenly, as expected (34 to 28). The theoretical norm is 33 to 33. The total number of stresses also conforms closely to the theoretical norm. 168 stresses divided by 66 cola or 33 (hypothetical) bicola yields 2.55 stresses per colon or 5.09 stresses per bicolon. The expected norms are 2.5 and 5, which would result from 165 stresses. We conclude that although there is deviation from the 3′2 pattern among the verses, overall the poem corresponds to this pattern.

*Distribution of Syllables*

| Syllables | | Cola | | Total Syllables |
|---|---|---|---|---|
| 3 | × | 1 | = | 3 |
| 4 | × | 5 | = | 20 |
| 5 | × | 12 | = | 60 |
| 6 | × | 15 | = | 90 |
| 7 | × | 12 | = | 84 |
| 8 | × | 12 | = | 96 |
| 9 | × | 4 | = | 36 |
| 10 | × | 3 | = | 30 |
| 11 | × | 1 | = | 11 |
| 12 | × | 1 | = | 12 |
| TOTALS | | 66 | | 442 |

No colon is less than 3 or more than 12 syllables in length. Most of the cola are 5 to 8 syllables, 51 of 66 cola (77%). The syllable distribution conforms to what was seen in the stress distribution: 27 cola are 5 to 6 syllables (= 2-stress cola) and 24 cola are 7 to 8 syllables (= 3-stress cola). The theoretical norm for a 3′2 stress pattern would be 6.68 syllables per colon or 13.35 syllables per bicolon (2.67 syllables per stress; see Freedman 1972d; 1986). The count of 442 syllables conforms almost exactly to the theoretical norm—6.697 syllables per colon or 13.394 syllables per bicolon (hypothetically 33 bicola).

### 2.1.4.3 *Strophes*

42.2    Second person references to the deity.

3    Third person references to the deity.

4    Minor refrain A as in 42.11. The four cola are joined by syntax and the repetition of יום.

5    אלה in v.5a refers to the following cola (c-f) which are joined by syntax.

7    The last two cola are prepositional phrases dependent on 42.7b.

8    The associated lexical items of 'deep', 'shafts', 'breakers', and 'rollers' unite this strophe.

9    Third person references to the deity.

10    Minor refrain B as in 43.2.

11    Minor refrain A′ as in 42.4.

43.1    After a major refrain and before minor refrain B′. The imperatives and injunctive prefixing verb unite the four cola.

2    Minor refrain B′ as in 42.10.

3    The imperative and jussives unite this strophe.

4    The repetition of אלהים and the synonym אל unify this strophe.

### *Length of Strophes*

|       | verses | cola | syllables | stresses |
|-------|--------|------|-----------|----------|
| 42.2  | 1      | 2    | 21        | 8        |
| 3     | 2      | 4    | 23        | 10       |
| 4     | 2      | 4    | 27        | 10       |
| 5     | 3      | 6    | 37        | 15       |
| 7     | 2      | 4    | 24        | 10       |
| 8     | 2      | 4    | 27        | 10       |
| 9     | 1      | 3    | 24        | 10       |
| 10    | 2      | 4    | 23        | 10       |
| 11    | 2      | 4    | 27        | 9        |
| 43.1  | 2      | 4    | 28        | 10       |
| 2     | 2      | 4    | 26        | 10       |
| 3     | 2      | 4    | 31        | 10       |
| 4     | 2      | 4    | 29        | 10       |

The strophic lengths range from two to six cola, from 21 to 37 syllables, and from 8 to 15 stresses. Ten of the thirteen strophes have 4 cola.

### 2.1.4.4 *Refrains*. The poem contains three major refrains and two pairs of minor refrains:

| Major refrains | — | 42.6, 12; 43.5 |
| Minor refrains A and A′ | — | 42.4; 11 |
| Minor refrains B and B′ | — | 42.10; 43.2 |

The three major refrains are structurally distinct from the stanzas (so also Wahl 1976: 215). Only in the major refrains is נפשי ('my soul') addressed in the second person. The contrast is particularly evident in 42.6-7, since in v. 7 נפשי is third person. The contrast between second and third person in reference to 'God' also serves to isolate these refrains:

| 42.6 | — | 'God' | = | third person (refrain) |
| 7 | — | 'God' | = | second person |
| 12 | — | 'God' | = | third person (refrain) |
| 43.1 | — | 'God' | = | second person |
| 4c-d | — | 'God' | = | second person |
| 5 | — | 'God' | = | third person (refrain) |

Finally, only in these refrains is there an exhortation to hope.

The minor refrains, on the other hand, are structurally part of their respective stanzas (so also Wahl 1977: 215). 42.4 (minor refrain A) continues the imagery of 42.2-3. Instead of drinking from the water of life (God), the psalmist's tears are his food. God is third person in 42.4 as in 42.3 and 5. (The enemies' question in 42.4d amounts to a third person reference to God, i.e. 'where is he?') 'El, my Rock' (minor refrain B; 42.10a) is third person as in the previous verse (42.9c). 42.11 (minor refrain A′) continues the third person, parallel to 42.4. In refrain B′ (43.2) 'God' is second person as in 43.1 and 3. The fact that the opening line of minor refrain B (42.10) uses the third person but the opening of minor refrain B′ (43.2) alters the line to the second person illustrates how the psalmist considered these minor refrains to be a part of their respective stanzas.

The minor refrain A occurs in the first (42.4) and the second (42.11) stanzas, and minor refrain B occurs in the second (42.10) and third (43.2) stanzas. The order of minor refrain A-B is reversed in the middle stanza. This serves to interlock the middle stanza with the first and third:

| Minor refrain A | — | 42.4 |
| Major refrain | — | 6 |
| Minor refrain B | — | 10 |

| | | |
|---|---|---|
| Minor refrain A′ | — | 11 |
| Major refrain | — | 12 |
| Minor refrain B′ | — | 43.2 |
| Major refrain | — | 5 |

Each minor refrain varies considerably from its partner. The first two cola of A (42.4a-b) and A′ (42.11a-b) are altogether different. The last two cola of each are identical (except for באמר without the suffix in 42.4c but with the suffix in 42.11c—באמרם). The initial cola of B and B′ are also different, although סלעי (42.10a) and מעוזי (43.2a) are word pairs. The differences between the other cola of B and B′ are less noticeable: שכחתני (42.10b) vs. זנחתני (43.2b) and אלך (42.10c) vs. אתהלך (43.2c).

On the other hand, the major refrains are practically identical. The only variation is with 42.6. Verse 6b does not begin with ומה, in contrast to 42.12b and 43.5b. ישועות is written *plene* in 42.6e in contrast to ישעת in 42.12e and 43.5e. The *waw* is attached to פני and אלהי begins a new verse in 42.6e, but there can be little doubt that this represents a scribal error and should be brought into harmony with 42.12e and 43.5e.

**2.1.4.5** *Stanzas.* Psalms 42–43 are one poem with three stanzas, each of which is followed by the major refrain:

| | |
|---|---|
| 42.2-5 | Stanza I |
| 6 | Refrain |
| 7-11 | Stanza II |
| 12 | Refrain |
| 43.1-4 | Stanza III |
| 5 | Refrain |

The poem begins with an address to God. The rest of stanza I (42.3-5) refers to God in the third person. There is no inclusion for it. The second stanza begins by addressing God in the second person. The reference to God changes to the third person in 42.9 and continues that way to the stanza's end (except for the quote embedded in 42.10). Again there is no inclusion. It closes with a quote. (On the closure function of quotations, see Watson 1984: 165.) Stanza III is united by the Psalmist's petition (imperatives, jussives). אלהים forms an inclusion (43.1a... 4d).

*Length of Stanzas*

|          | strophes | vv. | bicola | tricola | cola | syllables | stresses |
|----------|----------|-----|--------|---------|------|-----------|----------|
| 42.2-5   | 4        | 8   | 8      | 0       | 16   | 108       | 43       |
| 7-11     | 5        | 9   | 8      | 1       | 19   | 125       | 49       |
| 43.1-4   | 4        | 8   | 8      | 0       | 16   | 114       | 40       |

As can be seen, all of these stanzas are about the same length. The first and third stanzas are practically identical in length in their number of cola and syllables, although the first stanza has three more stresses. The middle stanza, however, is longer than the others by 3 cola, 11 to 17 syllables, and 6 to 9 stresses. This is due to the added tricolon of 42.9, the only tricolon in the poem other than the three in the major refrains. Appropriately, 42.9 is the poem's middle verse.

The size of the strophes creates an interesting pattern. Stanza I begins with a bicolonic strophe. This is followed by two tetracolonic strophes and one hexacolonic strophe. Stanza II has two tetracolonic strophes at each end and a tricolonic strophe in the middle. Stanza III has four tetracolonic strophes. The last seems to be the basic pattern. It is supplemented in Stanza II by an extra tricolon in the middle. Stanza I alters it by reducing the opening strophe and lengthening the final strophe.

2.1.4.6 *Sections*. Psalm 42–43 is tripartite with each major refrain completing a section: 42.2-6, 7-12; 43.1-5. Although there is a minor break before 42.6, 12, and 43.5, the major breaks come after each major refrain. Whereas in 42.6 'my soul' is addressed in second person, in 42.7 it occurs in third person. Also the change in mood between 42.6 and 7 is very noticeable. In 42.6 the psalmist reproaches his 'soul' for being downcast and exhorts it to hope—'Wait for God, for again I will praise him'—but in 42.7 he reaffirms his despair—'Within me my soul is cast down'. The other major break occurs between 42.12 and 43.1. The latter begins petitions addressed to God.

*Length of Sections*

|          | vv. | bicola | tricola | cola | syllables | stresses |
|----------|-----|--------|---------|------|-----------|----------|
| 42.2-6   | 10  | 9      | 1       | 21   | 139       | 55       |
| 7-12     | 11  | 9      | 2       | 24   | 157       | 61       |

| 43.1-5 | 10 | 9 | 1 | 21 | 146 | 52 |
|---|---|---|---|---|---|---|

One would expect each section to be 22 cola since the total is 66. Instead, the first and third sections are each one less and the middle section is two more. Possibly this is simply for the sake of variety. At any rate, it is the extra tricolon in the middle section that makes the difference. (42.9 is roughly the middle of the poem—29 cola before and 34 cola after.)

**2.1.4.7 *Views of Structure*.** Most scholars recognize the tripartite structure of Psalms 42–43 (Kirkpatrick 1902: 227; Briggs 1906: 365-66; Kissane 1953: 185; Weiser 1962: 347; Wahl 1977: 217; Alonso Schökel 1976; Beaucamp 1976: 188-90; Kraus 1978: 472; van der Lugt 1980: 474; Auffret 1981: 100; Trublet–Aletti 1983: 74; Craigie 1983: 325; Gerstenberger 1988: 178-82). Some of them distinguish structurally between the refrains and the stanzas (Briggs, Wahl, Beaucamp, Craigie, Gerstenberger).

Segal (1935: 129-31) attempts to reconstruct two different original psalms on the basis of the different types of refrains.

| Psalm I | 42.2-3 | | |
|---|---|---|---|
| | [Refrain] | | |
| | 42.5 | | |
| | 42.6 | = | Refrain |
| | 42.7-8 | | |
| | 42.12 | = | Refrain |
| | 43.3-4 | | |
| | 43.5 | = | Refrain |
| Psalm II | 42.4 | = | Refrain A |
| | 42.9 | | |
| | 42.10 | = | Refrain B |
| | 42.11 | = | Refrain A |
| | 43.1 | | |
| | 43.2 | = | Refrain B |

In contrast, we believe one should distinguish between minor and major refrains in the one psalm. Needless to say, most scholars no longer find this type of radical rewriting of the text convincing.

Girard (1984: 338-51) proposes his own schema. He understands the poem to consist of two overlapping panels: 42.2-11 and 42.6–43.5. Each panel is shaped chiastically:

| | | | |
|---|---|---|---|
| A --- 42.2-4 | | C -- 42.6 | |
| B -------- 42.5 | | D ------ 42.7-9 | |
| C ------------ 42.6 | | E ---------- 42.10-11 | |
| B -------- 42.7-8 | | F ------------------ 43.1 | |
| A --- 42.9-11 | | E ---------- 43.2 | |
| | | D ------ 43.3-4 | |
| | | C -- 43.5 | |

In general, Girard structures the poem on the basis of repeated words or word-pairs. When a word in one verse is repeated in another verse, those two verses are parallel. However, the results are not very convincing. How does 42.2 relate to 42.9-11, or 42.10 to 42.2-4 on the left panel? Why is 42.11 considered parallel to 43.2 on the right panel? The major weakness of his proposal is his view that the refrain in 42.12 was interpolated later when Psalms 42 and 43 were separated. The basis for this hypothesis, as he admits, is that 42.12 does not fit into his diptychic structure (348). In our opinion his proposal imposes a preconceived structure on the text.

Lund (1942: 117) followed by Alden (1974: 25-26) also offers a double chiastic outline, although without overlapping:

| | |
|---|---|
| A | 42.2-4 |
| B | 42.5 |
| C | 42.6 |
| B′ | 42.7-8 |
| A′ | 42.9-11 |
| A″ | 42.12 |
| B″ | 43.1-2 |
| C′ | 43.3 |
| B‴ | 43.4 |
| A‴ | 43.5 |

The parallels are made on the basis of repeated words. Again the results are not very convincing. It is difficult to see how the following verses are related: 42.2 and 42.9-11; 42.10 and 42.2-4; 42.8 and 42.5. The major refrains are located in the middle of the first section (C) and at the beginning and end of the section (A″, A‴). The parallel between 42.10 and 43.2 is unaccounted for. Lund's proposal, like Girard's seems to be forcing the text into a chiastic pattern.

*2.1.5 Repetition.* The poem's repetitions and minor refrains serve to interlock the three stanzas together. The following displays these connections:

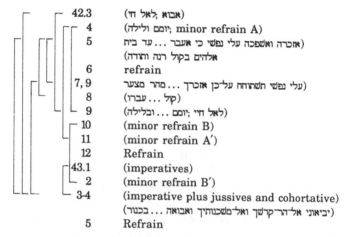

| | |
|---|---|
| 42.3 | (אבוא ;לאל חי) |
| 4 | (יומם ולילה; minor refrain A) |
| 5 | (אזכרה ואשפכה עלי נפשי כי אעבר ... עד בית |
| | אלהים בקול רנה ותודה) |
| 6 | refrain |
| 7, 9 | (עלי נפשי תשתוחח על־כן אזכרך ... מהר מצער |
| 8 | (קול ... עברו) |
| 9 | (לאל חיי ;יומם ... ובלילה) |
| 10 | (minor refrain B) |
| 11 | (minor refrain A') |
| 12 | Refrain |
| 43.1 | (imperatives) |
| 2 | (minor refrain B') |
| 3-4 | (imperative plus jussives and cohortative) |
| | (יביאוני אל־הר־קדשך ואל־משכנותיך ואבואה ... בכנור) |
| 5 | Refrain |

The first and second stanzas have points of contact at 42.3, 4, 5 and 42.7, 8, 9, 11. The second and third stanzas have points of contact at 42.7, 10 and 43.3 and 2. There are points of contact between the first and third at 42.3, 5 and 43.3-4. 42.3 and 43.3-4 form an inclusion for the whole poem: the psalmist's question in 42.3, 'when will I go' (אבוא), becomes his prayer in 43.3-4, 'let them bring me... Then I will go' (יביאוני ... ואבואה). One should also note the connections between 42.9 and the rest of the psalm, which argue for the integrity of 42.9. (See Rowley 1940: 45-50 for a survey of suggested emendations.)

We wish to highlight two repetitions which serve to reinforce the psalmist's dominant concern, his *soul's* longing for his *God.* נפשי occurs seven times (42.2b, 3a, 5b, 6a, 7a, 12a; 43.5a). *'ĕlōhîm*, its suffixed forms, and *'ēl*, total 21 occurrences (3 × 7). Yhwh is used once for a total of 22 references to the deity. This appropriately corresponds to the acrostic nature of the poem with its 66 cola.

*'ĕlōhîm*    —    10

| | | |
|---|---|---|
| 'ĕlōhê | — | 1 |
| 'ĕlōheykā | — | 2 |
| 'ĕlōhāy | — | 4 |
| 'ēl | — | 4 |
| | | 21 |

The locations of these references to God in the poem form a symmetrical pattern.

| Stanza I | 42.2 | 'ĕlōhîm—(vocative) |
|---|---|---|
| | 3 | 'ĕlōhîm |
| | | 'ēl ḥāy |
| | | 'ĕlōhîm |
| | 4 | 'ĕlōheykā |
| | 5 | 'ĕlōhîm |
| Refrain | 6 | 'ĕlōhîm |
| | | 'ĕlōhay |
| Stanza II | 9 | yhwh |
| | | 'ēl ḥayyāy |
| | 10 | 'ēl salʿî |
| | 11 | 'ĕlōheykā |
| Refrain | 12 | 'ĕlōhîm |
| | | 'ĕlōhāy |
| Stanza III | 43.1 | 'ĕlōhîm—(vocative) |
| | 2 | 'ĕlōhĕ māʿûzzî (vocative) |
| | 4 | 'ĕlōhîm |
| | | 'ēl |
| | | 'ĕlōhîm—(vocative) |
| | | 'ĕlōhāy—(vocative) |
| Refrain | 5 | 'ĕlōhîm |
| | | 'ĕlōhāy |

The first and third stanzas each have 6 references to God whereas the second stanza has 4. The three refrains total 6, 2 in each. In the first stanza 'ēl is in the third position whereas in the third stanza 'ēl is positioned third from the end. The other two references to 'ēl are in the middle of the second stanza, bracketed by יהוה and 'ĕlōheykā. Thus 'ēl is located symmetrically in the psalm: third position in the first stanza, middle of the second stanza, and third from the end of the last stanza. Also, the only instance of יהוה occurs roughly in the middle of the poem (29 cola before and 34 cola after 42.9).

### 2.1.6 *Thought Progression*

This psalm is generally recognized as an individual lament or complaint (Sabourin 1974: 239-40); Gerstenberger 1988: 181). Most of the elements of this genre are found here: address to God, complaints, petition, expression of trust, and vow of praise. It is important, however, to observe how these elements express themselves in the poem's structure. First, we will focus on each stanza and then on the movement of the whole poem.

**2.1.6.1 *Stanzas*.** The psalmist begins by expressing his longing for God. He pants and thirsts for God and longs to go and see God's face (42.2-3). Instead of enjoying the waters of life, his tears are his drink (42.4). While others taunt him with the question, 'Where is your God?', he remembers how he used to joyfully make pilgrimages to the temple (42.4-5).

The second stanza begins with the psalmist's explanation of why his soul is cast down. He remembers God (42.7b) and how God used to commission his חסד toward the psalmist (42.9). But now he is in a distant land far away from the temple (42.7c-d). He is drowning in Sheol, as it were, under God's rollers and breakers (42.8). In the past he used to respond to God's חסד with singing (42.9), but now he laments to God, 'Why have you forgotten me?' (42.10). The enemies' taunting question, 'Where is your God?', causes a breaking of his bones (42.11).

The third stanza is dominated by petitions. He prays to be vindicated and delivered from his taunters (43.1). 43.2 explains why God should help him: because God is his fortress and because the psalmist is being oppressed. 43.3-4 then continue the petitions. He prays that God will send his messengers of light and truth that they may bring him to God's presence at the temple. Then he will praise God again.

**2.1.6.2 *Poem*.** The poem is tripartite. Each part culminates in the major refrain. Each part reveals a movement from despair expressed in the stanza to hope and assurance expressed in the refrain (Ridderbos 1976). The refrains unify the poem 'as three equal columns might function to support and unify a decorative frieze...' (Alonso Schökel 1977: 61).

Yet, it is not as if each part stands independently. There is a definite movement from stanza to stanza. In stanza I the psalmist's distress consists of his longing and thirsting for God. 'When will I go and see the face of God?' he asks. No emphasis is put on his enemies. He only briefly mentions their question, 'Where is your God?'

In the second stanza his lament is presented much more radically. It is no longer just a problem of longing for God. Now God is the problem, the reason for his present distress. God's breakers and rollers are drowning him in the waters of chaos. Now he has his own question, one which is more serious, 'Why have you forgotten me?' The enemies also are highlighted. In 42.4 we did not know if the enemy was one or many (באמר), but now we see the plural (חרפוני צוררי באמרם—42.11). We discover that they are 'oppressing' (42.10) and 'taunting' (42.11) him. The second stanza heightens his distress and lament.

In the third stanza the lament is displaced by his petition. His double complaint of 'why... why?' (43.2) is no longer only an expression of deep agony. The petitions which bracket it have changed its function. Now the complaint is designed to motivate God to intervene and bring him to the temple. Also in this section we have the fullest description of his enemies. They are an 'impious nation, deceitful and perverse men' (43.1). Now for the first time the psalmist petitions God to deliver him from these his enemies. The laments of the first two stanzas have been succeeded by petitions in the third stanza.

There are other variations between the stanzas which should be noted. Except for the opening couplet, the poet refers to God objectively in the third person in stanza I. He switches to second person in the first two verses of stanza II (42.7-8) and then reverts back to the third person (42.9-11). The third stanza finds the poet consistently addressing God in the second person until near the end where it switches to third person (43.4a-b) and then back to second person (43.4c-d).

The poet's recollections of the past vary. In 42.5 his recollection focuses on himself. The psalmist remembers how he used to rejoice with the crowd keeping festival. But in 42.9 he remembers Yahweh and Yahweh's חסד. His past communion with God makes the present all the more agonizing (42.10). In the third stanza there is no recollection. The poet instead con-

centrates on the future and prays that he might go to the
temple as he did in the past.

Finally, the use of water imagery varies (Alonso Schökel
1976: 4-8). In the first stanza the poet longs for and thirsts
after the waters of life, i.e. God (42.2-3). Instead of the waters
of life, his tears have become his food (42.4). In the second
stanza, however, the waters represent death (42.7-8).

> The poet who desperately seeks water, finds it, but it is not life-
> giving water—it is destructive. God *sends* water, overwhelming,
> destructive of life. God, who was to have been the life of the
> psalmist, has become his death; he has become an elemental
> force, oceanic, irresistible (p. 7).

The water imagery is omitted from the third stanza. In the
place of 'your breakers and your rollers' (42.8) is substituted
the phrase 'your light and your truth' (43.3). He prays that
God's light might lead him out of the dark deadly waters.

The whole poem reaches its climax in the third movement.
Whereas the second stanza heightens the lament, the third
stanza finally introduces the petitions. The stanza's end (43.3-
4) speaks the most of the joyous future. In it a progression can
be seen from the 'holy mountain' to God's 'dwelling' to God's
'altar' to 'El' himself. The psalmist's question in 42.4, 'When
will I go and see the face of God?', is now his prayer. Once
there, he vows to praise God with a lyre.

In conclusion, the poem exhibits a thought progression
which corresponds to its formal format.

## 2.2 Psalm 46

### 2.2.1 Text

| | Text | Syllables | | Total | Stresses |
|---|---|---|---|---|---|
| 46.1 | למנצח לבני־קרח על־עלמות שיר | | | | |
| 2a. | אלהים לנו מחסה ועז | 3+2+2+2 | = | 9 | 4 |
| b. | עזרה בצרות נמצא מאד | 2+3+2+2 | = | 9 | 4 |
| 3a. | על־כן לא־נירא בהמיר ארץ | 2+1+2+3+1 | = | 9 | 4 |
| b. | ובמוט הרים בלב ימים | 3+2+2+2 | = | 9 | 4 |
| 4a. | יהמו יחמרו מימיו | 2+3+2 | = | 7 | 3 |
| b. | ירעשו־הרים בגאותו | 3+2+4 | = | 9 | 3 |
| c. | [יהוה צבאות עמנו] | 2+3+3 | = | 8 | 3 |
| d. | [משגב־לנו אלהי יעקב] סלה | 2+2+3+2 | = | 9 | 4 |
| 5a. | נהר פלגיו ישמחו עיר־אלהים | 2+3+4+1+3 | = | 13 | 4 |
| b. | קדש משכני עליון | 2+3+2 | = | 7 | 3 |
| 6a. | אלהים בקרבה בל־תמוט | 3+3+1+2 | = | 9 | 3 |
| b. | יעזרה אלהים לפנות בקר | 4+3+2+1 | = | 10 | 4 |
| 7a. | המו גוים מטו ממלכות | 2+2+2+3 | = | 9 | 4 |
| b. | נתן בקולו תמוג ארץ | 2+3+2+1 | = | 8 | 4 |
| 8a. | יהוה צבאות עמנו | 2+3+3 | = | 8 | 3 |
| b. | משגב־לנו אלהי יעקב סלה | 2+2+3+2 | = | 9 | 4 |
| 9a. | לכו־חזו מפעלות יהוה | 2+2+3+2 | = | 9 | 4 |
| b. | אשר־שם שמות בארץ | 2+1+2+2 | = | 7 | 3 |
| 10a. | משבית מלחמות עד־קצה הארץ | 2+3+1+2+2 | = | 10 | 4 |
| b. | קשת ישבר וקצץ חנית | 1+3+3+2 | = | 9 | 4 |
| c. | עגלות ישרף באש | 3+2+2 | = | 7 | 3 |
| 11a. | הרפו ודעו כי־אנכי אלהים | 2+3+1+3+3 | = | 12 | 4 |
| b. | ארום בגוים ארום בארץ | 2+3+2+2 | = | 9 | 4 |
| 12a. | יהוה צבאות עמנו | 2+3+3 | = | 8 | 3 |
| b. | משגב־לנו אלהי יעקב סלה | 2+2+3+2 | = | 9 | 4 |
| TOTALS | | 25 cola | | 222 | 91 |

### 2.2.2 Translation

1. For the musical director. Of the sons of Korah.
   According to Alamoth. A song.

2a. God is for us a refuge and protection.
  b. As a help in troubles the Mighty One lets himself be found.
3a. Therefore we will not fear though the earth change,
  b. and though the mountains totter into the heart of the seas.
4a. Let its waters roar and foam!
  b. Let the mountains shake at its haughtiness!

## REFRAIN

c. *[Yahweh of hosts is with us;*
d. *the God of Jacob is a fortress for us.]* SELAH

5a. There is a river whose streams make glad the city of God,
b. the holiest of the dwellings of the Most High.
6a. God is in her midst, she will not totter.
b. God helps her at the break of dawn.
7a. Nations roar, kingdoms totter.
b. He gives forth his voice, the earth trembles.

## REFRAIN

8    *Yahweh of hosts is with us;*
*the God of Jacob is a fortress for us.* SELAH

9a. Come, see the deeds of Yahweh,
b. how he wrought devastations on the earth.
10a. He is about to make wars cease to the ends of the earth.
b. The bow he will break and he will shatter the spear.
c. War-wagons he will burn in the fire.
11a. 'Desist and know that it is I who am God;
b. (that) I am exalted among the nations; I am exalted on the earth.'

## REFRAIN

12a. *Yahweh of hosts is with us;*
*the God of Jacob is a fortress for us.* SELAH

### 2.2.3 *Translation Notes*

v. 2a. ועז—'and protection'
On this word's meaning of 'protection, stronghold', see Craigie (1972: 145-46) and Dahood (1965a: 173).

v. 2b. נמצא מאד—'the Mighty One lets himself be found'
On the basis of Isa. 55.6; 1 Chron. 28.9; and 2 Chron. 15.2, 4, 15, we parse נמצא as a niphal participle rather than a qal prefixing verb. The preposition לנו in A is gapped. Cf. 1 Chron. 28.9; 2 Chron. 15.2, 4, 15 where the preposition ל accompanies the Niphal of מצא.

Dahood (1970a: xxvi) and Freedman (1973) suggest reading *mā'ēd*, 'the Mighty One', for MT *mĕ'ōd*. (On the disputed Ugaritic *mid*, see Marcus 1974 and Loretz 1974a.) We prefer to retain the MT *mĕ'ōd* and understand it as the substantive 'power, might' as in Deut. 6.5 and 2 Kgs 23.25. It would then be a noun used as a divine title, 'the Mighty

One', much as *'ōz* is used elsewhere. In this case the divine appellatives of אלהים ... מאד bracket the bicolon. However, it is also possible to
understand מאד as an adverb, 'he is very accessible' (cf. Ps. 47.10d).

**v. 3a.** בהמיר ארץ—'though the earth change'
בהמיר is parsed here as an intransitive hiphil infinitive of מור. As the following three lines clarify, the imagery is that of the earth reverting to
chaos (cf. Ps. 104.6; Jer. 4.23-24; Weiss 1961: 274-75). Dahood (1959: 167-
68; 1965a: 278-79) translates, 'we will not fear the gorge/jaws of the
nether world', on the basis of Ugaritic *hmry / mhmrt* (Hebrew: מהמרות)
'watery depths'. However, this interpretation does not fit well with the
context. The threat is not the underworld but the reversion of the created order to chaos. ארץ never denotes 'the underworld' in this psalm
(vv. 7b, 9b, 10a, 11c). In v. 3 ארץ is clarified by הרים and ימים.

**v. 4a.** יהמו יחמרו מימיו—'Let its waters roar and foam'
There is a change in syntax between v. 3 and v. 4a-b. Verse 3 employs
the preposition ב plus infinitive construct to express concessive
clauses, but v. 4 has prefixing verbs. Therefore, we understand יהמו,
יחמרו, and ירעשו as jussives (so also Delitzsch 1871 and Kissane 1953). By
expressing it this way the psalmist reinforces the declaration of v. 3a,
i.e. 'Let the world return to chaos, we still will not fear'.
 The antecedent of the suffix of מימיו is ימים in v. 3b. ימים may be parsed
as a plural of extension (GKC 124b) or as the singular *yām* with
enclitic *mēm*. Either can explain the singular suffix.

**v. 4b.** בגאותו—'at its haughtiness'.
The antecedent of the suffix of בגאותו, as also of the suffix of מימיו, is ימים
in v. 3b.
 Verse 4 expands on v. 3b. The order הרים ... ימים in v. 3b is reversed in
v. 4, מימיו ... הרים. Verse 4b is parallel to v. 3b:

|  |  |  |
|---|---|---|
| 3b | — | במוט הרים בלב ימים |
| 4b | — | ירעשו הרים בגאותו |

This indicates that the 'haughtiness' is that of the 'sea'. The
'haughtiness' of the sea is also mentioned in Ps. 89.10 (גאות הים) and Job
38.11 (גאון גליך) (cf. Ezek. 47.5).
 The imagery is that of the chaotic waters flooding the earth and ris-
ing above the mountains (cf. Ps. 104.6; Weiss 1961: 275-82). When the
defiant waters 'roar and foam', even the mountains, the symbol of stability and durability (Ps. 30.7-8), shake at the sea's arrogant swelling
and totter into its midst.

**v. 4d.** סלה—'SELAH'
The presence of 'SELAH' at the end of v. 4b in the MT seems out of place,
since in vv. 8 and 12 it appears after the refrains (cf. also Ps. 39.6, 12,
where it appears after the refrains). We follow the view of most com-

mentators that the refrain was accidently omitted by a copyist and that
*selāh* originally followed this refrain. For a comparable example of a
refrain-line which fell out by scribal mistake, compare Num. 24.4 with
v. 16.

v. 5b. קדש משכני עליון—'the holiest of the dwellings of the Most High'
This colon is a famous *crux interpretum*. The singular adjective קדש is
in construct followed by the plural construct noun משכני. Consequently,
some follow the variant readings. For example, Weiser (1962: 365) and
Kraus (1978: 494) follow the LXX: *qiddēš miškānô 'elyôn*, 'The Most
High has sanctified his dwelling'. Others suggest emendations. Kruse
(1949) breaks the first colon at עיר־אל, begins the second colon with הים
(revocalized to *hayyām*), and reads a piel *qiddēš*: 'The river, its
streams make glad the city of God; the sea sanctifies the dwellings of
the Most High'. Dahood (1965a: 280) attaches נהר פלגיו to v. 4b and reads
*sālāh*, 'heap up', for *selāh*. He follows the LXX in reading *qiddēš* and
understands the *yodh* of משכני as a third person singular suffix:

| | | |
|---|---|---|
| v. 4b | — | Though . . . the river and its channels |
| | | stand in a heap, |
| v. 5a | — | God brings happiness to his city, |
| v. 5b | — | the Most High sanctifies his habitation. |

Still others follow the MT but understand v. 5 as a nominal sentence.
Kissane (1953: 203) takes נהר as the subject and קדש משכני עליון as the
predicate, 'A river whose streams rejoice the city of God, is the sanctuary, the dwelling of the Most High'. Junker (1962) reverses the subject and predicate.

We, too, prefer to follow the MT but we believe that קדש משכני עליון is in
apposition to עיר אלהים. Both of these phrases are the direct object of ישמח
with נהר פלגיו serving as a double subject. There are three possible ways
to understand the phrase קדש משכני עליון.

1. *mškny* is an epexegetical genitive or a genitive of specification
   after the bound form of the adjective *qĕdōš*: 'the holy dwelling'
   (Williams 46; GKC 132c). A similar phenomenon occurs in Ps.
   65.5, *qĕdōš hêkālekā*, 'your holy temple'. In this case משכני is a
   plural of majesty or of extent or of amplification (GKC 124 a-f; cf.
   Ps. 43.3; 84.2; 132.5, 7, which however read משכנות).
2. *mškny* is an appositional genitive, 'the holy place which is the
   dwelling of the Most High' (Williams 42; GKC 130e). *qādōš* is an
   adjective used as a noun as in Isa. 57.15, 'holy place'. The plural,
   משכני, is explained the same way as above.
3. The bound structure, *qĕdōš miškĕnê*, expresses the superlative
   (Williams: 78; GKC 133g). This could be understood in one of two
   ways:

a. qĕdōš refers to the Holy of Holies in the Temple, 'the holiest place of/in the dwelling of the Most High' (Junker: 1962). The plural משכני is explained the same way as in no. 1 above.

b. qĕdōš refers to the temple which is the holiest sanctuary of all the other previous or contemporary dwellings of God. This would understand the plural משכני to be a numerical plural, 'the holiest of the dwellings of the Most High' (cf. Ps. 87.2).

The difficulty with the first two options is that they do not explain the distinction between the singular adjective קדש and the plural noun משכני. Psalm 65.5 is not a perfect parallel because it has a *singular* noun after the bound form of קדש. Therefore, we prefer the third option and take the bound structure as a superlative. We are unable to decide between options 3a and 3b since both are defensible.

The image of v. 5 contrasts with vv. 3-4. Whereas the unruly waters of chaos create fear and cause even stable mountains to shake and collapse, a gentle river with its channels gives joy to God's city and sanctuary.

The image of the river probably operates on several levels. (For a convenient summary of views, see Weiss 1961: 282-83.) A comparison with Isa. 8.6 suggests that the metaphor received its concrete historical inspiration from the Siloam conduit whose 'channels' would irrigate the valley below (Shanks 1985: 22-38, especially 34-35; McCarter 1985: 951-53). Or the allusion might be to the later tunnel of Hezekiah (Neve 1974: 244). There probably is also an allusion to Canaanite mythology in which El's throne is located at the head of two streams (Kraus 1978: 104-108). No doubt one should also think of the river of Eden (Gen. 2.10) and the eschatological river flowing from Jerusalem's temple (Ezek. 47.1-12; Joel 4.18; Zech. 14.8).

v. 6b. לפנות בקר—'at the break of dawn'
This phrase indicates the time at which the sun first appeared on the horizon (cf. Judg. 19.26-27; McCurley 1983: 41-43). The background of the phrase is Yahweh's victory over the enemies at the break of dawn (Isa. 17.12-14; Exod. 14.27; cf. Ziegler 1950).

v. 7. המו גוים מטו ממלכות—'Nations roar, kingdoms totter'.

נתן בקולו תמוג ארץ—'He gives forth his voice, the earth trembles'.
The first colon echoes vv. 3-4. Just as the waters of chaos 'roar' and cause fear, so do 'nations'. Just as mountains become unstable and 'totter into the heart of the seas', so human kingdoms are unstable and 'totter'. The B colon asserts that God's power is even more awesome and fearful. Whereas nations and kingdoms create fear and uneasiness by their roaring and instability, God causes the whole earth to tremble simply by uttering with his voice.

The reference of נתן בקולו is probably to God's thunder and theophany that cause the earth to tremble (cf. Pss. 29; 18.8, 14; 77.19; Joel 2.10-11; 4.16). A study of מוג reveals that it has more the sense of 'tremble' or 'shake' than of 'melt' (cf. Exod. 15.15; 1 Sam. 14.16; Nah. 1.5; Job 30.22; Ps. 107.26-27).

**v. 9a. לכו־חזו—'Come, see'**
This and the imperatives in v. 11a are addressed to the nations mentioned in v. 7. When speaking of Jerusalem the psalm uses the first person plural or the third person singular.

**v. 9b. אשר־שם שמות בארץ—'how he wrought devastations on the earth'**
אשר is used as a conjunction to introduce an object-clause after the imperatives of 9a (GKC 157). Its function is similar to that of כי in v. 11a. The phrase שׂים שמות does not occur elsewhere. However, similar phrases indicate that it means 'to lay waste, to make as a devastated wasteland' (cf. Isa. 13.9; Jer. 4.7; 18.16; 51.29; Joel 1.7; Zech. 7.14—שׂים לשמה; Josh. 8.28; Jer. 6.8; 10.22; Mic. 1.7; Mal. 1.3—שׂים שממה; Jer. 12.11; Zeph. 2.13—שׂים לשממה). It refers to the historical deeds of judgment which God has made against cities and nations in the past.

**v. 10. משבית . . . ישבר וקצץ . . . ישרף—'He is about to make cease . . . he will break and he will shatter . . . he will burn'**
The participle and three finite verbs are interpreted here as future (cf. Isa. 2.4; 9.4; Jer. 49.35; Ezek. 39.9f.; Hos. 2.20; Mic. 4.3).

**v. 10c. עגלות—'war wagons'**
עגלה regularly means 'wagon, cart'. If that is true here, it would refer to wagons used to carry weapons (Craigie 1983: 342). Also possible is Dahood's suggestion of 'shields', based on a Qumran text (1965a: 281).

## 2.2.4 *Structure*
### 2.2.4.1 *Versification.* Psalm 46 has 25 cola, 23 according to the MT. (We follow most commentators in restoring the refrain after v. 4b.) It consists of 12 verses (counting the extra refrain) which include 11 bicola and 1 tricolon. The tricolon (v. 10) occurs in the middle of the third stanza (vv. 9-11). The other two stanzas are vv. 2-4b and 5-7. Each stanza is followed by a refrain (vv. [4c-d], 8, 12).

| | |
|---|---|
| v.2 | Bicolon—אלהים and מאד are a word pair which bracket the verse (see under Notes). |
| v.3 | Bicolon—The phrases בהמיר ארץ in A and במוט הרים in B are parallel. Both are concessive clauses following the main clause לא־נירא in A. |

v. 4a-b    Bicolon—The third person plural prefixing verbs and the third person singular suffixes (בנאותו, מימיו) tie the two cola together.

v. 4c-d    Bicolon (reconstructed)—This bicolon consists of a chiasm: משׂגב־לנו parallel (b) עמנו ...(a) יהוה צבאות (b)... אלהי יעקב (a).

v. 5    Bicolon—The B colon is in apposition to עיר־אלהים in A. We count עיר־אלהים as one stress.

v. 6    Bicolon—The repetition of אלהים and the third person feminine suffixes (בקרבה ... יעזרה) tie the two cola together.

v. 7    Bicolon—The nouns ממלכות ... גוים in A and ארץ in B are paired.

v. 8    Bicolon—Same as v. 4c-d.

v. 9    Bicolon—The B colon is an object clause coordinated with לכו־חזו in the A colon. מפעלות in A and שמות in B are a word pair.

v. 10a-c    Tricolon—The nouns מלחמות in A, חנית ... קשׁת in B, and עגלות in C form word pairs. Also, the verbs in B and C are parallel.

v. 11    Bicolon—Verse 11b is to be taken as one colon similar to vv. 7a, b, 10b. The B colon is an object clause, with כי gapped, coordinated with הרפו ודעו in the A colon (cf. v. 9b). The first person pronoun אנכי in A and the first person verbs in B also connect the two cola.

v. 12    Bicolon—Same as v. 4c-d and v. 8.

### 2.2.4.2 *Stress and Syllable Counts*

| Verse | Syllables | | Totals | Stresses | | Totals |
|---|---|---|---|---|---|---|
| 2 | 9 + 9 | = | 18 | 4 + 4 | = | 8 |
| 3 | 9 + 9 | = | 18 | 4 + 4 | = | 8 |
| 4a-b | 7 + 9 | = | 16 | 3 + 3 | = | 6 |
| 4c-d | 8 + 9 | = | 17 | 3 + 4 | = | 7 |
| 5 | 13 + 7 | = | 20 | 4 + 3 | = | 7 |
| 6 | 9 + 10 | = | 19 | 3 + 4 | = | 7 |
| 7 | 9 + 8 | = | 17 | 4 + 4 | = | 8 |
| 8 | 8 + 9 | = | 17 | 3 + 4 | = | 7 |
| 9 | 9 + 7 | = | 16 | 4 + 3 | = | 7 |
| 10 | 10 + 9 + 7 | = | 26 | 4 + 4 + 3 | = | 11 |
| 11 | 12 + 9 | = | 21 | 4 + 4 | = | 8 |
| 12 | 8 + 9 | = | 17 | 3 + 4 | = | 7 |
| TOTALS | 12 verses/25 cola | | 222 | | | 91 |

### Distribution of Stresses

| Cola | Bicola | Tricola |
|------|--------|---------|
| 2″—0 | 3″3—1 | 4″4″3—1 |
| 3″—9 | 3″4—4 | |
| 4″—16 | 4″3—2 | |
| | 4″4—4 | |

The stress pattern seems to be a mixture of 4″4 and 3″3. In the first stanza there are two 4″4 bicola and one 3″3 bicolon (vv. 2-4b). In the second stanza the pattern varies. The first two verses are 4″3 (v. 5) and 3″4 (v. 6). Taken together these two verses are equivalent to one 4″4 and one 3″3. The third verse (v. 7) is 4″4. The third stanza is similar to the second. The first two verses (4″3—v. 9; 4″4″3—v. 10) when taken together are equivalent to one 4″4″4 tricolon and one 3″3 bicolon. The third verse is a 4″4 bicolon (v. 11). Thus each stanza has the equivalent of two 4″4 verses and one 3″3 verse. This mixture is then reflected in the refrains which are 3″4. The distribution of the colon-types and the total number of stresses also indicate a combination of 4″4 and 3″3 patterns. Nine cola are 3-stress and sixteen cola are 4-stress which indicates that the poem is not based on a consistent 3″3 or 4″4 pattern. The first two stanzas have 22 stresses, each of which is equivalent to two 4″4 verses plus one 3″3 verse (vv. 2-4b, 5-7). The third stanza has 26 stresses which is equivalent to one 4″4 bicolon plus one 4″4″4 tricolon plus one 3″3 bicolon (vv. 9-11). Put differently, the first and second stanzas each have four 4-stress cola and two 3-stress cola. The third stanza with its extra colon has five 4-stress cola and two 3-stress cola.

### Distribution of Syllables

| Syllables | | Cola | | Total Syllables |
|-----------|---|------|---|-----------------|
| 7 | × | 4 | = | 28 |
| 8 | × | 4 | = | 32 |
| 9 | × | 13 | = | 117 |
| 10 | × | 2 | = | 20 |
| 11 | × | 0 | = | 0 |
| 12 | × | 1 | = | 12 |
| 13 | × | 1 | = | 13 |
| TOTALS | | 25 | | 222 |

No colon is less than 7 or more than 13 syllables long. Most of the cola are 7–9 syllables (21 out of 25, 84%). Nine syllable cola are the most frequent (13). Seventeen cola are 9–13 syllables and eight cola are 7–8 syllables. The first stanza has five 9-syllable cola and one 7-syllable colon. The second stanza has four 9–13-syllable cola and two 7–8-syllable cola. The third stanza with its extra colon has five 9–12-syllable cola and two 7-syllable cola. These statistics also indicate that there is a mixture between 3-stress cola (= 7–8 syllables) and 4-stress cola (= 9–13 syllables) with four 9–13-syllable cola plus two 7–8-syllable cola in each stanza. Again the refrains match this imbalance with 8 syllables in the first colon and 9 syllables in the second colon.

2.2.4.3 *Strophes.* The strophes and stanzas coincide in this psalm. We will discuss them under the heading of Stanzas.

2.2.4.4 *Refrains.* The refrain occurs three times: vv. 4c-d (reconstructed), 8, and 12. The refrain in v. 12 is clearly isolated structurally. In v. 11 God speaks but in v. 12 the psalmist speaks of God in the third person. Verse 8 is also structurally isolated. Verse 9 begins with two imperatives addressed to the nations mentioned in v. 7, whereas v. 8 is a statement that 'Yahweh of hosts is *with us*'. The city is spoken of in the third person in vv. 5-6, but in v. 8 the first person plural is used. On this basis one can infer that the refrain is also isolated between v. 4a-b and v. 5. Only in the refrains the phrases יהוה צבאות and אלהי יעקב occur. Except for v. 9a, the refrains contain the only mention of *Yhwh*.

The refrains are identical in wording and spelling. It is noteworthy that the refrains contain the only chiastic bicola in the poem:

| | | |
|---|---|---|
| יהוה צבאות עמנו | — | a b |
| משׂגב־לנו אלהי יעקב | — | b a |

2.2.4.5 *Stanzas.* The structure of the poem is tripartite:

| | |
|---|---|
| vv. 2-4b | Stanza I |
| [v. 4c-d | Refrain] |
| vv. 5-7 | Stanza II |

| v. 8 | Refrain |
| vv. 9-11 | Stanza III |
| v. 12 | Refrain |

There are several features which unify each stanza. In the first stanza v. 3 is connected with v. 2 by syntax (על־כן in v. 3a) and by the first person plural reference (לנו—v. 2a; נירא—v. 3a). Verse 4 is joined to v. 3 by the suffixes on מימיו and בגאותו and the reversed order of ימים... הרים (v. 3b) to הרים... מימיו in v. 4. There is no inclusion.

In the second stanza the suffixes of בקרבה (v. 6a) and יעזרה (v. 6b) point back to עיר in v. 5a, thereby joining those two verses. The repetition of מוט unites vv. 6 and 7. There is no inclusion.

Inclusion unifies the third stanza however. Both vv. 9 and 11 begin with two plural imperatives and both end with בארץ. ארץ is also repeated in v. 10a. The subject of the verbs in v. 10 is יהוה, mentioned in v. 9a, which connects those two verses. The stanza ends with a change of speaker, Yahweh (cf. Watson 1984: 165).

In terms of verses, the first and second stanzas each consist of three bicola. The pattern is changed in the third stanza. It begins with a bicolon which is followed by a tricolon and it ends with a bicolon.

*Length of Stanzas*

| | vv. | bicola | tricola | cola | syllables | stresses |
|---|---|---|---|---|---|---|
| vv. 2-4b | 3 | 3 | 0 | 6 | 52 | 22 |
| vv. 5-7 | 3 | 3 | 0 | 6 | 56 | 22 |
| vv. 9-11 | 3 | 2 | 1 | 7 | 63 | 26 |

The first two stanzas are the same length. The third stanza has one extra colon. The syllable and stress counts confirm that the third stanza is one colon longer.

2.2.4.6 *Sections.* Psalm 46 is tripartite with the refrains completing each section: vv. 2-4d (v. 4c-d = reconstructed), 5-8, 9-12. Clearly the last verse of the psalm (v. 12) completes the third section. Also, v. 4c-d completes the first section. The use of the first person plural in the first refrain and in the first stanza ties those two together. So also v. 8 should be construed with

vv. 5-7 more than with the following on the basis of the analogy of the other two refrains.

*Length of Sections*

|  | *vv.* | *bicola* | *tricola* | *cola* | *syllables* | *stresses* |
|---|---|---|---|---|---|---|
| vv. 2-4d | 4 | 4 | 0 | 8 | 69 | 29 |
| vv. 5-8 | 4 | 4 | 0 | 8 | 73 | 29 |
| vv. 9-12 | 4 | 3 | 1 | 9 | 80 | 33 |

The first two sections are the same length, but the third section is one colon longer.

2.2.4.7 *Views of Structure.* Most scholars recognize the poem's tripartite structure (Kirkpatrick 1902: 255; Briggs 1906: 393; Segal 1935: 131; Kissane 1953: 202-203; Weiser 1962: 367; Beaucamp 1976: 201-202; Kraus 1978: 495; Craigie 1983: 343). Gerstenberger (1988: 190-95) is similar except that he puts v. 4 with vv. 5-7, which in our opinion is against the close connection between v. 4 and v. 3. Briggs, Segal, Beaucamp, and Gerstenberger distinguish structurally between the refrains and the stanzas. Four scholars offer other views.

P. van der Lugt (1980: 474) suggests that the poem consists of two stanzas: vv. 2-7; 8-12. The first stanza has two strophes: vv. 2-4, 5-7. The second stanza contains a refrain (v. 8), a strophe (vv. 9-11) and a refrain (v. 12). He counts verses and concludes that each stanza has six verses. There are problems with this proposal. There is no convincing reason why vv. 5-7 should be joined with vv. 2-4 to form the first half. Verse 7 can just as easily be joined with the second half. The גוים of v. 7 are addressed in vv. 9-11 and mentioned in v. 11b. Verses 5-7 have as much of a unified character as do vv. 8-12. Also, to arrive at a symmetry of length he divides vv. 8-12 into six verses by counting two verses in v. 10, which is doubtful.

Alden (1974: 26-27) outlines the psalm in one large chiastic structure:

| A. | v. 2 God is refuge |
|---|---|
| B. | v. 3 No fear |
| C. | vv. 4-5 God rules over natural calamities |
| D. | v. 6 God is here |
| E. | v. 7a Nations rage |
| E. | v. 7b God speaks |

> D.              v. 8 God is here
> C.              vv. 9-10 God rules over political calamities
> B.       v. 11 Be still
> A.   v. 12 God is refuge

This proposal is really quite forced. Why should the refrain in
v. 8 not be labelled 'A' as in v. 12? Verse 11 is not parallel to v. 3.
הרפו in v. 11a is an imperative addressed to the nations urging
them to 'desist' from their raging, quite unlike the first person
verb לא־נירא of v. 3.

Girard (1984: 373-76) offers a third option based on repeated
words and phrases. He argues for a bipartite structure with
v. 8 serving as a hinge: vv. 2-8; 8-12. Both halves are symmetrical. Verses 2-8 follow as ABCD/C⁻¹/DCBA structure and
vv. 8-12 follow an AB/C/BA structure. (Trublet–Aletti 1983: 37
has a similar view.)

| | |
|---|---|
| A | v. 2 (אלהים לנו מחסה ועז) |
| B | v. 3a (מור ארץ) |
| C | v. 3b (מים) |
| D | v. 4a (יהוה) |
| C⁻¹ | vv. 5-6 (בל־ימוט) |
| D | v. 7aα (המה) |
| C | v. 7aβ (מים) |
| B | v. 7b (מת ארץ) |
| A | v. 8 (משגב־לנו אלהים) |
| | |
| A | v. 8 (יהוה צבאות עמ משגב־לנו אלהי יעקב) |
| B | vv. 9-10a (impv. of הזה, ארץ, משביח 'make cease', ארץ) |
| C | v. 10b-c |
| B | v. 11 (רפה 'cease', impv. of ידע, ארץ) |
| A | v. 12 (same as v. 8) |

Girard's analysis does successfully display the interconnec-
tions which exist between the lines on the level of word repetition. However, he has overlooked a few repetitions which create difficulties for his schema. גוים is repeated in v. 7a (D) and
v. 11b (B); עזר is repeated in v. 2b (A) and v. 6b (C⁻¹); יהוה occurs
in v. 9a (B) as well as vv. 8 and 12 (A); and אלהים occurs in vv. 5-
6 (C⁻¹) and v. 11a (B) as well as vv. 2, 8, and 12 (A). It is also
dubious to connect v. 10a with v. 9 and to parallel משביח (v. 10a)
with הרפו in v. 11a. Girard's proposal is similar to that of van
der Lugt and has the same problem. Why include v. 7 with 2-6
instead of with 8-12?

Tsumura (1980) suggests a chiastic structure for vv. 2-8 which is similar to Girard's.

| | |
|---|---|
| A | 'God is our strong refuge' (2a) |
| B | Presence of a 'mighty Help(er)' (2b) |
| | THEREFORE 'we will not fear' (3a) |
| C | 'the earth' splits (3b) |
| D | 'The sea' shakes mountains (3c-4) |
| E | 'The river' gladdens the City (5) |
| E´ | 'God's Presence' helps the City (6) |
| D´ | 'God' shakes nations (7a-c) |
| C´ | 'The earth' melts (7d) |
| B´ | Presence of 'the LORD of Hosts' (8a) |
| A´ | 'God of Jacob is our stronghold' (8b) |

Generally he parallels v. 2 with v. 8, vv. 3-4 with v. 7, and v. 5 with v. 6. As such this is fairly convincing. However, there are a few difficulties. Verse 6 (E´) also parallels v. 2 (A-B) and v. 8 (A´-B´). (The root עזר occurs in v. 6b and v. 2b.) There is a contrast between the mountains 'tottering' in v. 3 (D—מוט) and the city's not 'tottering' in v. 6 (E´—מוט). There are close connections between vv. 2-4 and vv. 5-8, to be sure, but not in such a precise chiastic arrangement. Finally, vv. 9-11 also relate to the previous verses. Verse 7 connects with vv. 3-4. The statement 'I am exalted on the earth' in v. 11b hearkens back to vv. 2-4. In conclusion, none of the above chiastic arrangements is totally convincing.

## 2.2.5 *Repetition*

Before proceeding to the poem's thought progression, one should recognize the importance repetition has for this psalm. The poet likes to repeat a key word or concept five times. God is identified as a 'refuge' (v. 2a), 'protection' (v. 2a), and 'fortress' (vv. 4d [reconstructed], 8b, 12b) five times. The noun ארץ is repeated five times (vv. 3a, 7b, 9b, 10a, 11b). אלהים occurs five times in the stanzas—refrains not included—and is positioned at the beginning of the first stanza (v. 2a), the end of the last stanza (vv. 11a), and twice in the middle of the second stanza (vv. 6a, b), plus one occurrence in the genitive in v. 5a. Including the refrains and the other references to God, God is mentioned 14 times, a multiple of 7 which is common in the Psalter (אלהים—v. 2a, 4d [reconstructed], 5a, 6a, b, 8b, 11a, 12b; מאד—

v. 2b; יהוה—vv. 4c [reconstructed], 8a, 9a, 12a; עליון—v. 5b).
These repetitions summarize well the theme of the psalm: *God
is our refuge and the lord over the earth.*

### 2.2.6 *Thought Progression*
Psalm 46 is usually regarded as a Song of Zion (Sabourin 1974:
206-208). The psalm does exhibit close similarities with the
songs of Zion, but it lacks an introductory exhortation to praise
and any explicit reference to Zion (Craigie 1983: 342). Krinetzki (1962: 27), followed by Gerstenberger (1988: 194), prefers
to see it more as a collective Song of Confidence. The psalm
also has connections with prophetic literature (Neve 1974).
No one Gattung captures the tripartite character and the
thought progression of the Psalm. We will first focus on each
stanza and then on the movement of the whole poem.

2.2.6.1 *Stanzas*. The first stanza begins with the dominant
theme of the poem: God is our refuge and help in troubles.
Verses 3-4 derive the consequences from that thesis: therefore
we will not fear though the earth revert to chaos. Verses 3b-4
focus and specify what would happen if the earth would
change to chaos. The sea would rage in anger and cause even
the stable, strong, and enduring mountains to shake and slide
into it. But God is lord even over the sea. The community
expresses its confidence in God's ability to help. The use of the
first person plural dominates this stanza.

The second stanza continues the water imagery of the first
stanza. The city and sanctuary of God are gladdened by a
gently flowing river. Verse 6 leaves off the metaphorical language and expresses more straightforwardly why the city is
safe. Because God is in Jerusalem's midst, she cannot totter
but will be quickly helped by God. Verse 7 expands on v. 6 in
two ways. In contrast to Jerusalem's assured stability, other
kingdoms can totter. And if nations can defiantly roar causing
fear, how much more does the earth itself tremble in fear
when God simply utters with his voice. Verse 7 illustrates
God's power to help Jerusalem in the face of roaring nations.
The second stanza focuses on Jerusalem's gladness and
security because of God's presence. Not even the nations can

terrify the city. Here the psalmist speaks of Jerusalem in the third person.

The final stanza is addressed to the nations. The nations are exhorted to observe what Yahweh has done and how he has devastated other nations in the past. The nations are to be terrified by Yahweh's power. The mood changes to a more positive one in v. 10. Yahweh is the one who will end all war. Such a prospect should encourage the nations to acknowledge Yahweh gladly. Verse 10b focuses on the particulars which are subsumed under the general reference to wars in v. 10a. The stanza climaxes with a direct address to the nations from God. God calls the nations to cease from their warring plans and to acknowledge that Yahweh is God and Lord. The thrust of stanza III is universal. The focus is on Yahweh and the nations.

2.2.6.2 *Poem.* The poem exhibits a movement in three stages. Weiser (1962: 367) captures well the three-fold progression: 'creation–history–eschatology'. The first stanza emphasizes that God is a powerful fortress in the midst of the created order. Therefore, the community need not fear even if the world should revert to chaos. In the second stanza, God's presence historically located in Jerusalem is highlighted. This guarantees the city's stability and security in the face of warring nations and falling kingdoms. The third stanza has a universal outlook. The nations are summoned to behold the historical devastations which Yahweh has enacted in the past. The promise of a future universal peace is set forth. This leads up to v. 11 where God himself exhorts the nations to cease from their warring and to acknowledge Yahweh's present lordship. The third stanza is not totally dominated by eschatology, however, as Weiser's suggestion might intimate. Rather, the movement is from Yahweh's past deeds (v. 9) to his future actions (v. 10) to his present lordship (v. 11). Verse 11 serves as the poem's climax, since only here does God speak in the first person. God's lordship 'among the nations' (v. 11b) effectively summarizes the thrust of stanzas II-III, and his lordship 'on the earth' (v. 11b) summarizes stanza I. Thus the nations are urged to join in confessing Yahweh as Jerusalem does in the refrains and in v. 2.

There is also an interesting progression in terms of speakers. In stanza I the community in Jerusalem speaks in first person plural. In stanza II the psalmist speaks of Jerusalem in the third person. In the third stanza there is no mention of 'we' or of Jerusalem. Now the psalmist addresses the nations and speaks of their relationship with Yahweh. This culminates in Yahweh's direct address to the nations. Intersecting this progression comes the community's confession—'we' form—in the refrains.

The final bicola of the first and second stanzas are picked up by the first bicola of the second and third stanzas respectively. Verse 5 continues the water imagery of v. 4a-b. The 'river...its streams' in v. 5a contrasts with 'seas... its waters' in vv. 3b-4a. In contrast to the raging waters of chaos which terrify even the mountains, there is a gently flowing river which gladdens Jerusalem. Verse 9a picks up v. 7a. The nations which roar and fall are addressed in v. 9ff. The roaring nations are called to recognize how Yahweh has devastated nations in the past (v. 9). And, one might argue, the terrified and tottering kingdoms are encouraged to hope in Yahweh who will make all wars cease (v. 10).

One should also observe how stanza II picks up on the vocabulary of stanza I. In contrast to the mountains which 'totter' (מוט) and shake because of the sea's 'roaring' (המה) in vv. 3-4b, Jerusalem will not 'totter' (מוט) even though other kingdoms 'totter' (מוט) and 'roar' (המה) (vv. 6-7).

Finally, one should recognize how the refrain serves as a climax for each stanza. Although the refrain is identically repeated three times (v. 4c-d is reconstructed), each occurrence is accented and colored differently by its preceding stanza (cf. Weiser 1962: 366-74). The accent is on the phrase, 'the God of Jacob is a fortress for us' (v. 4d) in light of v. 2. In the face of the threat of chaos, the community will not fear because God is their protecting fortress. In the second refrain (v. 8), the stress falls on the prepositional phrase 'with us'. Verses 5-6 emphasize that God's dwelling is in the midst of the community. The third stanza causes the reader to focus on the phrase 'Yahweh of hosts' in v. 12. The nations are called to see the historical deeds and devastations that God has exacted against defiant nations. Verse 10 highlights that he is a conquering warrior who will eliminate war.

In conclusion, the poem's thought progression corresponds well with its tripartite structure.

## 2.3 Psalm 49

### 2.3.1 Text

| | Text | Syllables | | Total | Stresses |
|---|---|---|---|---|---|
| 1. | למנצח לבני־קרח מזמור (על־מות?) | | | | |
| 2a. | שמעו־זאת כל־העמים | 2+1+1+3 | = | 7 | 3 |
| b. | האזינו כל־ישבי חלד | 3+1+3+1 | = | 8 | 3 |
| 3a. | גם־בני אדם גם־בני־איש | 1+2+2+1+2+1 | = | 9 | 3 |
| b. | יחד עשיר ואביון | 1+2+3 | = | 6 | 3 |
| 4a. | פי ידבר חכמות | 1+3+2 | = | 6 | 3 |
| b. | והגות לבי תבונות | 3+2+3 | = | 8 | 3 |
| 5a. | אטה למשל אזני | 2+3+2 | = | 7 | 3 |
| b. | אפתח בכנור חידתי | 2+3+3 | = | 8 | 3 |
| 6a. | למה אירא בימי רע | 2+2+2+1 | = | 7 | 4 |
| b. | עון עקבי יסובני | 2+3+4 | = | 9 | 3 |
| 7a. | הבטחים על־חילם | 4+1+2 | = | 7 | 2 |
| b. | וברב עשרם יתהללו | 3+2+4 | = | 9 | 3 |
| 8a. | אח לא־פדה יפדה איש | 1+1+2+2+1 | = | 7 | 4 |
| b. | לא־יתן לאלהים כפרו | 1+2+3+2 | = | 8 | 3 |
| 9a. | ויקר פדיון נפשם | 3+2+2 | = | 7 | 3 |
| b. | וחדל לעולם | 3+3 | = | 6 | 2 |
| 10a. | ויחי־עוד לנצח | 2+1+2 | = | 5 | 2 |
| b. | לא יראה השחת | 1+2+2 | = | 5 | 2 |
| 11a. | כי יראה חכמים ימותו | 1+2+3+3 | = | 9 | 3 |
| b. | יחד כסיל ובער יאבדו | 1+2+2+3 | = | 8 | 4 |
| c. | ועזבו לאחרים חילם | 4+4+2 | = | 10 | 3 |
| 12a. | [קברם] בתימו לעולם | 3+3+3 | = | 9 | 3 |
| b. | משכנתם לדר ודר | 4+2+2 | = | 8 | 3 |
| c. | קראו בשמותם עלי אדמות | 3+3+2+3 | = | 11 | 4 |
| 13a. | ואדם ביקר בל־ילין | 3+2+1+2 | = | 8 | 3 |
| b. | נמשל כבהמות נדמו | 2+4+2 | = | 8 | 3 |
| 14a. | זה דרכם כסל למו | 1+2+1+2 | = | 6 | 3 |
| b. | ואחריהם בפיהם ירצו סלה | 4+3+2 | = | 9 | 3 |
| 15a. | כצאן לשאול שתו | 2+2+2 | = | 6 | 3 |
| b. | מות ירעם | 1+2 | = | 3 | 2 |
| c. | וירדו בם ישרים לבקר | 3+1+4+2 | = | 10 | 3 |
| d. | וצירם לבלות שאול מזבל לו | 3+3+2+3+1 | = | 12 | 4 |
| 16a. | אך־אלהים יפדה נפשי | 1+3+2+2 | = | 8 | 3 |
| b. | מיד־שאול כי יקחני סלה | 2+2+1+4 | = | 9 | 3 |
| 17a. | אל־תירא כי־יעשר איש | 1+2+1+2+1 | = | 7 | 3 |
| b. | כי־ירבה כבוד ביתו | 1+2+2+2 | = | 7 | 3 |
| 18a. | כי לא במותו יקח הכל | 1+1+3+2+2 | = | 9 | 3 |
| b. | לא־ירד אחריו כבודו | 1+2+2+3 | = | 8 | 3 |
| 19a. | כי־נפשו בחייו יברך | 1+2+3+3 | = | 9 | 3 |
| b. | ויודך כי־תיטיב לך | 4+1+2+1 | = | 8 | 3 |

| | | | | | |
|---|---|---|---|---|---|
| 20a. | תבוא עד־דור אבותיו | 2+1+1+3 | = | 7 | 3 |
| b. | עד־נצח לא יראו־אור | 1+1+1+2+1 | = | 6 | 3 |
| 21a. | אדם ביקר ולא יבין | 2+2+2+2 | = | 8 | 3 |
| b. | נמשל כבהמות נדמו | 2+4+2 | = | 8 | 3 |
| TOTALS | | 44 cola | | 340 | 132 |

### 2.3.2 *Translation*

1. For the musical director. Of the sons of Korah. A song (regarding death?).

2a. Hear this, all you peoples;
 b. listen, all you inhabitants of the passing world,
3a. both lowly and noble,
 c. rich and poor alike.
4a. My mouth shall speak wisdom,
 b. and the muttering of my heart understanding.
5a. I will incline my ear to a comparison;
 b. I will disclose my riddle with a lyre.
6a. Why should I fear in evil days,
 b. when the iniquity of those slandering me surrounds me,
7a. those who trust in their wealth
 b. and in the greatness of their riches boast?
8a. A brother a noble certainly cannot ransom;
 b. nor pay to God a ransom for himself.
9a. Though the ransom money for their life be considered valuable,
 b. it/he will cease forever.

10a. Let him continue to live forever!
 b. Will he not see the pit?
11a. For he should see that (even) the wise die.
 b. (Certainly) the fool and brute perish together,
 c. and leave to others their wealth.
12a. Graves are their homes forever,
 b. their dwelling places for generation after generation,
 c. though they invoked their own names on (their) lands.

### REFRAIN

13a. *Yes, a human in splendor does not remain through the night,*
 b. *but is like the cattle that perish.*

14a. This is the destiny of those who have foolish self-confidence,
 b. and that of their followers who delight in their words. SELAH
15a. Like sheep they are appointed for Sheol.
 b. Death will shepherd them.

    c. The upright will trample upon them in the morning.
    d. Their form is for consumption by Sheol from its palatial abode.
16a. But God will ransom my life
   b. from the hand of Sheol; surely he will take me. SELAH

17a. Do not fear that a noble becomes rich,
   b. that the glory of his house increases.
18a. For in his death he cannot take anything;
   b. his glory cannot descend after him.
19a. Though he blesses his soul in his lifetime,
   b. (saying), 'They praise you for you do good to yourself',
20a. it will go to the generation of his fathers
   b. who will never see the light.


## REFRAIN

21a. *A human in splendor, yes, does not understand,*
   b. *but is like the cattle that are dumb.*

## 2.3.3 *Translation Notes*

v. 1. עַל־מוּת—'regarding death'
Possibly עַל־מוּת at the end of 48.15 has been displaced from the title of Psalm 49.

v. 2b. יֹשְׁבֵי חָלֶד—'inhabitants of the passing world'
In its four other occurrences (Ps. 17.14; 39.6; 89.48; Job 11.17) the noun *ḥeled* carries the connotation of what is limited and time-bound (F. de Meyer 1979: 160). In Psalm 39.6 it is collocated with *ḥādēl*, *yāmay*, and *hebel*. In Ps. 89.48 it is parallel to *šāwě*', 'remember how I am *temporal*, for what *vanity* you have created all the sons of man'. The same connotation applies in Job 11.17 as can be seen by its parallel line: 'Brighter than noonday (your) *passing life* will rise, (its) darkness will be like the morning'. 'Already here there is an allusion to the solution (of the riddle); a clue is given to the attentive reader' (F. de Meyer 1979: 160). The rich are inhabitants of a passing world.

v. 3a. גַּם־בְּנֵי אָדָם גַּם־בְּנֵי־אִישׁ—'both lowly and noble'
The use of גַּם. . .גַּם and the contrast made in v. 3b indicate that there is a contrast here. בְּנֵי־אִישׁ refers to the noble in conformity with the usage of אִישׁ in v. 8 and v. 17 (cf. Ps. 62.10; *TWAT* I.684).

v. 6b. עֲקֵבַי עָוֹן—'when the iniquity of those slandering me'
*ăqēbay* is understood here as a verbal adjective formed from the verb עָקַב (BDB). It is also possible to follow Origen, *akobbai* = *'ăqubay* (cf. Jer. 17.9), or a proposed qal participle *'ōqěbay*. The result in transla-

tion would be the same. Dahood (1965a: 297, 251-52) demonstrates that
עקב can have the nuance 'to slander' on the basis of Jer. 9.3 and Ps.
89.52. However, the Ugaritic evidence that he marshalls should be
removed (see Craigie 1983: 319 and the literature cited there). This
nuance fits well here since the psalm discusses the arrogant rich who
would no doubt mock the pious poor.

Casetti (1982: 177f., 293) translates עקבי עון as 'die Schuld meiner Ver-
gangenheit' and argues that v. 6 quotes the words of 'those who trust in
their wealth' (v. 7), and that it expresses the confidence of the arrogant
rich, 'Why need I fear?' However, v. 17 indicates that the *psalmist* and
the pious are the ones tempted to 'fear'. Also, the reader expects the
psalmist to be the speaker in v. 6 following the first person singular of
vv. 4-5. Such an abrupt change of speakers in v. 6 would be indicated in
the text. The other occurrences of the first person singular are the
suffixes in v. 16 which refer to the psalmist, as Casetti acknowledges.

v. 6b. יסובני—'surrounds me'
Casetti (1982: 176) argues convincingly that there is no need to emend
the singular to a plural verb. עון is often the subject of finite verbs (cf.
Prov. 5.22; 1 Sam. 28.10; Ps. 40.13; 2 Kgs 7.9; Isa. 6.7; 64.5; Ps. 38.5;
Ezra 9.6; also cf. Ps. 32.10b).

v. 7a. הבטחים על-חילם—'those who trust in their wealth'
Verse 7 clarifies the identity of those mentioned in v. 6b. They are the
arrogant, self-sufficient, unbelieving rich (cf. Pss. 52.9; 62.11; 73.12).

v. 8a. אח לא-פדה יפדה איש—'A brother a noble certainly cannot ransom'
The direct object את is placed forward for emphasis. איש refers to the
noble rich as in v. 3a and v. 17a. There is no need to read with a few
manuscripts *'ak* and then to emend the qal *yipdeh* to a niphal
*yippādeh* as many commentators do (Weiser 1962: 384-85; Kraus 1978:
517; Craigie 1983: 356-57). Nor is it necessary to understand *'aḥ* as an
interjection (*contra* Dahood 1965a: 298; F. de Meyer 1979: 158; Casetti
1982: 188-90). The MT makes perfect sense as it stands with איש as the
subject, יפדה as a transitive qal, and את as the direct object (van der
Ploeg 1963: 147-48; Gross 1972). The sequence of אח ... איש occurs quite
often (2 Kgs 7.6; Isa. 3.6; 9.18; 19.2; Jer. 13.14; 23.35; Ezek. 24.23; 33.30;
cf. Gross 1972: 67-68).

v. 8b. לא-יתן לאלהים כפרו—'Nor pay to God a ransom for himself!'
The antecedent of the suffix of כפרו is איש at the end of the previous
colon.

v. 9a. ויקר פדיון נפשם—'Though the ransom money for their life be considered valuable'
We follow Casetti (1982: 202) in understanding v. 9a as a concessive
clause. *wĕyēqar* is a qal prefixing form written defectively. Here the

meaning of the verb is 'to be honored, considered valuable in the eyes of others' (cf. Isa. 43.4; Zech. 11.13; 1 Sam. 26.21; 18.30; 2 Kgs 1.13-14; Ps. 72.14). The sense is: 'even though the money he lays down be considered great'.

v.9b. וחדל לעולם—'it/he will cease forever'
This phrase is the main clause following the previous concessive clause. The basic meaning of חדל is 'to cease' or 'to withdraw' and can be translated either actively or passively (*TWAT* II.748). Since this 'riddle' contains much irony, it might be best to understand this phrase as polysemous. The surface meaning is to take פדיון, the subject of יקר, as the subject of חדל. In that case it would yield the meaning, 'the ransom money will be lacking or fail forever' (cf. Job 19.14; Prov. 10.19). The deeper meaning is that 'he, the man of v.8, will cease living forever' (cf. Ps. 39.5; Job. 3.17; 14.7, 10; cf. *TWAT* II.753).

v.10a. ויחי־עוד לנצח—'Let him continue to live forever!'
This colon is difficult. There are basically three options (for a survey of views, see Casetti 1982: 196, 202-204).

1. Construe v.10a with 9b, 'he will desist forever from continuing to live' (e.g. Calès 1936: 496).
2. Verse 10a is a purpose clause to be construed with v.8 and v.9 is a parenthesis, 'Nor can he pay to God a ransom for him... so that he might continue to live forever' (so Kraus 1978: 516-17; Craigie 1983: 356-57). A simple *waw* plus a precative often introduces a purpose clause in Hebrew (Williams 518).
3. Understand the verb as a jussive after a simple waw, 'Let him continue to live forever!' (Freedman, p.c.). Sometimes a jussive occurs after a simple waw when purpose is not intended (Williams 185).

The first option is not grammatically possible. When חדל means 'to desist from an activity' or 'to stop doing something', it is followed by a *min* or an infinitive (BDB). The second option is possible grammatically, but it seems too complicated. We prefer option three because it is the simplest and because it corresponds to the usage of *wîḥî* elsewhere. Psalm 69.33 reads, 'Let your hearts revive' (*wîḥî lĕbabkem*), and Ps. 72.15 reads, 'Let (the king) live' (*wîḥî*). We understand v.10a as a mocking wish, a taunt, 'Let him continue to live forever (if he can)!'

v.10b. לא יראה השחת—'Will he not see the pit?'
This colon cannot be a continuation of the previous wish since יראה is an imperfect, not the apocopated jussive form. We take it as a question which is not introduced by the interrogative particle (GKC 150a). The following colon indicates that it is a question, 'Will he not see the pit?

## 2. The Texts: Psalm 49    73

(Yes, he will see it.) *For* he should see that even the wise die.' (So also
Casetti 1982: 202-205.)

v. 11b. יאבדו—'perish'
Possibly there is a contrast between ימות in v. 11a and יאבדו. Whereas the
wise 'die', the foolish rich and the stupid 'perish' forever. The latter
and not the former receive the focus of the following cola.

v. 11c. ועזבו לאחרים חילם—'and leave to others their wealth'
The subject of the verb and the antecedent of the pronominal suffix is
the 'fool and the brute' of v. 11b, since the focus is on the wealthy. (Cf.
v. 12c).

v. 12a. קברם—'graves'
We follow LXX τάφοι and read *qĕbārim*, written defectively, on the
assumption that a metathesis has occurred. Although *qereb* (MT) can
mean 'inward thought' (Ps. 5.10; 64.7), it is never followed by indirect
discourse, which would yield 'their inward thought is that their
homes are forever'.

v. 12c. קראו בשמותם עלי אדמה—'though they invoked their own names on
(their) lands'.
The idiom *šēm niqrā"l*, 'name has been called upon' (2 Sam. 12.28; 1
Kgs 8.43; Isa. 4.1; Amos 9.12) seems to be the basis of this phrase. The
idiom refers to ownership. The phrase then means that the rich claim
ownership of many lands. This understanding fits well with v. 11c,
and with v. 12a-b: though the rich claimed to own in their own name
many lands, they will leave their wealth to others and graves will be
their permanent homes.
However, possibly the phrase is polysemous here. The idiom קרא בשם,
'to invoke the name of', is usually used of invoking Yahweh's name
(Gen. 4.26; 12.8; 13.4; 1 Kgs 18.24; Isa. 41.25; 64.6; etc.). In contrast, the
wicked rich invoke their own names. They put their trust in themselves rather than in Yahweh (v. 7; cf. Dahood 1965a: 299 and Casetti
1982: 78-82; Dahood, However, understands the subject of the verb to be
their heirs and Casetti considers it impersonal, 'others').

v. 13a. ואדם ביקר—'Yes, a human in splendor'
We take the *waw* to be emphatic (Williams no. 438; Casetti 1982: 294).
The noun *yĕqar* is polysemous. (Cf. F. de Meyer 1979: 159). It means
both 'preciousness, wealthiness' and 'honor, high status' (BDB, 430).
*bîqār* also contains a sound play on the noun *bāqār*, 'cattle'. Dahood
(1965a: 299) translates יקר 'the Mansion' and interprets it as a name of
the nether world. To do this he understands בל in the affirmative sense
'indeed'. However, the parallel in v. 21 indicates that בל is a negative
(on Dahood's view, see Casetti 1982: 86-87).

**v. 13b. נדמו—'that perish'**
Since the verb נדמו is parallel to ילין, it is the niphal of דמה II (or III?)
which sometimes means 'to be destroyed, perish' (cf. Jer. 47.5; Hos.
10.7, 15; Obad. 5; Zeph. 1.11; *TWAT* II.280-81). It makes a fitting parallel to ילין, since such 'perishing' happens at night (Isa. 15.1; Hos. 10.15;
Obad. 5; cf. Casetti 1982: 93).

**v. 14a. כסל—'foolish self-confidence'**
The noun *kēsel* occurs five other times with this meaning. In Ps. 78.7
and Prov. 3.26 it means 'confidence' that is in God. In Job 8.14 it
denotes 'self-confidence' and in Job 31.24 'confidence' is put in gold.
However, the connotation in Eccl. 7.25 is that of 'folly', parallel to *sik-
lût*. Our translation 'foolish self-confidence' attempts to capture the
above meanings, especially since *kēsel* is colored by *kĕsîl* in v. 11b. The
translation 'foolish self-confidence' should be understood to include
confidence in their riches as in v. 7 and Job 31.24.

**v. 14b. ואחריהם בפיהם ירצו—'and that of their followers who delight in
their words'**
The preposition plus suffix (אחריהם) could indicate place, i.e. those who
walk behind them, or time, i.e. their successors (BDB). We take it both
ways and thus translate it, 'their followers'.

**v. 15a. שתו—'they are appointed'**
The verb שתו, a by-form of שית (GKC no. 67ee), is used in an intransitive
sense, 'to be set, appointed' (cf. Ps. 3.7; Isa. 22.7; Hos. 6.11; Casetti
1982: 118-19). The subject of the verb is both the fools and their followers
mentioned in v. 14.

**v. 15b. מות ירעם—'Death will shepherd them'**
In contrast to Yahweh the 'shepherd' (Ps. 23), Death will shepherd
them. The verb may suggest also that Death will 'feed upon them' (cf.
v. 15d; Ps. 80.14; Ezek. 34.10; cf. F. de Meyer 1979: 161).

**v. 15c. וירדו בם ישרים לבקר—'The upright will trample upon them in the
morning'**
This is a notoriously difficult colon. Among the various possibilities,
five are worth mentioning. (For a survey of views, see Casetti 1982: 132-
40.)

1. Follow the MT and translate, 'The upright will trample upon
   them in the morning'. The verb רדה is taken in the sense 'to tread,
   trample' as in Joel 4.13. The idea is that the upright trample upon
   the wicked's graves (cf. Mal. 3.21 and possibly Hab. 3.19c). The
   temporal reference, 'in the morning', is in contrast with the verb
   ילין in v. 13a. Whereas the wicked rich do 'not remain through the
   night' (בל-ילין, v. 13a), the righteous triumph over them 'in the
   morning' (see also Exod. 34.25; Deut. 16.4; Ps. 30.6; and 1 Chron.

9.27 where לין and בקר are contrasted). Often in the Hebrew Bible 'the morning' is the time of reversal from suffering to good fortune and vindication (Ziegler 1950: 281-88).

2. Follow the MT and translate, 'they will rule over them, being docile, in the morning'. The subject of the plural verb וירדו is 'Death' and 'Sheol' mentioned in v. 15a-b. Both 'Death' and 'Sheol' are personified in this verse, 'Death' as a shepherd in v. 15b and 'Sheol' as a consumer in v. 15d, and thus they serve as an appropriate subject of the verb רדה (in Ezek. 34.4 false *shepherds* 'rule'—רדה). ישרים is in apposition to the suffix of בם. Casetti (1982: 136-38) argues that ישרים designates the wicked rich who 'walk straight on the way', allowed to turn neither to the right nor to the left as sheep being shepherded by Death. (One should compare especially 1 Sam. 6.12 as well as Prov. 9.15; 29.27; Ps. 37.14; and Mic. 2.7.) The temporal reference, 'in the morning', is understood as in option one above. Or possibly one should repoint to *lĕbāqār*, 'as cattle' (so Dahood 1965a: 300). Then the piont would be that they go 'straight as cattle' under the rulers of Death and Sheol (*bāqār* would be parallel with *ṣōʾn* in v. 15a, a common word pair).

3. Emend *bām yĕšārîm* to *bĕmêšārîm* and translate, 'They will rule (them) with equity in the morning'. The subject of the verb is 'Death' and 'Sheol' as in option two above. The suffix of ירעם in the previous colon is ellipsed. The preposition ב plus noun מישרים is used ironically. Usually this prepositional phrase applies to the way in which Yahweh judges the world, i.e. 'with equity' (Pss. 9.9; 96.10; 98.9). Just as 'Death will shepherd them' instead of Yahweh, so also Death and Sheol will rule them 'with equity' instead of Yahweh. (A similar phrase occurs in Ezek. 34.4, 'with force you [the false shepherds] have ruled them and with harshness'.) Again, *labbōqer* could be emended to *lĕbāqār*.

4. Emend *wayyirdû* to *wayyērĕdû* and *labbōqer* to *lĕbāqār* and translate, 'The upright will descend with them as cattle'. 'As cattle' is parallel to 'as sheep' and 'will descend' is parallel to 'are set for Sheol' in v. 15a. Or one could keep *labbōqer*, 'The upright will descend with them in the morning'. The point of the colon is that even the 'upright' go to Sheol. How much more certainly will the wicked go there (cf. Isa. 34.7; Jer. 50.27).

5. Emend *wayyirdû* to *wayyērĕdû*; *bām yĕšārîm* to *bĕmêšārîm*; and *labbōqer* to *lĕbāqār* and translate 'They will descend straightway as cattle' (so Dahood 1965a: 300 except that he translates *bĕmêšārîm* 'into his gullet'). The subject of the verb is the wicked rich of v. 15a. The use of במישרים is similar to that of Prov. 23.31, '(wine) goes down smoothly' (במישרים יהלך), i.e. it flows smoothly, without difficulties. Again, one could keep MT's *labbōqer*.

It is difficult to decide among these five alternatives. The fifth option is doubtful because it emends *wayyirdû* to *wayyērĕdû*, and yet *yērēd* is written correctly in v. 18. The fourth option is also weak because the four cola of v. 15 describe the destiny of the fools and their followers as introduced in v. 14. That the upright die is not in view in this context, although it is certainly true. Also, the idiom ב ירד is never used to indicate accompaniment, 'to descend along with others'. This is expressed by ירד עם/את (e.g. Gen. 42.38; 46.4; 1 Sam. 26.6; Isa. 34.7; Ezek. 31.17; etc.). The third option is weak because the phrase רדה במישרים never occurs elsewhere. The difficulty with the second option is its understanding of ישרים. It seems forced to argue that ישרים indicates that the wicked rich like sheep are 'docile' and are forced to 'walk straight' under the rule of Death and Sheol. This would be indicated by phrases such as ישר דרך (Prov. 29.27), ישרי דרך (Ps. 37.14) and ישר הלך (Mic. 2.7). Also, it is doubtful that Sheol and Death would be the subject of the plural verb.

We therefore prefer to follow the MT in option one. The point of the colon, then, is that the foolish rich and their followers do not 'remain through the night' (v. 13a) but become corpses upon whom the upright trample in the morning. This idea is also picked up in v. 20b, 'who will never see the light (of day)'.

**v. 15d.** וצירם לבלות שאול.—'Their form is for consumption by Sheol'. וצירם is difficult. The *Kethib* is *wĕṣîrām* but the *Qere* reads *wĕṣûrām*. There are six possibilities:

1. Emend to *wĕṣûrātām* from the noun *ṣûrâ*, 'and their form, design' (Ezek. 43.11; cf. Syriac).
2. Emend to *wĕyiṣrām* from the noun *yēṣer*, 'and their shape'.
3. Follow the *Kethib* from the noun *ṣîr* IV, 'and their image', in the sense of the human body's form. This sense is related to the verb יצר, 'to shape, form' which is used in connection with the human body in Isa. 44.2; 49.5; etc. (Dahood 1965a: 300-301). In Isa. 45.16 *ṣîr* is used with *ḥārāš*, 'craftsman', and denotes 'idol'. It might also be a wordplay on *ṣîr* III, 'their pangs', alluding to the pangs they will experience in Sheol.
4. Follow the *Qere* from the noun *ṣûr* I, 'and their rock' (Casetti 1982: 145-46). Casetti interprets the *waw* plus noun as a question, 'und ihr Fels?' The noun refers to God (often designated as a 'rock') and the suffix 'their' includes all humans (v. 11). He further interprets the following noun שאול as the direct object of לבלות and translates, 'er [God] soll bereit sein die Scheol zu zermürben, von der Wohnung aus, die er hat'. He understands the sentence as asserting the absence of God in the face of death (pp. 147-53). To paraphrase: 'and their God? He should intervene from his lofty abode and destroy death when men face it. But he does not. Where

is he?' This amounts to a radical re-interpretation which is in line with his thesis that vv. 11-15 form an original pessimistic psalm to which the other verses were added later. There are two major difficulties with his interpretation. First, the antecedent of the suffix of צירם is the wicked rich mentioned in v. 14. These arrogant rich are godless; they trust in themselves and their wealth (vv. 7, 11c-12, 13a, 14a), not in Yahweh, the Rock. Second, the verb בלה 'to wear out, consume', is a most inappropriate word to express such a destruction of Sheol, a concept nowhere expressed in the Hebrew Bible (Delitzsch 1871: 117-18).

5. Understand *ṣûr* as an unattested noun from the verb צור III, 'to cast (metal)', yielding 'and their form' (cf. option 1 above).

6. Emend to *yĕṣûrām* the qal passive participle of יצר, 'and their shape', i.e. what has been shaped. Compare Job 17.7 where *yĕṣuray* seems to designate 'limbs'. Confusion of *yodh* and *waw* occurs frequently (cf. Freedman 1976a: 162-63).

The first possibility is weak because of the *masculine* singular suffix of the following לו. The second and the sixth are doubtful emendations, the fourth was rejected above, and the fifth is an unattested noun. The third possibility seems the most probable.

The sequence—noun plus *lĕ* plus the infinitive—implies a self-understood form of היה (GKC 114k[2]). The verb בלה means 'to consume, waste away' (Dahood 1965a: 301). 'Sheol' is the subject of the verb. Verse 15d is parallel to v. 15b: 'Death shepherds them' // 'Sheol consumes their form'.

v. 15d. מזבל לו—'from its palatial abode'
In Hab. 3.11 זבלה (read *zĕbulōh*) designates the palatial abode of the moon, Yahweh's divine mythological enemy. In its other three occurrences זבל designates Yahweh's palatial abode (1 Kgs 8.13; 2 Chron. 6.2; Isa. 63.15). In Ps. 49.15d it is used ironically to refer to Sheol's (and Death's) palatial abode. Sheol/ Death will become the wicked's god who will 'consume' them and 'shepherd' them 'from its palatial abode' (on the Ugaritic usage of *zbl*, see *TWAT* II.531-32).

v. 16b. כי יקחני—'surely he will take me'
The function of the particle כי is emphatic (Dahood 1965a: 301; Aejmelaeus 1986a: 208). The verb לקח with God as subject is used similarly in Gen. 5.24; 2 Kgs 2.3, 5, 9; and Ps. 73.24. The first two refer to an 'assumption' before death. The latter does not specify the manner of God's 'taking' the psalmist but it does occur *after* death: ואחר כבוד תקחני, 'and afterwards you will take me (to) glory'.

Ps. 49.16 also does not specify *how* God will 'ransom' and 'take' the psalmist. But this deliverance from Sheol does seem to occur after the psalmist's death. In v. 11a the psalmist probably would have included himself with the חכמים who die, since he identifies himself as 'wise' in v. 4a—חכמות. Also, the close relationship between Psalms 49 and 73 in other respects indicates that 49.16 should be interpreted in the light of 73.24.

Therefore, the contrast Psalm 49 makes between the pious poor and the wicked rich is not that the former do not die but the latter do. Rather, the contrast consists in this: the former die but are delivered from the power (*yad*) of Sheol; whereas the latter 'perish' in Sheol (v. 11b), 'cease forever' (v. 9b), have graves as their eternal homes (v. 12a-b), are destroyed like cattle (v. 13), have death as their shepherd (v. 15b), are consumed by Sheol (v. 15d), and 'never see the light' (v. 20b). What the latter cannot do (vv. 8-9), God can do for the former (v. 16). (For a survey of views, see Casetti 1982: 209-30.)

v. 17b. כבוד ביתו—'the glory of his house'
The noun כבוד denotes 'wealth' as well as its usual meaning of 'glory, honor' (Dahood 1965a: 302). Compare יקר in vv. 13a and 21a.

v. 19a. כי־נפשו בחייו יברך—'Though he blesses his soul in his lifetime'
כי introduces a 'circumstantial' clause which is translated concessively here (Aejmelaeus 1986a: 196-99). The piel of ברך is never construed with נפש elsewhere. The normal construction for reflexives is with the hithpael. The piel is employed here to form a contrast with the usual idiom 'to bless God'. Instead of blessing God 'in his lifetime' (Pss. 63.5; 104.33; 146.2), the wicked rich blesses himself (Casetti 1982: 244-45.)

v. 19b. ויודך כי־תיטיב לך—'(saying), "They praise you for you do good to yourself"'
We follow Casetti (1982: 245-47) who demonstrates that this phrase is a parody of a hymn:

> Der Reiche, der sich selbst in v. 19a wie einen Gott pries, sieht sich auch von den andern wie ein Gott angebetet. Dies drückt er in einem Satz aus, der nichts anderes ist, als die Parodie auf einen Hymnus (p. 246)

The line is in direct discourse expressing how he blesses himself. The subject of the verb יודך is the rich man's followers who delight in his words (v. 14b). The masculine suffix *kā* is parallel to נפש as in Ps. 3.3. The line parodies the common phrase 'praise Yahweh for he is good' (Pss. 106.1; 107.1; 118.1, 29; etc.). Instead of asserting 'for God does good to you' (cf. Exod. 1.20; Josh. 24.20; Judg. 17.13; 1 Sam. 25.31; Ps. 125.4), they admire how he does good to himself. Verse 19 thus expands on v. 7 (יתהללו).

v. 20a. תבוא—'it will go'
The feminine noun נפש is the subject of the verb.

v.21a. יבין ולא—'yes, does not understand'
The *waw* is emphatic as in v. 13a (Dahood 1965a: 303). Commentators
who emend יבין to ילין as in v. 13a miss an important aspect of the
'comparison' and 'riddle' (v. 5). The 'riddle' is implied in the refrains
of v. 13 and in v. 21: how are the wicked rich like the cattle they own?
The similarity is in two respects. They are slaughtered like cattle (v. 13)
and they lack understanding like cattle (v. 21). (Perdue 1974, offers a
helpful study of the riddle. However, he emends the text unnecessarily
at places.) The comparison between people and ignorant beasts is also
made elsewhere (cf. בער, v. 11b; Pss. 32.9; 73.22; 94.8a; Job 35.11; Isa.
1.3; etc.).

Verses 13a and 21a form an interesting sound pair (Berlin 1985:
124):

| | | |
|---|---|---|
| *bal yālîn* | — | v. 13 |
| *lōʼ yābîn* | — | v. 21 |

v.21b. נדמו—'that are dumb'
The niphal of דמה II carries the nuance 'to be dumb, speechless' in certain texts (cf. Isa. 6.5; Hos. 4.6; *TWAT* II.281). This nuance fits well
here (cf. v. 13b above. Perdue 1974: 538-39, recognizes this shift in
meaning from v. 13b, though he emends to *nādammû*).

### 2.3.4 *Structure*

2.3.4.1 *Versification.* Psalm 49 is based on a 'non-alphabetic'
acrostic structure with 44 cola (22 × 2; see Freedman 1986). It
has 21 verses according to our versification, with 19 bicola and
2 tricola (20 verses according to the MT's versification). The
two tricola conclude the first stanza (vv. 11, 12).

v. 2     Bicolon—The two imperatives and two vocatives
         are parallel to each other. The syllable count is 15
         which leads us to count זאת in our stress count—
         3″3.

v. 3     Bicolon—בני אדם parallels אביון and בני איש parallels
         עשיר to form a chiasm. Because the syllable count
         is 15 we count גם־בני־איש as one in our stress
         count— 3″3.

v. 4     Bicolon—The verb is gapped in B, פי parallels לבי
         and הכמה parallels תבונות, with the last two form-
         ing final rhyme.

v. 5     Bicolon—Both cola begin with a first person sin-
         gular prefixing verb. משל and חידתי are a word
         pair. Both cola exhibit initial alliteration and final
         rhyme.

**v. 6** Bicolon—The two cola are joined by syntax with the main clause in A and a temporal clause in B. רע and עון form a word pair.

**v. 7** Bicolon—הבמחים parallels יהללו and חילם parallels עשרם in a chiastic arrangement.

**v. 8** Bicolon—The subject (איש) is gapped in B. The verb יפרה in A parallels the phrase—יתן לאלהים—in B. The suffix on כפרו in B has איש in A as its antecedent. The object-verb//verb-object sequence forms a chiasm.

**v. 9** Bicolon—Syntax joins the two cola with A as a concessive clause and B as the main clause. Both cola exhibit final rhyme (*-ām*).

**v. 10** Bicolon—The two cola are semantically antithetical: to 'continue to live forever' is the positive way of saying to 'not see the pit'.

**v. 11** Tricolon—The third person plural prefixing verbs (ימותו ... יאבדו), located in final position in cola A and B, form a word pair. *Waw* begins colon C. The subject of עזבו in C is כסיל ובער in B.

**v. 12** Tricolon—The initial קברם (read *qĕbārim* instead of MT *qirbām*; see under Notes) is gapped in B; בתימו is parallel to משכנתם; and לעולם parallels לדר ודר. The initial *qop* in C alliterates with the initial *qop* in A. The third person plural suffix on בשמוחם in C matches the suffixes in B and A.

**v. 13** Bicolon—אדם in A is the subject of ילין in A and נמשל in B. *bîqār* in A constitutes a sound play with the noun *bāqār* ('cattle'). The latter forms a word pair with בהמות ('cattle') in B.

**v. 14** Bicolon—The first two words in A are gapped in B. *Waw* begins the B colon. The suffixes in B have the same antecedent as the suffixes in A.

**v. 15a-b** Bicolon—The noun צאן ('sheep') in A and the verb ירעם ('will shepherd them') in B are semantically paired. שאול in A and מות in B are a word pair. The antecedent of the suffix on ירעם in B is the subject of the verb שתו in A.

**v. 15c-d** Bicolon—*Waw* begins each colon. Colon A and colon B are semantically sequential: 'the upright trample upon them... their form is for consumption by Sheol'. The antecedent of the suffix on צירם in B is the same as that of בם in A.

| | |
|---|---|
| v. 16 | Bicolon—אלהים in A is the subject of יפדה in A and יקחני in B, and the latter two verbs form a word pair. Both cola have final rhyme (-*î*). We follow BHS in beginning the second colon with כי, an example of enjambement. |
| v. 17 | Bicolon—The כי clauses in A and B form object clauses after the initial vetitive אל תירא. The prefixing verbs in A and B parallel each other. The antecedent of the suffix on ביתו in B is איש in A. |
| v. 18 | Bicolon—The negative לא is repeated. The third person singular suffixes on אחריו כבודו in B match the suffix on במותו in A. The two words in final position (הכל ... כבודו) represent a 'general-specific' sequence. |
| v. 19 | Bicolon—The second colon, initiated with a *waw*, consists of the quote by which 'he blesses himself' (see under Notes). כי is repeated. The verbs (ברך, ידה) form a word pair. |
| v. 20 | Bicolon—The final word in A (אבותיו) is the subject of the verb יראו in B. עד is repeated. |
| v. 21 | Bicolon—This bicolon is the same as v. 13 except that the initial *waw* in v. 13 is internal in v. 21a and that בל־ילין in v. 13a has been altered to לא יבין in v. 21a. |

### 2.3.4.2 *Stress and Syllable Counts*

| Verse | Syllables | | Totals | Stresses | | Totals |
|---|---|---|---|---|---|---|
| 2 | 7 + 8 | = | 15 | 3 + 3 | = | 6 |
| 3 | 9 + 6 | = | 15 | 3+ 3 | = | 6 |
| 4 | 6 + 8 | = | 14 | 3+ 3 | = | 6 |
| 5 | 7 + 8 | = | 15 | 3 + 3 | = | 6 |
| 6 | 7 + 9 | = | 16 | 4 + 3 | = | 7 |
| 7 | 7 + 9 | = | 16 | 2 + 3 | = | 5 |
| 8 | 7 + 8 | = | 15 | 4 + 3 | = | 7 |
| 9 | 7 + 6 | = | 13 | 3 + 2 | = | 5 |
| 10 | 5 + 5 | = | 10 | 2 + 2 | = | 4 |
| 11 | 9 + 8 + 10 | = | 27 | 3 + 4 + 3 | = | 10 |
| 12 | 9 + 8 + 11 | = | 28 | 3 + 3 + 4 | = | 10 |
| 13 | 8 + 8 | = | 16 | 3 + 3 | = | 6 |
| 14 | 6 + 9 | = | 15 | 3 + 3 | = | 6 |
| 15a-b | 6 + 3 | = | 9 | 3 + 2 | = | 5 |
| 15c-d | 10 + 12 | = | 22 | 3 + 4 | = | 7 |
| 16 | 8 + 9 | = | 17 | 3 + 3 | = | 6 |
| 17 | 7 + 7 | = | 14 | 3 + 3 | = | 6 |

| 18 | 9 + 8 | = | 17 | 3 + 3 | = | 6 |
| 19 | 9 + 8 | = | 17 | 3 + 3 | = | 6 |
| 20 | 7 + 6 | = | 13 | 3 + 3 | = | 6 |
| 21 | 8 + 8 | = | 16 | 3 + 3 | = | 6 |
| TOTALS | 21 verses/44 cola | | 340 | | | 132 |

### Distribution of Stresses

| Cola | Bicola | Tricola |
|------|--------|---------|
| 2″ - 5 | 2″2 - 1 | 3″3″4 - 1 |
| 3″ - 34 | 2″3 - 1 | 3″4″3 - 1 |
| 4″ - 5 | 3″2 - 2 | |
| | 3″3 - 12 | |
| | 3″4 - 1 | |
| | 4″3 - 2 | |

The dominant stress pattern is 3″3. Of the poem's 19 bicola, 12 exhibit this pattern (63%). That the 3″3 stress pattern controls this psalm is confirmed by analyzing the distribution of cola and the total number of stresses. Thirty-four of the 44 cola are 3-stress cola (77%). The remaining 10 cola are distributed evenly between 2-stress (5) and 4-stress (5). The poem has a total of 132 stresses which yields an average of 3 stresses per colon. We conclude that although there is deviation from the 3″3 pattern among the verses, overall the poem corresponds to this pattern.

### Distribution of Syllables

| Syllables | | Cola | | Total Syllables |
|-----------|---|------|---|-----------------|
| 3 | × | 1 | = | 3 |
| 4 | × | 0 | = | 0 |
| 5 | × | 2 | = | 10 |
| 6 | × | 6 | = | 36 |
| 7 | × | 9 | = | 63 |
| 8 | × | 13 | = | 104 |
| 9 | × | 9 | = | 81 |
| 10 | × | 2 | = | 20 |
| 11 | × | 1 | = | 11 |
| 12 | × | 1 | = | 12 |
| TOTALS | | 44 | | 340 |

No colon is less than 3 or more than 12 syllables long. Most of the cola are 6–9 syllables, 37 out of 44 (84%). Eight-syllable cola are the most frequent (13) followed by 7-syllable and 9-

syllable cola (9 each). This group of 7–9 syllable cola, which averages 8 syllables per colon, comprises 31 of the 44 cola (70%). The total of 340 syllables yields an average of 7.73 syllables per colon. This approximates the norm of 8 syllables for a 3″3 stress-patterned poem (cf. Pss. 111-12, which average 7.7 syllables per colon, in Freedman 1972d: 387-88).

2.3.4.3 *Strophes*. Psalm 49 contains five strophes: vv. 2-5, 6-9, 10-12, 14-16, 17-20 (so also Beaucamp 1976: 214-15).

vv. 2-5    This clearly is a prelude. The root אזן brackets these verses (vv. 2b, 5a).

vv. 6-9    Verses 6-7 are united by syntax. Verses 8-9 give the reason for the statement in v. 6a that there is no need to fear the wicked rich.

vv. 10-12   The mocking wish of v. 10a followed by the question in v. 10b introduce the strophe. Verse 11 responds to the question. The subjects of the verbs in vv. 11c-12 are the two nouns in v. 11b, 'the fool and the brute'.

vv. 14-16   Verse 14 introduces their destiny which is explained in v. 15. Verse 16 provides a contrast with v. 15, 'Their destiny is... But God will ransom my life.'

vv. 17-20   The exhortation of v. 17 begins this strophe (cf. v. 6a). Verses 18-19 are joined by initial repetition of כי. Verse 18 states the reason for the exhortation of v. 17. Verses 19-20 are joined by syntax.

### Length of Strophes

|        | verses | cola | syllables | stresses |
|--------|--------|------|-----------|----------|
| 2-5    | 4      | 8    | 59        | 24       |
| 6-9    | 4      | 8    | 60        | 24       |
| 10-12  | 3      | 8    | 65        | 24       |
| 14-16  | 4      | 8    | 63        | 24       |
| 17-20  | 4      | 8    | 61        | 24       |

Each of the strophes is the same size in cola and stress length. There is a slight variation in syllable length (from 59 to 64).

2.3.4.4 *Refrains*. Psalm 49 contains a pair of refrains in v. 13 and v. 21. Verse 13 is formally isolated from its immediate context. Both v. 12 and v. 14 speak of the rich in the plural but

v. 13 uses the singular. Verse 21 is also formally isolated. In v. 20a נפשׁ is the subject of the verb but the subject changes to אדם in v. 21. Elsewhere in the poem the rich person is designated as אישׁ (vv. 8, 17, בני אישׁ in v. 3a). Only in v. 13 and v. 21 are the rich designated אדם ביקר.

The second colon of the refrain is identical in both cases. However, the first colon varies significantly. The *waw* is placed before אדם in v. 13 but before the negative לא in v. 21. Different negatives and verbs are used to form a sound play and to capture the different points of comparison for the implied riddle, 'How is he like cattle?'

**2.3.4.5 *Stanzas.*** The structure of Psalm 49 is clear:

| | |
|---|---|
| vv. 2-5 | Prelude |
| vv. 6-12 | Stanza I |
| v. 13 | Refrain |
| vv. 14-20 | Stanza II |
| v. 21 | Refrain |

The prelude contains an inclusion with the root אזן (vv. 2b, 5a). There is no inclusion for either stanza. *Selāh*, whose meaning is uncertain, occurs at the end of v. 14 and v. 16. Its structural significance is unclear. Possibly it marks the beginning of Stanza II in v. 14 and the middle of that stanza. Or it might not have any structural significance. (On *selāh*, see Craigie 1983: 76-77 and Casetti 1982: 40-42.) Repetition and word pairs serve to unify each stanza: stanza I—חילם (vv. 7a, 11c), the root פדה (vv. 8a, 9a), לעולם and לנצח and לדר ודר (vv. 9b, 10a, 12a, b), יראה (vv. 10b, 11a); stanza II—שׁאול (vv. 15a, d, 16b), the root מות (vv. 15b, 18a), לקח (vv. 16b, 18a), נפשׁ (vv. 16a, 19a), כבוד (vv. 17b, 18b).

*Length of Stanzas*

| | | Strophes | vv. | bicola | tricola | cola | syllables | stresses |
|---|---|---|---|---|---|---|---|---|
| vv. | 2-5 | 1 | 4 | 4 | 0 | 8 | 59 | 24 |
| vv. | 6-12 | 2 | 7 | 5 | 2 | 16 | 125 | 48 |
| vv. | 14-20 | 2 | 8 | 8 | 0 | 16 | 124 | 48 |

In terms of cola, syllables, and stresses, each stanza is virtually identical with the other. The opening prelude is half the size of a stanza. Only counting 'verses' would be misleading, since stanza I has 7 verses due to the two tricola but has 16 cola like stanza II. Counting verses according to the MT's versification also misleads, since each of the two stanzas has 7 verses but the prelude, which is half as long, has 4 verses.

2.3.4.6 *Sections.* After the introduction (vv. 2-5), the body of the poem is divided into two sections with the refrain completing each section: vv. 6-13, 14-21. The major break in the body of the psalm comes between v. 13 and v. 14. Verse 14 marks the beginning of the second section with the introductory sentence, 'This (i.e., 'the following') is the destiny of those who have foolish self-confidence, and that of their followers...' Also, v. 13 is connected with the preceding more than with the following because of the sound play between אדמה at the end of v. 12 and ואדם at the beginning of v. 13, and because of the initial *waw* for v. 13.

*Length of Sections*

|          | vv. | bicola | tricola | cola | syllables | stresses |
|----------|-----|--------|---------|------|-----------|----------|
| vv. 6-13 | 8   | 6      | 2       | 18   | 141       | 54       |
| vv. 14-21| 9   | 9      | 0       | 18   | 140       | 54       |

The length of each section is the same.

2.3.4.7 *Views of Structure.* Most scholars recognize that the psalm consists of a prelude plus two stanzas with two refrains (Kirkpatrick 1902: 268; Briggs 1906: 405-406; Segal 1935: 131-32; Kissane 1953: 212; Weiser 1962: 386; Beaucamp 1976: 212; F. de Meyer 1979: 158; Trublet–Aletti 1983: 76; Craigie 1983: 358; Girard 1984: 395; Gerstenberger 1988: 202-207). Some of them make a distinction in structure between the refrains and the stanzas (Briggs, Segal, Beaucamp, Trublet–Aletti, Girard, Gerstenberger).

Van der Lugt (1980: 474) goes his own way. He posits a structure with a prelude followed by three stanzas: vv. 2-5, 6-11, 12-15, 16-21. This schema ignores the structural significance of the refrains completely. Why begin a stanza with v. 12? (See 1.5.1 for a critique.)

Casetti (1982) argues that vv. 11-15 + 21 comprise the original psalm, which was later expanded by two strophes (vv. 6-10, 16-20) and the prelude (vv. 2-5) (cf. above under notes to v. 15d). He bases this hypothesis on two formal criteria. First, excluding the refrains, he argues that vv. 11-15 consist of four tricola (vv. 11, 12, 14-15a, 15b-d), whereas the rest of the psalm has bicola. In contrast we argue for only two tricola (vv. 11, 12) and see the rest as bicola. Second, vv. 6-10 and 16-20 stand out as closely related to each other but with little relation to vv. 11-15. In response we agree that vv. 6-10 and vv. 16-20 are closely related (see below). However, vv. 11-15 also exhibit connections with the rest of the psalm. Note the following:

a. כי יראה (v. 11a) picks up on לא יראה of the previous verse;
b. שאול (vv. 15a, d, 16a) connects v. 16 with v. 15;
c. numerous repetitions—זכם (vv. 11a, 4a), מות (vv. 11a, 15b, 18a), אחר (vv. 11c, 18b), חיל (vv. 11c, 7a), בית (vv. 12a, 17b), לעולם (vv. 12a, 9b), דר (vv. 12b, 20a), משל (vv. 13b, 21b, 5a), יקר (vv. 13a, 21a, 9a), פה (vv. 14b, 4a);
d. and the related cola of v. 11c and v. 18b. (On the unity of the Psalm, see F. de Meyer 1979.)

## 2.3.5 *Repetitions*

The many repeated elements of this psalm serve to unify the various parts of the two stanzas (compare the similar analysis of Girard 1984: 392-400). On the one hand, the first (vv. 6-9) and the fourth (vv. 17-20) strophes are related and so are the second (vv. 10-12) and the third (vv. 14-16). The first strophe is introduced with the question, 'Why should I fear?' (v. 6), and the fourth strophe begins with the exhortation, 'Don't fear' (v. 17). The second strophe begins with the mocking wish, 'Let him continue to live forever', followed by the rhetorical question, 'Will he not see the pit?' (v. 10). The beginning of the third strophe responds to v. 10, 'This is their destiny... Sheol and Death' (vv. 14-15).

| | | | |
|---|---|---|---|
| A | — | vv. 6-9 | אירא, ברב עשרם |
| B | — | vv. 10-12 | ימותו, כסיל לאחרים |
| B' | — | vv. 14-16 | מות, כסל, אחריהם |
| A' | — | vv. 17-20 | תירא, ירבה, יעשר |

On the other hand, there are connections between the first and the third strophes and between the second and the fourth. Especially clear are the parallels between vv. 8-9 and 16, and between vv. 10 and 20.

| vv. 8-9 | אח לא פדה יפדה איש<br>לא יתן לאלהים כפרו<br>ויקר פדיון נפשם | v. 16 | אך אלהים יפדה נפשי<br>מיד שאול כי יקחני |
|---|---|---|---|

(אח and אך represent a sound pair.)

| v. 10 | ויחי עוד לנצח<br>לא יראה השחת | v. 20b | עד נצח לא יראו אור |
|---|---|---|---|

In addition to these repetitions, it is significant that the nouns for 'wealth' and for 'death' each occur seven times in the body of the psalm (vv. 6-21). The nouns that designate wealth are: עשר (v. 7b), חיל (vv. 7a, 11c), כבוד (vv. 17b, 18b), and יקר (vv. 13a, 21a). The nouns that designate the grave are: מות (v. 15b), שאול (vv. 15a, d, 16b) שחת (v. 10b), קברם (v. 12a), and דור אבותיו (v. 20a). These two key-word groups provide a good summary of the psalm's theme: the wicked *rich* perish in the *grave*.

### 2.3.6 *Thought Progression*

The genre of Psalm 49 is generally recognized to be a wisdom psalm (Kuntz 1974: 204-205; Gerstenberger 1988: 206 labels it 'Meditation and Instruction'). However, elements of other genres also have been employed by the psalmist. Verses 6-7 resemble a lament, v. 16 contains the sounds of a thanksgiving song, and vv. 17f. imitate the form of a salvation oracle (Kraus 1978: 518-19). These various elements have been united to form an expanded discussion of the 'mashal' and 'riddle' found in vv. 13 and 21.

2.3.6.1 *Stanzas*. The prelude (vv. 2-5) begins with a call to listen addressed to all people, the lowly and noble, the rich and poor. The psalmist is about to utter wisdom and to disclose a riddle.

The first stanza opens with a rhetorical question, 'Why should I fear' the wicked rich? Verses 8-9 give the reason why one need not fear: the rich man's money cannot save him. Verse 10 mocks him with a wish, 'Let him live forever!', and then asks the question which dominates the rest of the stanza, 'Will he not see the pit?' Yes, he will, and he should recognize the fact. For he should see that since even the wise die, certainly the fool and brute (i.e. the foolish rich) will perish. They will leave their wealth to others, and graves will become their eternal homes, though they own much property (vv. 11c-12c).

The second stanza begins by asserting the destiny of these foolish rich and their followers: death will shepherd them like sheep; they will be trampled upon and will waste away in Sheol (vv. 14-15). The psalmist then contrasts his own fate— God will redeem him from Sheol (v. 16). He concludes with instruction for the listeners. One need not fear when the rich grow in wealth and power (v. 17). Two reasons follow. First, the rich cannot take his money with him to the grave (v. 18). Second, though he is honored in this life he will join his fathers who will never again see the light of life.

2.3.6.2 *Poem*. After the introduction, the body of the poem begins with a rhetorical question, Why should I fear when the iniquity of the arrogant rich surrounds me? There is no need to fear, for the rich cannot ransom a life with his money (vv. 6-9). Verse 10a forms a transition to the next stage of the discussion, 'Let him continue to live forever if he can!' Verse 10b then introduces the following with a question, 'Will he not see the pit?' Yes, he will. If even the wise die, certainly the arrogant rich will perish with graves as their eternal homes and abandon their wealth to others (vv. 11-12). The first movement then peaks with the refrain of v. 13. The arrogant rich will not survive the night. They are like the cattle (which they probably own) in that they will both perish.

The second movement begins with the introduction, 'The following is their destiny and that of their followers' (v. 14). Death and Sheol will shepherd them, consume them, and be their gods (v. 15). But in contrast to their fate, God will ransom the psalmist from Sheol (v. 16). This is another reason why he need not fear (v. 6). The psalmist then exhorts his listeners not to fear when the rich get richer (v. 17). Two reasons follow: they cannot take their wealth with them and they will never see the light of day again. The second movement then climaxes with the refrain of v. 21. The arrogant rich lack understanding. They are like cattle in that they will be speechless and silenced forever.

The second stanza expands on the things said in the first stanza. First it broadens the two groups—the wicked rich and the pious. Whereas the first stanza speaks only of the rich themselves, the second stanza includes their followers (v. 14b) and fathers (v. 20). In the first stanza only the psalmist is unlike the wicked rich (v. 6). But the second stanza adds an exhortation to the wise hearer (v. 17) in addition to a statement concerning the psalmist (v. 16). Second, their respective fates are heightened and expanded in the second stanza. The first stanza informs us that the wicked rich 'perish' (v. 11b) and have graves as their eternal homes (v. 12a-b). The second stanza intensifies the evil fate that awaits them, 'Death will shepherd them' (v. 15b), Sheol will consume them (v. 15d), and they 'never will see the light' (v. 20b). We also learn more of the fate of the pious in the second stanza. In stanza I the psalmist tells us he need not fear (v. 6a). But the wise do die, which apparently includes the psalmist (v. 11a). The second stanza expands and clarifies. In contrast to the wicked rich who will never see the light (v. 20b), God will redeem and take the psalmist from the hand of Sheol, i.e., give him life after death (v. 16). The wise hearer by implication will receive the same fate since he need not fear (v. 17a).

Thus we see a movement and a progression from stanza to stanza. The poet formally structured the poem in two parts plus an introduction. The introduction to each stanza (vv. 6, 14) sets the tone for each half. The content and thought progression correspond to and justify this formal structure.

Finally, one should observe how the poet closes the poem by expanding on the beginning, a sort of inclusion. Verse 19 clarifies v. 7. The rich 'boast' in their wealth (v. 7) by 'blessing' themselves and rejoicing in the praise they receive from others (v. 19).

## 2.4 *Psalm 56*

### 2.4.1 *Text*

| | Text | Syllables | | Total | Stresses |
|---|---|---|---|---|---|
| v. 1. | למנצח על־יונת אלם רחקים לדוד מכתם באחז אתו פלשתים בגת | | | | |
| 2a. | חנני אלהים | 3+3 | = | 6 | 2 |
| b. | כי־שאפני אנוש | 1+4+2 | = | 7 | 2 |
| c. | כל־היום לחם ילחצני | 1+2+2+4 | = | 9 | 3 |
| 3a. | שאפו שוררי כל־היום | 3+3+1+2 | = | 9 | 3 |
| b. | כי־רבים לחמים לי מרום | 1+2+3+1+2 | = | 9 | 4 |
| 4a. | יום אירא אני | 1+2+2 | = | 5 | 3 |
| b. | אליך אבטח | 3+2 | = | 5 | 2 |
| 5a. | באלהים אהלל דברו | 3+3+3 | = | 9 | 3 |
| b. | באלהים בטחתי לא אירא | 3+3+1+2 | = | 9 | 3 |
| c. | מה־יעשה בשר לי | 1+2+2+1 | = | 6 | 3 |
| 6a. | כל־היום דברי יעצבו | 1+2+3+4 | = | 10 | 3 |
| b. | עלי כל־מחשבתם לרע | 2+1+4+2 | = | 9 | 3 |
| 7a. | יגורו יצפינו המה | 3+3+2 | = | 8 | 3 |
| b. | עקבי ישמרו | 3+3 | = | 6 | 2 |
| c. | כאשר קוו נפשי | 3+2+2 | = | 7 | 3 |
| 8a. | על־און פלט־למו | 1+1+2+2 | = | 6 | 3 |
| b. | באף עמים הורד אלהים | 2+2+2+3 | = | 9 | 4 |
| 9a. | נדי ספרתה אתה | 2+3+2 | = | 7 | 3 |
| b. | שימה דמעתי בנאדך | 2+3+4 | = | 9 | 3 |
| c. | הלא בספרתך | 2+5 | = | 7 | 2 |
| 10a. | אז ישובו אויבי אחור | 1+3+3+2 | = | 9 | 4 |
| b. | ביום אקרא | 2+2 | = | 4 | 2 |
| c. | זה־ידעתי כי־אלהים לי | 1+3+1+3+1 | = | 9 | 4 |
| 11a. | באלהים אהלל דבר | 3+3+2 | = | 8 | 3 |
| b. | ביהוה אהלל דבר | 3+3+2 | = | 8 | 3 |
| 12a. | באלהים בטחתי לא אירא | 3+3+1+2 | = | 9 | 3 |
| b. | מה־יעשה אדם לי | 1+2+2+1 | = | 6 | 3 |
| 13a. | עלי אלהים נדריך | 2+3+4 | = | 9 | 3 |
| b. | אשלם תודת לך | 3+2+1 | = | 6 | 3 |
| 14a. | כי הצלת נפשי ממות | 1+3+2+2 | = | 8 | 3 |
| b. | הלא רגלי מדחי | 2+2+3 | = | 7 | 3 |
| c. | להתהלך לפני אלהים | 4+2+3 | = | 9 | 3 |
| d. | באור החיים | 2+3 | = | 5 | 2 |
| TOTALS | | 33 cola | | 249 | 96 |

## 2.4.2 *Translation*

1. For a musical director. According to 'The Dove on Distant Tere-binths'. Of David. A Miktam. When the Philistines seized him in Gath.

2a. Be gracious to me, O God.
  b. For man hounds me;
  c. all day long the one warring oppresses me.
3a. My adversaries hound (me) all day long.
  b. For many are those warring against me from on high.
4a. On the day when I fear,
  b. in you I put my trust.

### REFRAIN

5a. *In God whose word I will praise,*
  b. *in God I trust, I will not fear.*
  c. *What can flesh do to me?*

6a. All day long they find fault (with me) with words against me;
  b. all their thoughts are for evil against me.
7a. They are hostile; they hide.
  b. They watch my steps
  c. just as they have waited for my life.
8a. In spite of (their) wickedness is there escape for them?
  b. In (your) wrath bring down the peoples, O God.

9a. May you keep count of my tossings.
  b. Put my tears in your bottle.
  c. Are they not in your book?
10a. Then my enemies will turn back.
  b. On the day when I call out,
  c. this is what I know, that God is for me.

### REFRAIN

11a. *In God whose word I will praise,*
  b. *in Yahweh whose word I will praise,*
12a. *in God I trust, I will not fear.*
  b. *What can humans do to me?*

13a. Binding upon me, O God, are my vows to you.
  b. I will pay (my) thank offerings to you.
14a. For you have delivered my life from death,
  b. yea, my feet from stumbling,
  c. that I may walk before God
  d. in the light of the life.

### 2.4.3 *Translation Notes*

v. 1. על־יונת אלם רחקים—'According to "The Dove on Distant Terebinths"'
The MT reads 'according to The Silent Dove among the Far-off', if we
understand *'ēlem* to be a noun from אלם, 'silence'. However, its only
other occurrence is in Ps. 58.2 where there is little doubt that it should
be read *'ēlim*, either 'gods' (cf. Ps. 82; cf. Kraus 1978: 574) or 'rams—
leaders' (Dahood 1968a: 57). Therefore, it is probably better to read with
most commentators *'ēlim* from *'ayil*, 'terebinth, mighty tree'. It seems
to be the title of a song.

v. 1. לדוד—'Of David'
The meaning of the *lamed* is, of course, a much discussed problem (for
a convenient summary of views, see Craigie 1983: 33-35). Here the historical note in the title indicates that it is intended as a *lamed auctoris*.
The defective spelling of *dāwîd* indicates either a pre-exilic date for the
title or an archaism (Freedman 1983).

v. 1. מכתם—'A Miktam'
Psalms 15; 56–60 are all titled 'a Miktam'. The meaning of *miktām* is
uncertain (see Craigie, 1983: 154, for a survey of views). The most likely
interpretation is to postulate a Hebrew root כתם 'to inscribe', related to
כתב, 'to write'. We might compare Isa. 38.9 which has *miktāb*, 'inscription'. An interchange of ב and ם is possible, for example *bārî'/
mĕrî*. In Jer. 2.22, *niktām 'ăwōnēk lĕpānay* should probably be translated 'your iniquity is *inscribed* before me'.
If this is correct, a *miktām* Psalm might have been published by
being engraved on a stone slab, according to the practice of the ancient
Near East (Ginsberg 1945). The inscription on stone could have con-
sisted of the whole poem or of a prominent part of the poem. Delitzsch
(1871: 218-19) suggests the latter since Pss. 56, 57 and 59 contain
refrains and Pss. 16, 58, and 60 contain significant quotes introduced
by אמר or דבר.

v. 1. באחז אתו פלשתים בגת—'When the Philistines seized him in Gath'
The historical reference is to 1 Sam. 21.10-15.

v. 2b. כי־שאפני אנוש—'For man hounds me'
The כי clause introduces the reason why the psalmist needs help: he is
under attack from his enemies. Usually a כי clause following an
imperative states the reason for *saying* the petition and not the cause
for *what* is prayed. (On the function of כי in prayers see Aejmelaeus
1986b: 68-79; *contra* Dahood 1968a: 42.)
שאף usually means 'to pant after, long for' (Ps. 119.131; Job 7.2; 36.20;
Isa. 42.14; etc.), although BDB suggests שאף II 'to trample' as in Amos
2.7. In light of vv. 6-7, however, the emphasis seems to be more on the
enemies' *desire* for the psalmist.

v.2c. לחם ילחצני—'the one warring oppresses me'
Although לחם I, 'to do battle', usually appears in the niphal, it does
appear in the qal in Ps. 35.1, as is the case here and in v.3b. לחם parallels אנוש in the chiasm of v.2b-c. Therefore, we should not follow
Dahood's (1968a: 42) reconstruction of a dual accusative *lĕḥēm*, 'with
both jaws'.

v.3b. לחמים לי מרום—'those warring against me from on high'
מרום is difficult. Kraus (1978: 565-66) omits it. Jacquet (1977: 220) connects it with v.4a, 'dès le point du jour'. Briggs (1907: 30), Dahood
(1968a: 43), *et al.* also connect it with v.4a but read it as a vocative, 'O
Most High'. In light of the parallel between v.4a and v.10b, אקרא
יום אירא/ביום, מרום should be construed with v.3b. It could be a vocative
divine appellative as in Ps. 92.9. However, since God is mentioned ten
times in this poem (אלהים nine times, יהוה once), it is doubtful that there
would be an eleventh. We prefer to understand it as an adverbial
accusative (as in Isa. 22.16; 33.5; 37.23; 40.26, etc.), which is similar in
meaning to *mimmārôm*, 'from on high'. (Cf. Ps. 73.8).

v.4a. יום אירא אני—'On the day when I fear'
This clause is a concise temporal clause parallel to ביום אקרא in v.10b
(GKC 155l). In light of the post-positive pronoun אתה in v.9a, we include
אני in v.4a rather than 4b.

v.4b. אליך אבטח—'in you I put my trust'
Usually בטח takes the preposition ב as in vv.5 and 11-12, but it can also
take אל (Pss. 4.6; 31.7; 86.2; etc.). אל is used here probably for the sake of
alliteration.

v.5a. באלהים אהלל דברו—'In God whose word I will praise'
   b. באלהים בטחתי—'in God I trust'
This verse is a good example of 'staircase parallelism' in which a sentence is started, then interrupted (here with a relative clause), and
then resumed from the beginning and completed (see Watson 1984:
150f.). Three factors indicate this: (1) The piel of הלל almost never takes
the preposition ב (Ps. 44.9 is the only exception but the verb there has
no second object); (2) the pronominal suffix on דברו is resumptive to an
ellipsed relative (the relative אשר is rare in poetry); (3) the verb בטח takes
the preposition ב. Consequently, there is no need to understand דברו as
a second object of הלל (*contra* Briggs 1907: 34) or to emend (*contra*
Dahood 1968a: 43).

v.6a. דברי יעצבו—'they find fault (with me) with words against me'
The MT is usually translated, 'they vex my words', i.e. they twist and
misrepresent what the psalmist says. The parallel indicates that the
psalmist's enemies plot against him. Verse 7 pictures them lying in
wait for him. The thought of falsely accusing the psalmist and mis-

representing his statements does not fit this context very well. We prefer to understand the suffix of דברי as an objective genitive, 'with words against me' (see GKC 135 for examples of the objective genitive). Possibly one should read a plural participle with suffix—*dōbĕray* (Dahood 1968a: 43). Or one might understand the י of דברי as dittography with the following יעצבו. At any rate the words are being spoken by the enemies in their plotting against the psalmist (cf. Prov. 15.1; Ps. 35.20). The verb יעצבו here means 'to find fault with' as also in 1 Kgs 1.6.

### v.7a. יגורו—'they are hostile'

We follow Kellermann's suggestion that גור II, usually translated 'to attack', is simply a specialized use of גור I, 'to sojourn'. He suggests that 'fremd sein' and 'feind sein' can be two different manifestations of the same person (*TWAT* I.980).

### v.7a. יצפינו המה—'they hide'

The *Kethib* reads a hiphil; the *Qere* reads a qal. It might be possible to read a hiphil, 'they set up spies'. The subject of the following verb could then refer to the spies whom they placed, 'They (the spies) watch my steps' (Delitzsch 1871: 168; cf. Ps. 59.1; 1 Sam. 19.11; Judg. 9.25). However, since the two occurrences of the hiphil have an object suffix (Exod. 2.3; Job 14.13) and the closest parallel reads a qal (Prov. 1.18), we prefer to follow the *Qere*. We join the pronoun המה to v.7a in conformity with the position of אתה in v.9a. The emphatic pronoun המה serves to contrast the enemies and the psalmist, 'They... my steps'.

### v.7b. עקבי ישמרו—'They watch my steps'

'They watch my steps' is similar to the following phrases: 'those who watch (שמר) for my life' (Ps. 71.10); 'those who watch (שמר) for my fall' (Jer. 20.10); and 'they mock the footsteps (עקבות) of your anointed' (Ps. 89.52). Thus there is no need to read with Dahood *ʿōqĕbay* 'my maligners'.

### v.7c. כאשר קוו נפשי—'just as they have waited for my life'

Since the previous four verbs in vv.6-7b are prefixing verbs, the suffixing verb קוו probably is significant here. They now lie in wait for the psalmist just as they have done in the past. (Cf. Zech. 10.8b; Pss. 71.10; 119.95.)

### v.8a. על־און פלטלמו—'In spite of their wickedness is there escape for them?'

This is a difficult clause. There are at least five possible interpretations. The first two emend the text but the other three keep the MT.

1. Some follow LXX (ὑπὲρ τοῦ μηθενός) and read *ʾayin* for MT *ʾāwen*, 'on no account let them escape' (e.g. NIV).

2. Many emend *palleṭ* to *palles*, 'weigh out to them/requite them' (RSV; Briggs 1907: 35; Kissane 1953: 244; Jacquet 1977: 225) or 'observe' (Kraus 1978: 566).

3. A third approach considers פלם an imperative but understands the prepositions differently. Dahood (1968a: 44) suggests understanding על as 'from' and למו as the preposition plus a first person plural suffix, 'from their malice deliver us'. However, the verb פלם is normally construed with מן and never with על (cf. v.14a, 'you delivered my life from death', ממות). Also, it is doubtful that למו is a first person plural suffix.

   Possibly one could construe למו, a possessive *lamed* plus the normal third person plural suffix, with על און and understand נפשׁי at the end of v.7 to be gapped, 'from their wickedness rescue my life'. Wahl (1977: 255) suggests that the ל of למו might be a 'privative' (or rather, 'separative') *lamed*, 'because of (their) iniquity deliver (us) from them'. However, the fact that פלם is normally construed with מן and never with על or a separative *lamed* argues against these proposals.

4. A fourth possibility is to understand *palleṭ* as an imperative but with an ironical meaning. פלם can mean 'to carry away safe, bring forth to safety' (Isa. 5.29; Mic. 6.14; Job 21.10) much like נצל, 'to carry away as plunder', and משׁך, 'to carry off'. In that case we might understand the clause as an ironical play on this meaning; instead of 'bring them into safety' it reads 'carry them away unto misfortune'. However, this seems forced.

5. Finally, the traditional view, which we prefer, considers the clause to be a question, 'In spite of (their) wickedness is there escape for them?' (Delitzsch 1871: 169; Weiser 1962: 421). The verb *palleṭ* is parsed as an infinitive construct as in Ps. 32.7, 'you surround me with the shouts of deliverance' (*rānnê palleṭ*). Interrogative clauses are often introduced without *hē* interrogatives (GKC 150a). A good parallel is found in 1 Sam. 16.4 which also has an infinitive construct, 'Is your coming in peace?' (*šālōm bô'ekā*). Compare also 2 Kgs 5.26. Examples of פלם plus *lamed* of advantage are found in 2 Sam. 22.2 and Ps. 144.2.

v.8b. באף עמים הורד אלהים—'In (your) wrath bring down the peoples, O God'

This colon is the midpoint of the psalm (16 cola, 45 stresses, 120 syllables before and 16 cola, 47 stresses, 120 syllables after). This fact indicates its importance. It clarifies who the enemies are, namely the foreign armies who are attacking the psalmist. The prayer is that God 'bring down' the peoples who are warring against the psalmist 'from on high' (v. 3b). (On the significance of אלהים here, see under 2.4.5.)

v. 9a. ‏נדי ספרתה אתה‎—'May you keep count of my tossings'
The noun *nōd* occurs only once elsewhere, as the place name of the
region where Cain wandered (Gen. 4.16). There the name 'Nod' is
obviously based on the meaning of the verb ‏נוד‎, 'to wander as a fugitive'.
If *nōd* has that sense here, then the psalmist is praying that God keep
a record of his 'fugitive existence', its length and many temporary
abodes (cf. Lam. 1.7; 3.19). However, the verb ‏נוד‎ also denotes 'to show
grief by shaking the head' (*TWAT* V.292). The nouns *nîd*, *nîdâ*, and
*mānôd* are related to this meaning. Therefore, *nōd* might refer to the
psalmist's laments, 'the bowing and shaking of the head in penitential
rites' (Eaton 1967: 149). In that case, the prayer is that God should
count the times the psalmist has shaken his head in grief. This
understanding fits well with the next colon which speaks of the
psalmist's 'tears'. The latter meaning seems the best, although possibly it is deliberately polysemous. At any rate, *nōd* forms a sound pair
with *nō'd* in the next colon.

In this context of imperatives, ‏ספרתה‎ should probably be understood
as a precative perfect (so Dahood 1968a: 45). For this image of the
divine record keeper, see Pss. 87.6; 139.16; Neh. 13.14 and numerous
references to the book of life.

v. 9b. ‏שׂימה דמעתי בנאדך‎—'Put my tears in your bottle'
The verb ‏שׂימה‎ is accented as an imperative and not as a passive participle (cf. 1 Sam. 8.5). The imperative is appropriate in this context of
petitions. In v. 9 the psalmist uses two vivid images to beseech God to
record and keep track of the psalmist's suffering and grief. Other
examples of this basic motif, though less picturesque, are found in 2
Kgs 20.5//Isa. 38.5 where God 'sees' Hezekiah's tears and in Ps. 39.13
where the psalmist prays, 'Don't be deaf to my tears'.

The noun *nō'd*, a sound pair with *nōd* in v. 9a, usually denotes a con-
tainer made of animal skin, a wineskin (Josh. 9.4, 13; 1 Sam. 16.20) or
milkskin (Judg. 4.19). Some authorities opt for that meaning here
(Honeyman 1939: 77; Kelso 1948: 43 n. 105). However, Richards (1985)
argues that it denotes a 'tear vase' made of terra-cotta, faience, or
highly decorated glass, such as is known especially from Egyptian
tombs.

v. 10a. ‏אז ישׁובו אויבי אחור‎—'Then my enemies will turn back'
The adverb ‏אז‎ introduces the logical sequence after the rhetorical question of v. 9c (cf. Isa. 58.7-8 for the same sequence). The relationship
between vv. 9c and 10a can be paraphrased: 'If (and since) you have
taken note of my tears and grief, then in that case I know that my
enemies will turn back'.

v. 10c. זה־ידעתי כי־אלהים לי—'this is what I know, that God is for me'
This clause is an expression of confidence with close parallels in Pss.
54.6; 73.25; 118.6-7; 124.1-2 (*contra* Dahood 1968a: 47). The object clause,
'that God is *for me*', echoes the rhetorical questions of vv. 5c and 12b,
'What can flesh/humans do *to me*?'

v. 11b. ביהוה אהלל דבר—'in Yahweh whose word I will praise'
This clause at first appears suspect since it creates a four cola refrain
in vv. 11-12 in contrast to the three cola refrain in v. 5. Also, it has the
only occurrence of 'Yahweh' in the poem. However, it should be kept
since the poem is based on an acrostic structure which would be dis-
torted if it were omitted (33 cola = 22 + 11). The fact that the total number of references to God equals ten counting יהוה (אלהים nine times, יהוה
once) is a further argument for retaining it. The third person suffix of
דברו in v. 5 is omitted in v. 11a-b but is to be assumed in translation.

v. 13a. עלי—'Binding upon me'
The preposition plus suffix, עלי, means 'incumbent on me as an obliga-
tion' as in 2 Sam. 18.11; Prov. 7.14; etc. (BDB).

v. 14a. כי הצלת נפשי ממות—'For you have delivered my life from death'
This verse states the reason for the psalmist's vow of praise in v. 13. It
also functions as the actual 'declarative' praise of God by the psalmist
(Westermann 1981: 64-81). We understand the perfect as a 'prophetic
perfect'. The psalmist is so certain that God has heard his prayer that
he speaks of the deliverance as past. Therefore he vows to thank God
(v. 13).

What accounts for this switch to a perfect, which occurs regularly in
laments? Two explanations seem possible. One is that a 'Heilsorakel'
was spoken to the suppliant by a priest which assured him that his
prayer was heard (Begrich 1934; cf. Pss. 12.6; 60.8f.). The fact that the
psalmist promises to praise God's word (vv. 5, 11) might indicate that
he expected a word of assurance from the priest.

The other is that a real, inward psychological change occurred
within the psalmist during the course of the psalm (so Weiss 1984: 313-
14, 442-44, who also gives a survey of views). As the Psalmist expressed
his confidence in God (vv. 5, 11-12), his mood changed from lament and
petition to certainty of deliverance.

v. 14b. הלא—'yea'
The interrogative ה plus negative expresses certainty here (GKC 150e).
Literally it reads, 'Is it not true (that you have delivered) my feet from
stumbling?' A close parallel to v. 14 is found in Ps. 116.8-9.

### 2.4.4 *Structure*

2.4.4.1 *Versification*. The poem is based on a 'non-alphabetic' acrostic structure with 33 cola (= 22 + 11; see Freedman 1986). There are 16 verses (13 verses according to MT): 1 monocolon, 13 bicola, and 2 tricola. The poem begins with a monocolon. The first refrain is a tricolon and the other is two bicola. The extra colon in the latter was probably added to produce the 33 cola structure. The other tricolon is located internally (v. 7).

| | |
|---|---|
| v. 2a | Monocolon—This initial imperative plus vocative seems to be isolated (cf. Ps. 57.2a. On the existence of monocola, see Watson 1984: 168-74). |
| v. 2b-c | Bicolon—The subjects and verbs are arranged chiastically. There is initial alliteration with כ. |
| v. 3 | Bicolon—The B colon expands on the enemies, now plural, mentioned in the A colon. There is final rhyme. |
| v. 4 | Bicolon—The two cola are joined by syntax: temporal clause plus main clause. Each colon has a first person singular prefixing verb. Four of the five words alliterate. |
| v. 5 | Tricolon—The first two cola represent 'stair-case parallelism' (Watson 1984: 150-56). באלהים is repeated in initial position in A and B. The C colon expands on the B colon, 'I will not fear./What can flesh do to me?' |
| v. 6 | Bicolon—כל is repeated. The B colon, 'all their thoughts are for evil against me', semantically parallels the phrase, 'they find fault with words against me', in A. |
| v. 7 | Tricolon—The plural verbs (three prefixing and one suffixing) which are semantically in sequence ('they are hostile, they hide... they watch... they waited') plus the word pair נפשי//עקבי unite the three cola. The sequence of object–verb in B is reversed in C. |
| v. 8 | Bicolon—The B colon responds to the question in A, 'Is there escape for them? No! Bring them down, O God'. למו and עמים are parallel. |

| v. 9a-b | Bicolon—The two cola are chiastic: object plus precative perfect//imperative plus object. The sound pair, $n\bar{o}d\hat{i}\ldots b\check{e}n\bar{o}'dek\bar{a}$, bracket the two cola. The objects, נדי and דמעתי, are paired semantically. |
|---|---|
| v. 9c-10a | Bicolon—Because ביום אקרא in v. 10b begins a new sentence as in v. 4a, we believe that v. 10a belongs with v. 9c. The adverb אז introduces the logical sequence after the question in the A colon. |
| v. 10b-c | Bicolon—The two cola are joined syntactically: temporal clause plus main clause (cf. v. 4). The prefixing verb in A and the suffixing verb in B are both first person singular. |
| v. 11 | Bicolon—Repetition and the word pair ביהוה ... באלהים connect these two cola. |
| v. 12 | Bicolon—B expands semantically on A, 'I will not fear. What can humans do to me?' |
| v. 13 | Bicolon—נדריך and תודח form a word pair. There is final rhyme of $k$. |
| v. 14a-b | Bicolon—The verb is gapped in B. נפש and רגלי are paired as are ממות and מדחי. |
| v. 14c-d | Bicolon—The prepositional phrase of B is syntactically dependent on A. |

## 2.4.4.2 *Stress and Syllable Counts*

| Verse | Syllables | | Totals | Stresses | | Totals |
|---|---|---|---|---|---|---|
| 2a | 6 | = | 6 | 2 | = | 2 |
| 2b-c | 7 + 9 | = | 16 | 2 + 3 | = | 5 |
| 3 | 9 + 9 | = | 18 | 3 + 4 | = | 7 |
| 4 | 5 + 5 | = | 10 | 3 + 2 | = | 5 |
| 5 | 9 + 9 + 6 | = | 24 | 3 + 3 + 3 | = | 9 |
| 6 | 10 + 9 | = | 19 | 3 + 3 | = | 6 |
| 7 | 8 + 6 + 7 | = | 21 | 3 + 2 + 3 | = | 8 |
| 8 | 6 + 9 | = | 15 | 3 + 4 | = | 7 |
| 9a-b | 7 + 9 | = | 16 | 3 + 3 | = | 6 |
| 9c-10a | 7 + 9 | = | 16 | 2 + 4 | = | 6 |
| 10b-c | 4 + 9 | = | 13 | 2 + 4 | = | 6 |
| 11 | 8 + 8 | = | 16 | 3 + 3 | = | 6 |
| 12 | 9 + 6 | = | 15 | 3 + 3 | = | 6 |
| 13 | 9 + 6 | = | 15 | 3 + 3 | = | 6 |
| 14a-b | 8 + 7 | = | 15 | 3 + 3 | = | 6 |
| 14c-d | 9 + 5 | = | 14 | 3 + 2 | = | 5 |
| TOTALS | 16 verses/33 cola | | 249 | | | 96 |

### Distribution of Stresses

| Cola | Bicola | Tricola |
|------|--------|---------|
| 2″ - 7 | 2″3 - 1 | 3″2″3 - 1 |
| 3″ - 22 | 3″2 - 2 | 3″3″3 - 1 |
| 4″ - 4 | 3″3 - 6 | |
| | 2″4 - 2 | |
| | 3″4 - 2 | |

The dominant stress pattern is 3″3. Of the poem's 13 bicola, 6 exhibit this pattern and 2 exhibit its variation, 2″4. One tricolon also has the same pattern. Thus, 9 out of the poem's 16 verses (56%) are based on a 3″3 pattern.

That this poem is based on a 3″3 stress pattern is further indicated by the distribution of cola and the total number of stresses. Twenty-two of the 33 total cola are 3-stress (67%). The other 11 cola are distributed fairly evenly between 2-stress cola (7) and 4-stress cola (4), one off the expected proportion of 6 to 5. This ratio of 22 3-stress cola to 11 2-stress plus 4-stress cola corresponds to the 'non-alphabetic acrostic' nature of the poem. The total of 96 stresses yields 2.9 stresses per colon (99 stresses would yield a perfect 3 stresses per colon). We conclude that although there is deviation from the 3″3 pattern among the verses, overall the poem corresponds to this pattern.

### Distribution of Syllables

| Syllables | | Cola | | Total Syll. |
|-----------|---|------|---|-------------|
| 4 | × | 1 | = | 4 |
| 5 | × | 3 | = | 15 |
| 6 | × | 6 | = | 36 |
| 7 | × | 5 | = | 35 |
| 8 | × | 4 | = | 32 |
| 9 | × | 13 | = | 117 |
| 10 | × | 1 | = | 10 |
| TOTALS | | 33 | | 249 |

No colon is less than 4 or more than 10 syllables in length. Most of the cola are 6–9 syllables, 28 of 33 cola (85%). The distribution reveals that the short cola (4–6 syllables) and the long cola (9–10 syllables) balance each other: 10 short to 14 long. There is an average of 7.5 syllables per colon. This is a little short of the usual length for a 3″3 stress pattern, i.e. 8 sylla-

bles, but it approximates the average per colon of Psalms 111
and 112, i.e. 7.7 syllables per colon (Freedman 1972d: 387).

2.4.4.3 *Strophes.* The poem has four strophes plus two refrains:
vv. 2-4 (5 = refrain), 6-8, 9-10 (11-12 = refrain), 13-14. The
first and the fourth strophes are a half-stanza each and the
middle two strophes together form a full stanza.

vv. 2-4    The reference to the deity is in the second person.
The vocative *'ĕlōhîm* in v. 2a and the preposition
*'ēleykā* in v. 4b form a semantic inclusion and a
phonological pair. The subject of the verbs in
vv. 2b-3b is the enemies. The four cola of vv. 2b-3b
are arranged in both a chiastic pattern and an
alternating pattern. In the chiastic pattern both
v. 2b and v. 3b begin with כי. Verse 2c begins and
v. 3a ends with כל־היום.

     ab:    ... כי (v. 2b)      כל־היום ... (v. 2c)
     ba:    כל־היום ... (v. 3a)      ... כי (v. 3b)

In the alternating pattern, v. 2b and v. 3a contain
the verb שאף, and v. 2c and v. 3b contain the participle of לחם.

     ab:    שאף + noun (v. 2b)      ... לחם ... (v. 2c)
     ab:    שאף + noun (v. 3a)      ... לחמים ... (v. 3b)

vv. 6-8    These cola are united by their discussion of the
enemies. The enemies are the subject of the verbs
in vv. 6-7, the antecedent of the pronominal suffixes in v. 6b (מחשבתם) and v. 8a (למו), and the object
of the imperative in v. 8b. Verses 6-7 describe their
hostile actions against the psalmist and v. 8 calls
for their punishment. Verse 8b, the middle colon
of the poem, also acts as a transition to the next
colon, since it begins the petitions to God.

vv. 9-10    Verse 9 expresses the psalmist's petition to God to
remember the psalmist. Verse 10b-c concludes
the petition, 'On the day when I call out, this is
what I know, that God is for me'. Note that the
final bicolon of this strophe begins with ביום אקרא
(v. 10b) which echoes the beginning of the final
bicolon in the first strophe, יום אירא (v. 4a). The repetition of the root ספר unites the two bicola of vv. 9a-
10a. The references to the deity are in the second
person in this strophe except for the final colon
where אלהים is third person (v. 10c). This switch

serves to prepare for the following refrain (vv. 11-12) where 'God' is also third person. Also אלהים serves to bracket this section if we include the transition colon of v. 8b.

vv. 13-14    'God' is in the second person except in v. 14c where אלהים is third person. (However, אלהים could be understood as a vocative, 'before you, O God'.) The switch seems to signal the end of the poem. אלהים brackets the strophe (vv. 13a and 14c). Verse 14 expresses the reason for the vow of v. 13 and is tied to it by the conjunction כי. The four cola of v. 14 are arranged chiastically: 'you delivered my life from *death*/*my feet* from stumbling/that *I may walk* before God/in the light of the *life*'. 'Death' is parallel to 'life' and 'my feet' parallels 'that I may walk'.

### Length of Strophes

|         | *verses* | *cola* | *syllables* | *stresses* |
|---------|----------|--------|-------------|------------|
| 2-4:    | 4        | 7      | 50          | 19         |
| 6-8:    | 3        | 7      | 55          | 21         |
| 9-10:   | 3        | 6      | 45          | 18         |
| 13-14:  | 3        | 6      | 44          | 17         |

Each of the first two strophes is 1 colon longer than each of the last two strophes. The range in syllable length is from 44 to 55. The range in stress length is from 17 to 21.

2.4.4.4 *Refrains*. The poem contains two refrains, v. 5 and vv. 11-12. Both refrains are structurally isolated from the stanzas. In vv. 2-4, אלהים is in the second person whereas in the refrain of v. 5 אלהים is third person. Verse 6 clearly begins a separate unit since the subject is the enemies. In vv. 8-10a and 13 אלהים is also in the second person in contrast to the third person references in the refrain of vv. 11-12. Verse 10c serves as a transition to the following refrain since אלהים is third person. It is best, however, to connect v. 10b-c with the previous strophe since v. 10b serves to conclude the petitions of vv. 8-10a, 'On the day when I cry out...' The following gives a summary view:

| vv. 2-4   | — | 'God' | = | second person          |
| v. 5      | — | 'God' | = | third person (refrain) |
| vv. 8-10a | — | 'God' | = | second person          |

| v. 10c | — | 'God' | = | third person (transition) |
| vv. 11-12 | — | 'God' | = | third person (refrain) |
| vv. 13 | — | 'God' | = | second person |

The refrains are the only places where we find 'stair-case parallelism'. They are not exactly alike however. Verse 5 reads דברו with a suffix but v. 11 reads דבר without a suffix. Verse 5 has the word 'flesh' (בשׂר) whereas v. 12 has the word 'humans' (אדם). Finally, v. 5 contains three cola whereas vv. 11-12 contain four cola. We believe that the extra colon (v. 11b) was included to bring the total number of cola to 33 (22 + 11) which follows a non-alphabetic acrostic pattern. The first and last half-stanzas together add up to 13 cola and the middle full-stanza has 13 cola. The sum of those is 26 cola. Two 3-cola refrains would bring the total of the psalm's cola to 32. Therefore, the extra colon produces the necessary 33 cola.

**2.4.4.5** *Stanzas.* The poem's structure consists of two half-stanzas and one full stanza separated by two refrains:

| vv. 2-4 | Half-stanza |
| v. 5 | Refrain |
| vv. 6-10 | Stanza |
| vv. 11-12 | Refrain |
| vv. 13-14 | Half-stanza |

The two half-stanzas are each one strophe whereas the middle full-stanza consists of two strophes (vv. 6-8, 9-10). (For comments concerning the two half-stanzas, see above under 2.4.4.3 *Strophes.*) The middle stanza is unified by its focus on the enemies. Verses 6-7 describe the enemies' activities and v. 8 contains a petition against them. Verse 10a is a statement of confidence that they will be defeated. Verse 10b-c concludes the petitions of vv. 8b-9b. There is semantic inclusion between v. 6b and v. 10c, 'all their thoughts are for evil *against me* (עלי)... God is for me (לי)'.

*Length of Stanzas*

| | strophes | vv. | monocola | bicola | tricola | cola | syllables | stresses |
|---|---|---|---|---|---|---|---|---|
| vv. 2-4 | 1 | 4 | 1 | 3 | 0 | 7 | 50 | 19 |
| vv. 6-10 | 2 | 6 | 0 | 5 | 1 | 13 | 100 | 39 |
| vv. 13-14 | 1 | 3 | 0 | 3 | 0 | 6 | 44 | 17 |

The two half-stanzas (vv. 2-4, 13-14) together have 13 cola like the middle full-stanza. The former approximate the latter in syllable count (94 to 100) and stress count (36 to 39). Counting 'verses' produces misleading results. The length of the two half-stanzas together is not larger than the middle stanza, which would be the case if one counted only 'verses'.

2.4.4.6 *Sections*. Psalm 56 has a tripartite structure with the refrains in v. 5 and vv. 11-12 completing the first two major sections: vv. 2-5, 6-12, 13-14. The major breaks in the psalm come between v. 5 and v. 6 and between v. 12 and v. 13. Verse 5 is an expression of trust, 'In God I trust, I will not fear'. It concludes with the rhetorical question, 'What can flesh do to me?' The answer is 'Nothing!' But then in v. 6 the psalmist complains about the enemies by describing their actions. The mood has changed to one of doubt and worry. The break after v. 12 is also evident in that v. 13 begins the vow of praise.

Although there are breaks before the refrains (see above under 2.4.4.4 *Refrains*), they are minor pauses. Verse 4 serves as a transition to the first refrain. The verb אירא in v. 4a is repeated in v. 5b except that in the latter it is negated. Also the prefixing verb אבטח in v. 4b anticipates the suffixing form בטחתי in v. 5b. Verse 10b-c also anticipates the refrain of vv. 11-12. The expression of confidence in v. 10c, 'This is what I know, that *God* is for me', prepares for the confidence expressed in vv. 11-12 where אלהים is also used in third person.

*Length of Sections*

|       | vv. | monocola | bicola | tricola | cola | syllables | stresses |
|-------|-----|----------|--------|---------|------|-----------|----------|
| vv. 2-5 | 5 | 1 | 3 | 1 | 10 | 74 | 28 |
| 6-12 | 8 | 0 | 7 | 1 | 17 | 131 | 51 |
| 13-14 | 3 | 0 | 3 | 0 | 6 | 44 | 17 |

Because of the extra colon in v. 11b, the middle section is one colon longer than the other two sections combined (17 to 16 cola). This extra colon in the refrain was included probably to bring the psalm's total to 33 (= 22 + 11) cola.

2.4.4.7 *Views of Structure*. Scholars differ in their analysis of the poem's structure. Only Briggs (1907: 30), Segal (1935: 132), and Jacquet (1977: 220-21) recognize that the refrains are structurally distinct from the surrounding strophes/ stanzas. However, they reconstruct additional refrains, one between v. 8 and v. 9 and the other at the end after v. 14:

vv. 2-4
v. 5—refrain
vv. 6-8
(refrain reconstructed)
vv. 9-11a
vv. 11b-12—refrain
vv. 13-14
(refrain reconstructed)

In an effort to keep the refrains the same length (3 cola), they include v. 11a with the previous section (Segal instead omits v. 11b). Both this move and the reconstructed refrains are dubious.

Other scholars see the refrains of vv. 5 and 11-12 as part of a strophe, usually at the conclusion of the strophe. They all agree that vv. 13-14 form a unit but they disagree regarding the other breaks. The following are some representative views. Similar to our view of the breaks is that of Kissane (1953: 243-45) and N. Ridderbos (1972: 34-35) who divide the poem into four strophes: vv. 2-5, 6-8, 9-12, 13-14. Some scholars divide the poem into six strophes: Kraus (1978: 566—vv. 2-3, 4-5, 6-7, 8, 9-12, 13-14); Trublet–Aletti (1983: 77—vv. 2-3, 4-5, 6-7, 8-9, 10-12, 13-14); Wahl (1977: 250-56—vv. 2-3, 4-5, 6-7, 8-10a, 10b-12, 13-14); and Gerstenberger (1988: 226-29—vv. 2-3, 4-5, 6-7, 8-9, 10, 11-14). Baumann (1945/1948: 169-73) organizes the poem so that the strophes are arranged symmetrically in length: vv. 2-4 (6 cola), 6-7b (4 cola), 7c-10b (8 cola), 10c and 11b-12 (4 cola), and 13-14 (6 cola). To achieve this pattern he omits vv. 5 and 11a and separates vv. 7c from 7b and 10c from 10b. This is hardly convincing.

Two scholars divide the poem into strophes and bigger units, i.e. stanzas: vv. 2-3 / 4-5, 6-7 / 8-9, 10-12 / 13-14 (Beaucamp 1976: 239-40); and vv. 2-3 / 4-5, 6-8 / 9-10a, 10b-12 / 13-14 (van der Lugt 1980: 474). The connection between the strophes in each stanza is not obvious. Why do vv. 6-7 or 6-8 go with vv. 4-5?

### 2.4.5 *Repetition*

Psalm 56 contains two significant repetitions which we would like to highlight. First, there are ten divine appellatives: אלהים occurs nine times and יהוה occurs once. Half of them are located in the refrains. The other five are located at the beginning of the first strophe (v. 2a), the end of the second (v. 8b) and third (v. 10c) strophes, and the beginning and end of the final strophe (v. 13a, v. 14c). Seven times the divine appellative occurs in the third person and three times as a vocative. The three vocatives are placed at the beginning of the first half-stanza (v. 2a), in the middle of the second stanza (v. 8b), and at the beginning of the final half-stanza (v. 13a). In fact, v. 8b which contains the second vocative is the middle colon of the poem. אלהים also forms an inclusion for the whole poem.

|  |  |  |  |  |
|---|---|---|---|---|
|  | v. 2a | אלהים | — | vocative |
| (Refrain) | v. 5 | אלהים ... אלהים | — | third person |
|  | v. 8b | אלהים | — | vocative |
|  | v. 10c | אלהים | — | third person |
| (Refrain) | vv. 11-12 | אלהים ... יהוה ... אלהים | — | third person |
|  | v. 13a | אלהים | — | vocative |
|  | v. 14c | אלהים | — | third person |

The other significant repetition is that of the psalmist's enemies. The enemies are explicitly mentioned seven times in nominal form: אנוש (v. 2b), לחם (v. 2c), שוררי (v. 3a), לחמים (v. 3b), המה (v. 7a), עמים (v. 8b), and אויבי (v. 10a). These repetitions highlight the two themes of the psalm, namely the psalmist's relationship with *God* as opposed to his relationship with his *enemies*.

### 2.4.6 *Thought Progression*

Psalm 56 is generally recognized as an individual lament or complaint (Sabourin 1974: 246-47; Gerstenberger 1988: 229). Most of the elements of this genre are found here: address to God, complaint, petition, expression of trust, and vow of praise. Yet, it is important that we see how this psalm expresses these features in its own unique manner. We will focus on the stanza level first and then on the movement of the whole poem.

2.4.6.1 *Stanzas*. The opening half-stanza of vv. 2-4 contains an address to God plus a brief petition, a description of the psalmist's enemies and their activities, and a statement of trust:

A.    Petition + address to God—v. 2a
B.    The enemies—vv. 2b-3b
C.    Statement of trust—v. 4

In other words, the first four elements of an 'individual lament' are found in this section.

In this context, the four cola dealing with the enemies serve the purpose of explaining why the psalmist needs God's intervention. The כי clauses explain the psalmist's needs, his distressful situation. The description of the enemies moves from general to specific and from singular to plural:

v. 2b 'man' (אנוש)—general/singular
v. 2c 'the one warring' (לחם)—specific/singular
v. 3a 'my adversaries' (שוררי)—general/plural
v. 3b 'Those warring against me' (לחמים לי)—specific/plural

There is also an intensification of the plurals in v. 3: 'my adversaries // many are those warring'. (On the chiastic and alternating patterns of these four cola, see above under 2.4.4.3.)

Verse 4 serves as a transition from the half-stanza to the refrain with v. 4a concluding the preceding and v. 4b anticipating the following. Verse 4a sums up the poet's reaction to the situation just described, 'On the day when I fear'. Verse 4b expresses his trust which anticipates the refrain of v. 5, 'I put my trust (אבטח) in you... In God I trust (בטחתי)'.

The middle full-stanza of vv. 6-10 contains a description of the enemies' activities, an address to God plus a lengthy petition, and a statement of trust:

B    The enemies—vv. 6-7
A    Petition + address to God—vv. 8-10a
C    Statement of trust—v. 10b-c

As can be seen, the same four elements of the first half-stanza are found in this stanza. However, the order is changed from ABC in vv. 2-4 to BCA in this section (so also Trublet–Aletti 1983: 77. For another example of an ABC/BAC outline, see Raabe 1985).

Five cola concerning the enemies appear at the beginning of this stanza. They are followed by a rhetorical question, 'In spite of (their) wickedness is there escape for them?', and a petition, 'In (your) wrath bring down the peoples, O God'. In this context the five cola dealing with the enemies function differently from those in vv. 2-3. Here the poet uses the description of the enemies to argue that they deserve to be punished and overcome by God. Also, the emphasis in this description of the enemies is different. Whereas vv. 2b-3 contain two different finite verbs (שאפני, ילחצני) and four nominal forms—two nouns and two participles (אנוש, לחם, שוררי, לחמים)—to describe the enemies, vv. 6-7 contain five finite verbs (ישמרו, יצפינו, יגורו, יעצבו, קוו) plus one noun (מחשבתם) and one pronoun (המה) to refer to the enemies. Thus the emphasis shifts to focus more on the enemies' activities than on their number or their character.

Verses 8-10a consist of six cola which are arranged symmetrically:

A   Question + petition against the enemies—v. 8a-b;
B   Two petitions that God be mindful of the psalmist— v. 9a-b;
A   Question + confidence of the enemies' defeat—v. 9c-10a.

Verse 10b-c serves as a transition from the preceding petitions and the following refrain. Verse 10b concludes the petitions, 'On the day when I call out'. Verse 10c anticipates the refrain, 'this I know, that God is for me (לי)... In God I trust, I will not fear. What can humans do to me (לי)?'

The third section (vv. 13-14), a half-stanza, contains an address to God, a vow of praise, and the reason for the vow:

address to God + vow of praise—v. 13
reason for the vow—v. 14

Here the poet thanks God for delivering him from death and from stumbling.

2.4.6.2 *Poem*. The poem exhibits three movements corresponding to its tripartite structure. The first movement (vv. 2-5) begins with a brief, general petition, 'Be gracious to me, O God'. This is followed by four cola, introduced by כי, which describe his need for God's help, i.e. he is being attacked by enemies. In v. 4 the poet expresses his feelings. He first expresses his reaction to his endangered situation, 'I fear'. He then expresses his trust in God (v. 4b). The first movement climaxes in the refrain of v. 5. Moving from v. 4 the reader focuses attention on the middle of the refrain (v. 5b), 'In God I trust, I will not fear'. Here the poet negates his earlier reaction of fear and affirms his trust in God.

The last colon of the refrain, 'What can flesh do to me?', prepares for the second movement (vv. 6-12). It begins with a lengthier description of the enemies' activities (vv. 6-7—five cola). Their devious actions show that they deserve God's judgment. Therefore, what follows is a lengthy prayer consisting of two rhetorical questions and three petitions (vv. 8-9). Verse 10a expresses the psalmist's confidence that God will answer and therefore the enemies will be defeated. Verse 10b concludes the prayer, 'when I call out', and v. 10c expresses the poet's confidence that 'God is for me'. This leads into the climax of the second movement which is also a refrain. In light of v. 10c, the reader focuses on the end of the refrain, 'I will not fear. What can humans do to me?'

In the third movement (vv. 13-14) the poet picks up on his promise to praise God found in the two refrains. He vows to offer God thank offerings. Verse 14 expresses the reason which is introduced by כי. God has delivered him from death so that he can continue to walk before God in the light of life. His promise to praise God followed by a כי clause harks back to the psalm's opening petition followed by a כי clause (vv. 2-3). Also, the chiastic arrangement of the four cola in v. 14 parallels the chiastic arrangement of the four cola in vv. 2b-3b; both sections are introduced by a כי (see above under 2.4.4.3 *Strophes*). In this way vv. 13-14 forms a fitting conclusion to the psalm. These verses express the resolution of his previous petitions. His trust in God has been vindicated and so he will offer thank offerings.

One can also see a tripartite progression in the poem's description of the enemies. We observed above that the first half-stanza focuses on the character and number of the enemies. The enemies are introduced with four nominal forms. They are described in a progression from singular to plural to an intensification of the plural, i.e. 'many'. The beginning of the middle stanza (v. 6) picks up where v. 3 left off by referring to the enemies in the plural. However, the focus is on their activities. The first two sections present their activities in a logical sequence:

> Man hounds me (v. 2b)... he oppresses me (v. 2c), they hound (v. 3a)... they find fault (with me) with words against me (v. 6a), all their thoughts are for evil against me (v. 6b), they are hostile, they hide (v. 7a), they watch my steps (v. 7b)... they wait for my life (v. 7c).

The sequence moves from their desire, words and thoughts to their hiding and watching. An unexpected change occurs in the third section (vv. 13-14). The enemies are not mentioned. Instead, the poet thanks God for delivering him from 'death' and his feet from 'stumbling'. This reveals the ultimate concern of the psalmist. It is a matter of life or death. To be delivered from the enemies is to be delivered from death.

In contrast to the enemies who are engaged in various activities against the psalmist, the psalmist himself is passive. He is the object of their attacks, not vice versa. The first person verbs reveal his response: he fears, trusts, will praise, will not fear, cries out, and vows thank offerings. His response reaches a climax at the end where he says that he will '*walk* before God in the light of the life' (v. 14).

Finally, one should note how the poet arranges the three 'actors' who interrelate in this psalm, and who are identified by the three personal pronouns in the poem (אני, המה, אתה). They are God, the enemies, and the psalmist ('I').

|  |  |  |
|---|---|---|
|  | God and 'I' | v. 2a |
|  | Enemies and 'I' | vv. 2b-3b |
|  | God and 'I' | v. 4 |
| REFRAIN | God and 'I' | v. 5a-b |
|  | Flesh and 'I' | v. 5c |
|  | Enemies and 'I' | vv. 6-7 |
|  | God and Enemies | v. 8 |
|  | God and 'I' | v. 9 |
|  | God and Enemies | v. 10a |
|  | God and 'I' | v. 10b-c |
| REFRAIN | God and 'I' | v. 11-12a |
|  | Humans and 'I' | v. 12b |

God and 'I'                                        vv. 13-14

The first half-stanza begins and ends with the relationship
between God and the psalmist. The focus of the middle stanza
alternates between the relationship of God and the enemies
and that of God and the psalmist. The middle colon (v. 8b)
identifies these enemies as hostile armies. The refrains deal
with both God and 'I' and humans and 'I'. The fact that the
refrains speak of 'flesh' and 'humans' rather than 'enemies'
reveals how the poet views his enemies. They are only part of
mortal 'humanity' (אדם) and weak 'flesh' (בשׂר) who will pass
away. 'Humanity' is set in contrast to God rather than the
psalmist. The refrains expand on the contrast set forth at the
psalm's beginning, 'Be gracious to me, O *God*. For *man* pants
after me' (note the alliteration,... אלהים אנושׁ). It is as if 'man'
and 'flesh' do pass away in the psalm since they are not mentioned in vv. 13-14. Only God and the psalmist remain at the
end.

## 2.5 *Psalm 57*

### 2.5.1 *Text*

| | Text | Syllables | | Total | Stresses |
|---|---|---|---|---|---|
| v. 1 | למנצח אל־תשחת לדוד מכתם בברחו מפני־שאול במערה | | | | |
| 2a. | חנני אלהים חנני | 3+3+3 | = | 9 | 3 |
| b. | כי בך חסיה נפשי | 1+2+3+2 | = | 8 | 3 |
| c. | ובצל־כנפיך אחסה | 3+4+2 | = | 9 | 3 |
| d. | עד יעבר הוות | 1+2+2 | = | 5 | 2 |
| 3a. | אקרא לאלהים עליון | 2+3+2 | = | 7 | 3 |
| b. | לאל גמר עלי | 2+2+2 | = | 6 | 3 |
| 4a. | ישלח משמים ויושיעני | 2+3+5 | = | 10 | 3 |
| b. | חרף שאפי סלה | 2+3 | = | 5 | 2 |
| c. | ישלח אלהים | 2+3 | = | 5 | 2 |
| d. | חסדו ואמתו | 2+4 | = | 6 | 2 |
| 5a. | נפשי בתוך לבאם | 2+2+3 | = | 7 | 3 |
| b. | אשכבה להטים | 3+3 | = | 6 | 2 |
| c. | בני־אדם | 2+2 | = | 4 | 2 |
| d. | שנידם חנית וחצים | 3+2+3 | = | 8 | 3 |
| e. | ולשונם חרב חדה | 4+1+2 | = | 7 | 3 |
| 6a. | רומה על־השמים אלהים | 2+1+3+3 | = | 9 | 3 |
| b. | על כל־הארץ כבודך | 1+1+2+4 | = | 8 | 3 |
| 7a. | רשת הכינו לפעמי | 1+3+3 | = | 7 | 3 |
| b. | כפף נפשי | 2+2 | = | 4 | 2 |
| c. | כרו לפני שיחה | 2+3+2 | = | 7 | 3 |
| d. | נפלו בתוכה סלה | 3+3 | = | 6 | 2 |
| 8a. | נכון לבי אלהים | 2+2+3 | = | 7 | 3 |
| b. | נכון לבי | 2+2 | = | 4 | 2 |
| c. | אשירה ואזמרה | 3+5 | = | 8 | 2 |
| 9a. | עורה כבודי | 2+3 | = | 5 | 2 |
| b. | עורה הנבל וכנור | 2+2+3 | = | 7 | 3 |
| c. | אעירה שחר | 3+1 | = | 4 | 2 |
| 10a. | אודך בעמים אדני | 3+3+3 | = | 9 | 3 |
| b. | אזמרך בל־אמים | 4+4 | = | 8 | 2 |
| 11a. | כי־גדל עד־שמם חסדך | 1+2+1+2+3 | = | 9 | 3 |
| b. | ועד־שחקים אמתך | 2+3+4 | = | 9 | 3 |
| 12a. | רומה על־שמם אלהים | 2+1+2+3 | = | 8 | 3 |
| b. | על כל־הארץ כבודך | 1+1+2+4 | = | 8 | 3 |
| TOTALS | | 33 cola | | 229 | 86 |

### 2.5.2 *Translation*

1. For the musical director. According to 'Do Not Destroy'. Of
   David. A Miktam. When he fled from Saul, in the cave.

2.a. Be gracious to me, O God, be gracious to me.
  b. For in you my soul has taken refuge;
  c. and in the shadow of your wings I will take refuge,
  d. until destruction passes by.

3a. I cry to God Most High,
  b. to El who avenges on my behalf.
4a. He will send from heaven and save me,
  b. though the ones hounding me taunt, SELAH
  c. God will send
  d. his steadfast love and his faithfulness.

5a. My life is in the midst of lions.
  b. I will lie down in the midst of those who are aflame,
  c. that is, the sons of man.
  d. Their teeth are a spear and arrows;
  e. and their tongue is a sharp sword.

## REFRAIN

6a. *Be exalted over the heavens, O God.*
  b. *Let your glory be exalted over all the earth.*

7a. A net they set for my feet.
  b. They bent down my life.
  c. They dug before me a pit—
  d. they fell into it! SELAH

8a. My heart is confident, O God,
  b. my heart is confident,
  c. so that I will sing and make music.
9a. Awake, O my 'self',
  b. awake, O harp and lyre,
  c. so that I can awaken the dawn.

10a. I will praise you among the nations, O Lord;
  b. I will make music to you among the peoples.
11a. For great to the heavens is your steadfast love;
  b. to the skies your faithfulness.

## REFRAIN

12a. *Be exalted over the heavens, O God.*
  b. *Let your glory be exalted over all the earth.*

### 2.5.3 *Translation Notes*

v. 1. אל־תשחת—'According to "Do Not Destroy" '
Apparently these words refer to a tune or melody (cf. Pss. 58.1; 59.1;
75.1). Possibly they are the opening words of the song to whose music
the psalm was set (so Dahood 1968a: 50).

v. 1. לדוד מכתם—'Of David. A Miktam'
See notes under Psalm 56.1.

v. 1. בברחו מפני־שאול במערה—'When he fled from Saul, in the cave'
The historical note refers to either 1 Samuel 22 or 24.

v. 2a. חני אלהים חני—'Be gracious to me, O God, be gracious to me'
The verb is repeated for emphasis (cf. Ps. 123.3). This is a good example of an 'ABA monocolon' (cf. Ps. 123.3a; Watson 1984: 172, 215).

v. 2b. כי בך חסיה נפשי—'For in you my soul has taken refuge'
נפשי is a periphrasis for the first person pronoun 'I' as also in vv. 5a and
7b (GKC 144m). The verb חסיה preserves the original third consonant
*yodh* (Dahood 1968a: 50). The כי clause gives the reason why the
psalmist appeals to God, i.e. because he trusts in him (cf. Pss. 16.1;
25.20; cf. Aejmelaeus 1986b: 72-77).

v. 2c. ובצל־כנפיך—'and in the shadow of your wings'
The image of God as a bird is found frequently. The function of God's
'wings' varies. Sometimes they serve to carry and transport Israel to
safety (Exod. 19.4; Deut. 32.11). Elsewhere, as here, they function as
protection or shelter (Ruth 2.12; Pss. 17.8; 36.8; 61.5; 63.8; 91.4). Some
scholars understand it as an allusion to the wings of the cherubim in
the temple (so Briggs 1907: 38; Kraus 1978: 190) or possibly to the
'wings' or roof of the temple (Keel 1978: 190). In Ps. 61.5 the setting
does seem to be the temple (cf. Ps. 27.5). Some hypothesize an incuba-
tion ritual in which the accused keeps vigil at the temple waiting for
vindication to come in the morning (H. Schmidt 1928: 22; Beyerlin 1970:
129f.; McKay 1979). However, the language is too vague and stylized to
posit such a specific setting. In our opinion, it is more likely that the
imagery of God's 'wings' represents a more general metaphor drawn
from nature rather than the temple (cf. Craigie 1983: 292; Ruth 2.12; on
this image in the Near East, see Dahood 1965a: 107-108; Keel 1978: 190-
92).

v. 2d. עד יעבר הוות—'until destruction passes by'
Discord between the subject and verb—here the feminine plural noun
הוות is construed with a third person masculine singular verb—often
happens when the verb precedes the subject (GKC 145o; Williams 228).
The noun usually occurs in the plural in the Psalter (Pss. 5.10; 38.13;
52.4; 55.12; 91.3; 94.20; with Ps. 52.9 being the only exception). הוות

refers to both the malicious desires and actions of the wicked (*TWAT* II.380-81). For the syntax of this clause compare Isa. 26.20.

v. 3b. גמר עלי—'who avenges on my behalf'
Dahood (1953c) convincingly argues that גמר has undergone a semantic development similar to that of גמל and שלם, both of which can denote 'to complete' or 'to recompense'. Thus גמר denotes 'to come to an end, cease' (Pss. 12.2; 77.9) or 'to avenge' (Pss. 7.10; 138.8). The latter is more appropriate here. However, in contrast to Dahood who understands עלי as a divine name, *'ēlî* 'Most High', we take עלי to be the suffixed preposition similar to בעדי in Ps. 138.8, 'on my behalf, for me' (cf. the related phrase גמל על in Pss. 13.6; 103.10; 116.7; etc.).

v. 4a. ישלח משמים ויושיעני—'He will send from heaven and save me'
Some scholars take the verbs in v. 4a and 4c as jussives, 'Let him send from heaven and save me... Let God send' (Weiser 1962: 425; Kraus 1978: 569; Auffret 1977: 60; *et al.*). In that case, vv. 2-4 would be understood as the petition. Three factors weigh against this view.

1. The similarity of sequence between vv. 2 and 3-4 indicates that v. 4 is a statement of confidence and not a petition. The petition in v. 2a is followed by a statement of confidence in v. 2b-d. Verse 3 describes the petition made in v. 2a, 'I cry to God Most High, to El who avenges on my behalf'. One therefore expects v. 4 to represent a statement of confidence as in v. 2b-d. In other words the sequence of v. 2—petition (2a) plus statement of confidence (2b-d)—is repeated in vv. 3-4—description of petition (3) plus expression of confidence (4) (cf. Pss. 3.5; 18.7f.).
2. The verbs in v. 4a and c expand on the participle in v. 3b, גמר. Thus one expects 'indicatives' to follow the participle of v. 3b and not jussives.
3. A close parallel is found Ps. 18.17, ישלח ממרום, where ישלח is also an 'indicative'.

For these reasons we translate the verbs in v. 4 as 'indicatives' (so also RSV, NIV, Dahood 1968a: 49).
   The object of ישלח in v. 4a is postponed until v. 4d, חסדו ואמתו. This amounts to a variation of 'staircase parallelism' in which a sentence is started, interrupted by an intervening word or clause, and then resumed from the beginning and completed (Watson 1984: 150-56). One should therefore understand v. 4 in the following way:

| Beginning of sentence | — | 'He will send from heaven' |
|---|---|---|
| Intervening material | — | 'and save me, though the one hounding me taunts' |
| Resumption and completion of sentence | — | 'God will send his steadfast love and his faithfulness'. |

Both משמים and אלהים are part of the one basic sentence which the poet has broken up, i.e. 'God will send from heaven his steadfast love and his faithfulness' (cf. O'Connor's treatment of the trope of 'coloration', 1980: 112-15).

v.4b. חרף שאפי—'though the ones hounding me taunt'
Since God is never the subject of the verb חרף, it is best to take the participle, a collective singular, as the subject of the verb (*TWAT* III.226, 228). On the meaning of שאף, 'to pant after, hound', see under Ps. 56.2.

The direct object is left unstated. It could be God as in Ps. 74.10 and Isa. 37.4, 23-24 or the psalmist as in Pss. 55.13 and 119.42. The clause is probably intentionally ambiguous so that both God and the psalmist are the objects of ridicule. A parallel is found in Ps. 42.11 where the enemies taunt the psalmist by asking, 'Where is your God?' The psalmist in our text expresses confidence that God will save him in spite of the enemies' taunt.

v.4d. חסדו ואמתו—'his steadfast love and his faithfulness'
These two nouns, a common word pair (Pss. 25.10; 40.11; 61.8; etc.), are the personified agents whom God sends to save the psalmist (cf. Ps. 43.3 where אמת is personified and Pss. 85.11 and 89.15 where both are personified). In v. 11 this word pair is split (cf. Melamed 1961; O'Connor 1980: 112-15).

v.5a. נפשי בתוך לבאם—'My life is in the midst of lions'
נפשי is a periphrasis for the first person pronoun 'I' (GKC 144m). It should not be construed with the verb אשכבה. The syntax is similar to that of 1 Kgs 3.8, 'your servant is in the midst of your people', and Ezek. 1.1, 'I (אני) was in the midst of the exiles'. The psalms often employ the metaphor of 'lions' to describe the enemies (cf. Pss. 7.3; 10.9; 22.14, 22; etc. On the MT's vocalization *lĕbā'im*, see Dahood 1968a: 52).

v.5b. אשכבה להטים—'I lie down in the midst of those who are aflame'
The cohortative אשכבה expresses strong resolution (cf. Ps. 4.9; GKC 108a-b). בתוך from the previous clause is ellipsed.

The qal participle להטים is difficult. Most commentators follow G.R. Driver (1931: 38-40) in understanding להם as a verb related to Arabic *lahaṭa*, 'to devour', and thus distinct from the Hebrew root להם whose common meaning is 'to be aflame'. In that case בני־אדם would serve as the direct object, i.e. 'among those who greedily devour the sons of man'. However, two factors weigh against this proposal.

1. להטים is accented *'oleh we-yored* which indicates that the Mas-soretes considered the main verse division to lie here and not after

בני אדם (cf. Yeivin 1980: 265). The versions unanimously agree (Delitzsch 1871: 175).

2. The Hebrew root consistently means 'to be aflame, burn'. When it takes a direct object it always occurs in the piel (Deut. 32.22; Isa. 42.25; Joel 1.19; 2.3; Mal. 3.19; Pss. 83.15; 97.3; 106.18). The qal occurs once but with no object (Ps. 104.4).

Therefore, we understand v.5a-c as a tricolon with בני־אדם in apposition to להטים.

The poet is working with two basic images regarding the enemies in v.5, lions and men. The 'teeth' and 'tongue' in v.5d-e refer to the lions' ferocious appetite, whereas the weapons belong to the 'sons of man'. Thus, the lions with their teeth and tongue are metaphorically equated with the human enemies with their weapons. The participle להטים applies to both. As it applies to the lions, it refers to the fiery appearance, the tawny body and magnificent mane of the male lion (Freedman, p.c.). As it applies to 'the sons of man', it designates their hot anger as well as their flashing swords.

v.6. רומה על־השמים אלהים—'Be exalted over the heavens, O God'
על כל־הארץ כבודך—'Let your glory be exalted over all the earth'
We understand this as an example of *syllepsis* (sometimes called *zeugma*), a kind of ungrammatical ellipsis. Here the imperative רומה, gapped in the second colon, belongs with both אלהים (grammatically) and כבודך (ungrammatically). Normally the latter would take the jussive form ירום. A close parallel is found in Ps. 113.4 where רום is also gapped in the second colon:

| רם על־כל־גוים יהוה | — | Yahweh is exalted over all the nations; |
| על השמים כבודו | — | his glory (is exalted) over the heavens. |

However, it is also possible to understand כבודך as a vocative divine title going with the gapped imperative, 'Be exalted over all the earth, Your Honor'.

In this context, v.6 functions as a prayer that God should manifest his majesty by saving the psalmist and intervening against the enemies (cf. Pss. 7.7 and 94.2 where הנשא functions the same way; also see Auffret 1977).

v.7b. כפף נפשי—'They bent down my life'
The MT is difficult. The feminine noun נפש should take a feminine verb if it is the subject, as in v.2b. However, כפף is vocalized as a third masculine singular suffixing verb. Also, when כפף is used intransitively, 'to be bent/bowed down', it is a qal passive participle (Pss. 145.14; 146.8). In Mic. 6.6, where it is used reflexively, the niphal occurs. In the only other occurrence, found in Isa. 58.5, the qal infinitive construct is used transitively, 'Is it to bend down one's head like a reed...'

Therefore, many scholars follow the LXX and read a third person plural—*kāpĕpû*, 'they bent down my life' (Jacquet 1977: 234; Kraus 1978: 570; *et al.*). We prefer to keep the consonants of the MT but to vocalize כפף as a qal infinitive absolute written defectively, *kāpōp* (Freedman, p.c.). The qal is used in a transitive sense with נפשׁי as its object (cf. Isa. 58.5). The infinitive absolute serves the same function as the other plural suffixing verbs (Williams 210). The colon expresses the attempt of the enemies to push the psalmist down into the pit where the net would entrap him.

**v. 8a-b.** נכון לבי אלהים נכון לבי—'My heart is confident, O God, my heart is confident'
This is a good example of a 'pivot pattern', in which the words in the first colon are repeated or paralleled in the second colon, but the final element of the first colon (usually a vocative) is gapped in the second colon (Watson 1984: 150, 214-21). נכון לבי means 'my heart is steadfastly confident in God' as the parallels in Pss. 78.37 and 112.7 indicate. Its opposite is 'to fear one's enemies' (Ps. 112.7-8).

**v. 8c.** אשׁירה ואזמרה—'so that I will sing and make music'
These two cohortatives are to be understood in sequence with the previous two cola (cf. GKC 108d; Ps. 30.13). The poet is so confident that God will save him that he intends to sing even before the dawn.

**v. 9.** עורה כבודי—'Awake, O my "self" ',
עורה הנבל וכנור—'awake, O harp and lyre',
אעירה שׁחר—'so that I can awaken the dawn'.
One might understand this verse in two different ways.

1. Read the text as follows:

| עורה כבודי עורה | — | Awake, O my honored one, awake! |
| הנבל וכנור | — | With harp and lyre |
| אעירה שׁחר | — | I will awaken (you) at dawn |

This view puts both imperatives in the same colon as also in v. 2a (so Auffret 1977). Elsewhere the imperative of עור is always addressed to someone else rather than to one's own self. Often the addressee is God (Pss. 7.7; 44.24; 59.5; Isa. 51.9). The vocative כבודי refers to God, 'my Honored One/my Glory', as in Ps. 3.4 and like כבודך in this psalm (vv. 6, 12). The implied object of אעירה is also God. The phrase הנבל וכנור is a prepositional phrase with an ellipsed ב. Thus, the psalmist is praying that God awaken from his sleep and intervene to save the psalmist. He plans to awaken the deity with his songs and musical instruments at dawn.

2. Read the text the traditional way. This view understands the first imperative to be addressed to the psalmist's own 'self'. Gevirtz (1981: 101-10) has demonstrated that כבוד denotes the 'belly' and, by

extension, the 'person, self' (cf. Pss. 7.6; 16.9; 30.13; 108.2; Gen.
49.6. It should not be emended to *kābēd*, 'liver', *contra* Dahood
1968a: 54). The second imperative is addressed to his 'harp and
lyre'. Like v.8c, the cohortative in v.9c should be understood in
sequence with the previous two cola. The noun שחר is the object of
the verb אעירה. (On the personification of 'dawn', see McKay 1970:
456-60.) The psalm is spoken in the early morning before the
dawn. The psalmist uses a powerful image to express his
confidence in God. The psalmist is so joyful that he cannot wait.
He exhorts himself and his instruments to wake up so that he can
awaken the slumbering sun with his music. This is similar to
Judg. 5.12, where Deborah is exhorted to awaken (עור) so that she
can sing a song. Usually the dawn awakens humans, but here
the psalmist reverses the sequence. Then in the morning he will
praise God in public among the peoples (v. 10).

While the first interpretation is possible, we prefer the second interpretation for the following reasons.

1. Understanding v.9 as a petition to God to wake up and intervene
   does not fit the context very well. Usually such petitions are spoken in the context of complaint and despair. But here the previous
   verse expresses the psalmist's confidence in God. The second
   interpretation fits this context better. The psalmist is so joyful that
   he wants to wake up early and sing and thereby, if possible, hasten the morning when he can praise God in public before others.
2. The nouns that follow imperatives in this psalm are all definite
   (vv.2a, 6, 9a, 12). Therefore, it is probable that the *hē* attached to
   נבל in v.9b marks a vocative. There are no instances in the Hebrew
   Bible where הנבל וכנור is a prepositional phrase with an ellipsed ב.
   When this phrase and similar phrases are used instrumentally,
   the preposition ב is always written (Pss. 33.2; 43.4; 49.5; 71.22; 98.5;
   144.9; 147.7; 149.3; 150.3; etc.).
3. The parallel text, Ps. 108.2-3, construes the second imperative עורה
   (the first imperative is omitted) with הנבל וכנור and כבודי with the
   preceding:

   > My heart is confident, O God.
   > I will sing and make music,
   > Yea, with my very 'self' (אף־כבודי).
   > Awake, O harp and lyre,
   > so that I can awaken the dawn.

In like manner, the MT accentuation of כבודי in Ps. 57.9, which
receives a *revia gadol*, indicates that it completes the final part of
the verse (Yeivin 1980: 267-68).

4. The time element, 'at dawn', is expressed with a preposition or a temporal phrase in the Hebrew Bible (so McKay 1970: 457; cf. Josh. 6.15; Judg. 19.25; 1 Sam. 9.26; Hos. 10.15; Neh. 4.15; Jon. 4.7). Therefore, one should probably take שׁחר to be the object of the verb אעירה.

v. 10b. בל־אמים—'among the peoples'
Read *ballĕʾummîm* for MT's *bal-ʾummîm* (cf. Pss. 44.15; 108.4; 149.7).

v. 12a. רומה על־שׁמים אלהים—'Be exalted over the heavens, O God'
On this verse, see under v. 6. However, in contrast to v. 6 which functions as a petition in that context, i.e. with perlocutionary force, v. 12 in this context functions as a doxology, i.e. with illocutionary force. After vowing to praise God in vv. 8-10, the psalmist now expresses his doxology. By uttering the imperative 'Be exalted', he is expressing his own praise rather than trying to move God to intervene. He is acknowledging that God is exalted over the heavens and earth (cf. Pss. 99.2; 113.4; 138.6; 148.13). The use of this imperative to praise God is also reflected in Ps. 21.14, רומה יהוה. Ps. 18.47 contains another close parallel where ירום, a jussive, functions as praise (see Mitchell 1987: 152). An analogy can be found in the *bārûk yahweh* formula, which is to be understood as an optative, 'May Yahweh be blessed/praised' (Mitchell 1987: 146-60). Just as the psalmist fulfills his vow to 'bless/praise' God (אברכה, Ps. 145.1) by uttering the *bārûk* formula, so he fulfills his vow to 'exalt' God (ארוממך, Ps. 145.1) by uttering the imperative רומה in Ps. 57.12.

### 2.5.4 *Structure*

2.5.4.1 *Versification*. The poem is based on a 'non-alphabetic' acrostic structure with 33 cola (= 22 + 11; see Freedman 1986). There are 15 verses (11 according to MT's versification) which include 1 monocolon, 10 bicola, and 4 tricola. The poem begins with a monocolon followed by a tricolon. The other three tricola are located internally, one near the end of the first stanza (v. 5a-c) and two in the middle of the second stanza (vv. 8-9). The two refrains (vv. 6, 12) are bicola.

| v. 2a | Monocolon—This represents an ABA monocolon (Watson 1984: 215). |
|---|---|
| v. 2b-d | Tricolon—The preposition ב and the root חסה are repeated in the first two cola. חסיה in A and אחסה in B represent the suffixing–prefixing verb sequence. The C colon is connected to B syntactically by עד. |

| | |
|---|---|
| v. 3 | Bicolon—The verb אקרא is gapped in the second colon. לאלהים and לאל are a word pair and sound pair. עליון and עלי are also a sound pair. |
| v. 4a-b | Bicolon—B is a concessive clause tied to A. A and B have final rhyme. |
| v. 4c-d | Bicolon—B is the direct object of the verb in A. |
| v. 5a-c | Tricolon—נפשי in A is grammatically parallel to the first person of the verb אשכבה in B and בתוך is gapped in B. לבאם in A and להטים in B alliterate and have final rhyme. בנ־אדם in C is in apposition to להטים (see under 2.5.3 Notes). |
| v. 5d-e | Bicolon—שניהם and לשונם, both with a plural suffix, are paired. תניח וחצים alliterates with חרב חדה. Both cola are verbless sentences. |
| v. 6 | Bicolon—The verb is gapped in B. על־השמים and על כל־הארץ are paired as are אלהים and כבודך. |
| v. 7a-b | Bicolon—The suffixing verb in A and the infinitive absolute in B (see under Notes) take the same subject. לפעמי and נפשי are paired. |
| v. 7c-d | Bicolon—Both cola begin with plural suffixing verbs. The antecedent of the suffix with בתוכה in B is שיחה in A and both have final rhyme. Semantically the two cola form a contrast. Instead of the psalmist, the enemies fall into the pit they dug. |
| v. 8 | Tricolon—The first two cola represent a 'pivot pattern' with אלהים gapped in B (Watson 1984: 216). The verbs in C are in sequence with the previous cola (see under Notes). |
| v. 9 | Tricolon—(On our colonic divisions, see under 2.5.3 Notes). עורה is repeated at the beginning of A and B and the same root begins C. כבודי in A and כור in B alliterate. The third colon is in sequence with the previous cola like v. 8c above. |
| v. 10 | Bicolon—This verse exhibits the 'pivot pattern'. Both cola match syntactically and semantically with אדני gapped in B. Also, there is initial alliteration. |
| v. 11 | Bicolon—The two cola match syntactically and semantically and exhibit final rhyme. Each of the word pairs of שחקים/שמים and אמתך/חסדך are split and נדל is gapped in B. |
| v. 12 | Bicolon—Compare v. 6. |

## 2.5.4.2 *Stress and Syllable Counts*

| Verse | Syllables | | Totals | Stresses | | Totals |
|-------|-----------|---|--------|----------|---|--------|
| 2a | 9 | = | 9 | 3 | = | 3 |
| 2b-d | 8 + 9 + 5 | = | 22 | 3 + 3 + 2 | = | 8 |
| 3 | 7 + 6 | = | 13 | 3 + 3 | = | 6 |
| 4a-b | 10 + 5 | = | 15 | 3 + 2 | = | 5 |
| 4c-d | 5 + 6 | = | 11 | 2 + 2 | = | 4 |
| 5a-c | 7 + 6 + 4 | = | 17 | 3 + 2 + 2 | = | 7 |
| 5d-e | 8 + 7 | = | 15 | 3 + 3 | = | 6 |
| 6 | 9 + 8 | = | 17 | 3 + 3 | = | 6 |
| 7a-b | 7 + 4 | = | 11 | 3 + 2 | = | 5 |
| 7c-d | 7 + 6 | = | 13 | 3 + 2 | = | 5 |
| 8 | 7 + 4 + 8 | = | 19 | 3 + 2 + 2 | = | 7 |
| 9 | 5 + 7 + 4 | = | 16 | 2 + 3 + 2 | = | 7 |
| 10 | 9 + 8 | = | 17 | 3 + 2 | = | 5 |
| 11 | 9 + 8/9 | = | 28 | 3 + 3 | = | 6 |
| 12 | 8 + 7/8 | = | 16 | 3 + 3 | = | 6 |
| TOTALS 15 Verses/33 cola | | | 229 | | | 86 |

### Distribution of Stresses

| Cola | Bicola | Tricola |
|------|--------|---------|
| 2″ - 13 | 3″2 - 4 | 3″2′2 - 2 |
| 3″ - 20 | 3″3 - 5 | 2′3″2 - 1 |
| 4″ - 0 | 2′2 - 1 | 3″3″2 - 1 |

The stress pattern is mixed. The 3″3 pattern and the 3″2 pattern are evenly distributed. The 3″3 pattern is represented by 5 bicola, 1 tricolon (3″3″2), and 1 monocolon (3″) for a total of 7 verses. The 3″2 pattern is represented by 4 bicola and 3 tricola for a total of 7 verses. Thus, 50% of the verses are in 3″3 and 50% in 3″2. 20 cola are 3-stress (61%) and 13 are 2-stress (39%). The average is 2.6 stresses per colon. However, this is misleading because the stress count is mixed.

### Distribution of Syllables

| Syllables | | Cola | | Total Syllables |
|-----------|---|------|---|-----------------|
| 4 | × | 4 | = | 16 |
| 5 | × | 4 | = | 20 |
| 6 | × | 4 | = | 24 |
| 7 | × | 7 | = | 49 |
| 8 | × | 7 | = | 56 |
| 9 | × | 6 | = | 54 |

| 10 | × | 1 | = | 10 |
|---|---|---|---|---|
| TOTALS | | 33 | | 229 |

No colon is less than 4 or more than 10 syllables in length. Twelve cola are 4–6 syllables and twenty cola are 7–9 syllables. This corresponds to the ratio of 2-stress to 3-stress cola (13–20). The modes are the 7-syllable and 8-syllable cola with 7 cola each.

Freedman (1986) has demonstrated that a colon of 8 syllables is often equivalent to a 3-stress colon even when it has only 2-stresses (e.g. Lam. 5.3b, 14b, 18b). Possibly there were secondary stresses or silent stresses (on the latter, see Watson 1984: 214-15). If we treat vv. 8c and 10b as equivalent to 3-stress cola, then Ps. 57 has 22 3-stress cola and 11 2-stress cola. This would correspond perfectly to its 'non-alphabetic' acrostic nature, just like Psalm 56.

2.5.4.3 *Strophes*. The poem consists of six strophes plus two refrains: vv. 2, 3-4, 5 (6 = refrain), 7, 8-9, 10-11 (12 = refrain).

| | |
|---|---|
| v. 2 | This strophe begins with a monocolon followed by a tricolon which is connected by an initial כי. The reference to the deity is in the second person. |
| vv. 3-4 | The reference to the deity is in the third person. The verbs in v. 4 expand on the participle in v. 3b (גמר). |
| v. 5 | Verse 5 is a complaint about the enemies with no reference to God. |
| v. 7 | This section is also a complaint about the enemies who are the subject of the four verbs. There is no reference to God. Verse 7a is chiastically parallel to v. 7c: |

ABC — רשת הכינו לפעמי 'A net they set for my feet.'

BCA — כרו לפני שיחה 'They dug before me a pit.'

לפעמי in A and לפני in C form a sound pair. Verse 7b and d give a contrast. The enemies tried to push the psalmist down into the pit but instead they fell into it:

כפף נפשי 'They bent down my life.'

נפלו בתוכה 'They fell into it.'

vv. 8-9      'God' is the second person, occurring as a vocative
             in the first colon. The two tricola exhibit similar
             structures. The double נטן לבי in v. 8a-b is balanced
             by the doubled עורה in v. 9a-b. The third colon of
             each tricolon begins with a cohortative, both of
             which form a sound pair (אשירה... אעירה). כבודי in
             v. 9a forms a word pair with לבי in v. 8a-b (cf. Ps.
             16.9).

vv. 10-11    The reference to 'God' in the vocative (אדני, v. 10a)
             introduces this strophe as it did in the previous
             strophe. The deity is in the second person also in
             v. 11. Verse 10 is further distinguished from the
             preceding by verbs with suffixes (אודך... אזמרך) in
             contrast to the non-suffixed verbs of v. 8 (אשירה
             ואזמרה ). כי connects v. 11 with v. 10.

### Length of Strophes

|       | verses | cola | syllables | stresses |
|-------|--------|------|-----------|----------|
| v. 2  | 2      | 4    | 31        | 11       |
| 3-4   | 3      | 6    | 39        | 15       |
| 5     | 2      | 5    | 32        | 13       |
| 7     | 2      | 4    | 24        | 10       |
| 8-9   | 2      | 6    | 35        | 14       |
| 10-11 | 2      | 4    | 35        | 11       |

The strophes vary in length. They range from 4 to 6 cola,
from 24 to 39 syllables and from 10 to 15 stresses. Yet the relationship of the strophes to each other seems to exhibit symmetry. Strophes I and VI approximate each other as do II and V.
Strophe III, however, is one colon longer than IV. The results
are the same regardless of the counting method except with
respect to 'verses'. Counting 'verses' would level the length of
the strophes.

2.5.4.4 *Refrains*. The poem contains two refrains, vv. 6 and 12.
Both refrains are structurally distinct from their respective
stanzas. Other than the imperatives at the beginning of the
poem (v. 2a), the refrains contain the only imperatives
addressed to God. Verse 6 is preceded and followed by complaints about the enemies with no references to God. Verse 12
is preceded by a כי clause (v. 11) which functions as the motive
for the vow in v. 10. Both vv. 6 and 12 are identical except that

the definite article is written in v. 6 (הַשָּׁמַיִם) but not in v. 12
(שָׁמַיִם). Both, however, are to be understood as definite nouns.

2.5.4.5 *Stanzas.* The structure of this poem consists of two
stanzas, each followed by a refrain:

|  |  |
|---|---|
| vv. 2-5 | Stanza I |
| v. 6 | Refrain |
| vv. 7-11 | Stanza II |
| v. 12 | Refrain |

The repetition of אֱלֹהִים (vv. 2a, 3a, 4c, and אֵל in 3b) and נֶפֶשׁ
(vv. 2b, 5a) serves to unify Stanza I. Also, the description of the
psalmist's dangerous situation in vv. 2d, 4b, and 5 contributes
to its unity. The repetition of זמר (vv. 8c, 10b) and the use of
near synonyms (אָשִׁירָה, v. 8c, אוֹדְךָ, v. 10a) serve to unify Stanza
II. Stanza II is further cemented by the psalmist's reference to
himself (לְפַעֲמִי, v. 7a, נַפְשִׁי, v. 7b, לְפָנַי, v. 7c, לִבִּי, v. 8a-b, כְּבוֹדִי, v. 9a)
and the mention of the deity in the second person (v. 8a, 10a).
Neither stanza exhibits inclusion.

Finally, it should be noted that *selāh* does not function as a
structural division marker in this poem. It occurs after v. 4b
and v. 7d, neither of which functions to mark the close of a
stanza. Possibly one could argue that the latter indicates the
beginning of Stanza II, and that the former marks the middle
of Stanza I. (For helpful discussions of *selāh*, whose meaning is
uncertain, see Craigie 1983: 76-77 and Casetti 1982: 40-42.)

*Length of Stanzas*

| | strophes | vv. | monocola | bicola | tricola | cola | syllables | stresses |
|---|---|---|---|---|---|---|---|---|
| vv. 2-5 | 3 | 7 | 1 | 4 | 2 | 15 | 102 | 39 |
| 7-11 | 3 | 6 | 0 | 4 | 2 | 14 | 94 | 35 |

The two stanzas are close to each other in length. The first
stanza is one colon longer than the second. The syllable and
stress counts confirm our colonic divisions, since the first
stanza is 8 syllables and 4 stresses longer than the second. By
only counting strophes, one misses the slight difference in
length between the two stanzas. Counting verses according to
the versification of the MT is even more misleading, since the
first stanza has four but the second stanza has five.

2.5.4.6 *Sections*. Psalm 57 is bipartite with the refrains completing each section: vv. 2-6, 7-12. The last verse of the psalm clearly completes the second half, although there is a pause between v. 11 and v. 12 (see above under 2.5.4.4 *Refrains*). The final rhyme (כבודך ... אמתך) and the repetition of שמים in v. 11 and v. 12 serve to tie the second refrain to the second stanza. The first refrain completes the first half. The imperatives in v. 6 and v. 2a bracket the first half. Verse 7 at first looks like a continuation of the complaints against the enemies in v. 5. However, the prophetic perfect in v. 7d, 'they have fallen into its midst', indicates that the petition of v. 6 has been answered and that the enemies have already been defeated—at least in the psalmist's mind. Therefore, the major break in the psalm comes between v. 6 and v. 7.

*Length of Sections*

|        | vv. | monocola | bicola | tricola | cola | syllables | stresses |
|--------|-----|----------|--------|---------|------|-----------|----------|
| vv. 2-6 | 8  | 1        | 5      | 2       | 17   | 119       | 45       |
| 7-11   | 7   | 0        | 5      | 2       | 16   | 110       | 41       |

The first section is one colon longer than the second which produces a psalm of 33 cola (22 + 11). The extra colon is probably the initial monocolon (v. 2a). Without it each section would have 5 bicola and 2 tricola.

2.5.4.7 *Views of Structure*. Most scholars recognize that vv. 2-6 and 7-12 are the two halves of the poem (Kirkpatrick 1902: 320-21; Baumann 1945/48: 173-76; Kissane 1953: 246; Auffret 1977; Wahl 1977: 257-63; Kraus 1978: 570-73; van der Lugt 1980: 474; Trublet–Aletti 1983: 38).

However, they differ on the strophic divisions. Wahl's divisions are the same as ours (vv. 2, 3-4, 5, 6 // 7, 8-9, 10-11, 12). Van der Lugt is similar except that he joins v. 3 with v. 2 rather than v. 4 (vv. 2-3, 4, 5, 6 // 7, 8-9, 10-11, 12). Kraus isolates v. 7 but not v. 5 (vv. 2, 3-6 // 7, 8-11, 12).

A few commentators divide the psalm after v. 5: Briggs (1907: 36-41—vv. 2, 3-4, 5 // 6, 7 = gloss, 8-9, 10-11, 12); Segal (1935: 132—vv. 2-5 + 7 // 6, 8-11, 12); Beaucamp (1976: 240-43—vv. 2, 3-4, 5 // 6, 7, 8-9a, 9b-10, 11-12); and Jacquet (1977: 231-40—vv. 2, 3-4b, 5, 4c-d // 6, 7, 8-9, 10-11, 12). The reason they divide it before v. 6 is because they consider v. 6 to be part

of the following hymnic section. In contrast, we believe v.6
functions as a petition which completes the first half. (For a
thorough discussion, see Baumann 1945/48: 173-76.)

Finally, Weiser (1962: 426) and Gerstenberger (1988: 229-
32) divide the poem after v.7 because they consider vv.2-7 to
be a complaint and vv.8-12 a hymnic section. In contrast, we
believe v.7 serves to introduce the following hymnic elements.

### 2.5.5 *Repetition*
Psalm 57 exhibits two significant repetitions which we wish to
highlight. First, there are nine divine appellatives. אלהים occurs
six times (vv.2a, 3a, 4c, 6a, 8a, 12a) and אל once (v.3b) making
a total of seven divine appellatives that alliterate אל. The other
two are עליון (v.3a) and אדני (v.10a). Second, the poet expresses
his confidence and vow of praise by using a first person singular verb or its equivalent seven times: חסיה נפשי (v.2b), אחסה
(v.2c), אשירה (v.8c), אזמרה (v.8c), אעירה (v.9c), אודך (v.10a), and
אזמרך (v.10b). These two repeated elements highlight the
dominant mood of the psalm, the poet's confidence in and
praise of God.

### 2.5.6 *Thought Progression*
Psalm 57 is generally recognized as an individual lament or
complaint (Sabourin 1974: 247-48; Gerstenberger 1988: 232).
Most of the elements of an individual lament are found here:
invocation, complaint about the enemies, petition, expression
of trust, and vow of praise. Yet, this psalm exhibits these features in its own unique way. Even though its Gattung is an
individual lament, the dominant tone is one of confidence and
praise rather than despair, much like Psalm 16. We will focus
on the stanza level first and then on the movement of the
whole poem.

### 2.5.6.1 *Stanzas*. 
Stanza I contains all the above elements of an
individual lament except the vow of praise. It begins with a
petition and address to God (v.2a). This is followed by an
expression of confidence in God which gives the reason for his
appeal to God (v.2b-c). In v.2d the psalmist alludes to his
enemies. He intends to trust in God 'until destruction passes
by'. Verses 3-4 recapitulate v.2. He asserts that he is praying to

God (v. 3) and then expresses his confidence that God will save him in spite of the enemies' taunts (v. 4). The relationship between vv. 2 and 3-4 can be summarized as follows:

| | | | |
|---|---|---|---|
| A | v. 2a | — | the actual petition—'Be gracious to me' |
| B | v. 2b-c | — | assertion of his trust—'For I take refuge in you' |
| C | v. 2d | — | reference to his enemies—'until destruction passes by' |
| A | v. 3 | — | assertion that he is petitioning God—'I call to God' |
| B | v. 4a | — | the object of his trust—'He will save me' |
| C | v. 4b | — | reference to his enemies—'Though those hounding me taunt' |
| B | v. 4c-d | — | the object of his trust—'God will send...' |

Verse 5 then expands on his dangerous situation in the midst of the enemies.

Stanza II begins with the description of the enemies, 'They set a net for my feet. They bent down my life. They dug a pit before me' (v. 7a-c). Verse 7d presents an unexpected reversal. Instead of the psalmist, his enemies fell into their own pit (נפלו, a prophetic perfect). The certainty of their demise leads into the psalmist's expression of his confidence in God (vv. 8-9). His heart is confident that he will praise God in public in the morning. In fact, so confident is he that he cannot wait until the morning comes. He rouses himself and his instruments from sleep so that he can awaken the slumbering dawn with his music. In vv. 10-11 the poet declares what he will sing about and why. He vows to praise God among the peoples because God's חסד and אמת are infinite (cf. Pss. 89.2-3; 103.11).

2.5.6.2 *Poem.* The poem exhibits two movements corresponding to its bipartite structure. The first movement begins with a petition to God. This is followed by an expression of confidence in God's protection (v. 2b-d) and in God's intervention on the psalmist's behalf (vv. 3-4). He then describes his dangerous situation. In the evening he lies down to sleep in the midst of enemies (v. 5). The first refrain (v. 6) in this context functions as a petition that God manifest himself as the exalted one over all, including these particular enemies. Verses 2a and 6 thus serve as the poem's petitions, which bracket the first movement.

The second movement begins by picking up on the complaint about the enemies (v. 7). Yet, the unexpected has happened. They fell into the pit they dug for the psalmist. In response to the certain demise of the enemies, the psalmist vows to sing a hymn. He is confident and eager to sing in the morning (vv. 8-9). Whereas he sleeps among the enemies at night (v. 5), in the morning he will praise God among the nations. In this context the second refrain (v. 12) functions as the beginning of the vowed doxology in contrast to the first refrain (v. 6) which functions as a petition.

The two movements can be outlined as follows:

> I.   Petition (v. 2a)
>      Confidence (vv. 2b-4)
>      Complaint about the enemies (v. 5)
>          Refrain—petition (v. 6)
> II.  Demise of the enemies (v. 7)
>      Vow to praise (vv. 8-11)
>          Refrain—doxology (v. 12).

The first movement is characterized by what the psalmist does at night. He prays, has confidence in God's protection and deliverance, and sleeps 'in the midst of enemies'. The second movement reveals what will happen in the morning. Because the enemies are already doomed, as it were, the psalmist is eager to praise God in public. In fact, he would like to hasten the appearance of the dawn to do so. Whereas the first movement is dominated by petition and trust, the second movement is dominated by praise.

The poem's description of the enemies also corresponds to this bipartite structure. The first stanza focuses on their character. They are lions and men who are aflame with anger. Their teeth and tongue are deadly weapons (v. 5). Their actions are only briefly mentioned, 'those hounding me taunt (me and God)' (v. 4b). The second stanza focuses on their actions. They set a net and dug a pit to capture the psalmist (v. 7). Whereas in the first stanza they are compared to animals, in the second stanza they are likened to hunters.

The location of the description of the enemies in the poem also reveals a contrast between the two stanzas. The strophe describing the enemies (v. 5) is placed at the end of the first stanza. It is preceded by a lengthy section in which the poet expresses trust in God. The second stanza begins with a strophe describing the enemies (v. 7) and is followed by a lengthy praise section. The different placement of these two strophes in their respective stanzas reveals that they serve different purposes. In the first stanza the poet expresses his trust in God *in spite of* his precarious situation in the midst of the enemies. In the second stanza the poet praises God *because of* the enemies' fall. In fact they fall not only in history, but they fall out of the poem too. The end of the poem (vv. 8-12) is characterized totally by the psalmist's praise of God's greatness. The poem began with imperatives expressing the psalmist's petition to God (v. 2a). It ends also with an imperative, but this time it expresses his doxology.

## 2.6 *Psalm 59*

### 2.6.1 *Text*

| | Text | Syllables | | Total | Stresses |
|---|---|---|---|---|---|
| 1. | למנצח אל־תשחת לדוד מכתם בשלח שאול וישמרו את־הבית להמיתו | | | | |
| 2a. | הצילני מאיבי אלהי | 4+4+3 | = | 11 | 3 |
| b. | ממתקוממי תשגבני | 5+5 | = | 10 | 2 |
| 3a. | הצילני מפעלי און | 4+4+1 | = | 9 | 3 |
| b. | ומאנשי דמים הושיעני | 4+2+4 | = | 10 | 3 |
| 4a. | כי הנה ארבו לנפשי | 1+2+3+3 | = | 9 | 3 |
| b. | יגורו עלי עזים | 3+2+2 | = | 7 | 3 |
| c. | לא־פשעי ולא־חטאתי יהוה | 1+2+2+3+2 | = | 10 | 4 |
| 5a. | בלי־עון ירוצון ויכננו | 2+2+3+5 | = | 12 | 4 |
| b. | עורה לקראתי וראה | 2+3+3 | = | 8 | 3 |
| 6a. | ואתה יהוה־אלהים צבאות | 3+2+3+3 | = | 11 | 4 |
| b. | אלהי ישראל | 3+3 | = | 6 | 2 |
| c. | הקיצה לפקד כל־הגוים | 3+2+1+3 | = | 9 | 3 |
| d. | אל־תחן כל־בגדי און סלה | 1+2+1+3+1 | = | 8 | 3 |
| 7a. | ישובו לערב יהמו ככלב | 3+2+2+2 | = | 9 | 4 |
| b. | ויסובבו עיר | 4+1 | = | 5 | 2 |
| 8a. | הנה יביעון בפיהם | 2+3+3 | = | 8 | 3 |
| b. | חרבות בשפתותיהם | 3+5 | = | 8 | 2 |
| c. | כי־מי שמע | 1+1+2 | = | 4 | 2 |
| 9a. | ואתה יהוה תשחק־למו | 3+2+2+2 | = | 9 | 3 |
| b. | תלעג לכל־גוים | 2+2+2 | = | 6 | 2 |
| 10a. | [עזי] אליך אשמרה | 2+3+3 | = | 8 | 3 |
| b. | כי־אלהים משגבי | 1+3+3 | = | 7 | 3 |
| 11a. | אלהי חסדי | 3+2 | = | 5 | 2 |
| b. | יקדמני אלהים | 5+3 | = | 8 | 2 |
| c. | יראני בשררי | 3+4 | = | 7 | 2 |
| 12a. | אל־תהרגם פן־ישכחו עמי | 1+3+1+3+2 | = | 10 | 4 |
| b. | הניעמו בחילך והורידמו | 4+4+5 | = | 13 | 3 |
| c. | מגננו אדני | 4+3 | = | 7 | 2 |
| 13a. | חטאת־פימו דבר־שפתימו | 2+2+2+4 | = | 10 | 4 |
| b. | וילכדו בגאונם | 5+3 | = | 8 | 2 |
| c. | ומאלה ומכחש יספרו | 4+3+4 | = | 11 | 3 |
| 14a. | כלה בחמה כלה ואינמו | 2+3+2+4 | = | 11 | 4 |
| b. | וידעו כי־אלהים | 4+1+3 | = | 8 | 3 |
| c. | משל ביעקב | 2+3 | = | 5 | 2 |
| d. | לאפסי הארץ סלה | 3+2 | = | 5 | 2 |
| 15a. | וישובו לערב יהמו ככלב | 4+2+2+2 | = | 10 | 4 |
| b. | ויסובבו עיר | 4+1 | = | 5 | 2 |
| 16a. | המה יניעון לאכל | 2+3+2 | = | 7 | 3 |
| b. | אם־לא ישבעו וילינו | 1+1+3+4 | = | 9 | 3 |
| 17a. | ואני אשיר עזך | 3+2+3 | = | 8 | 3 |

| | | | | | |
|---|---|---|---|---|---|
| b. | ואָרֹן לבקר חסדך | 4+2+3 | = | 9 | 3 |
| c. | כי־היית משגב לי | 1+3+2+1 | = | 7 | 3 |
| d. | ומנוס ביום צר־לי | 3+2+1+1 | = | 7 | 3 |
| 18a. | עזי אליך אזמרה | 2+3+4 | = | 9 | 3 |
| b. | כי־אלהים משגבי | 1+3+3 | = | 7 | 3 |
| c. | אלהי חסדי | 3+2 | = | 5 | 2 |
| TOTALS | | 46 cola | | 375 | 131 |

## 2.6.2 *Translation*

1.  For the musical director. According to 'Do Not Destroy'. Of David. A Miktam. When Saul sent (men) and they watched the house in order to kill him.

2a.  Deliver me from my enemies, O my God.
 b.  From those who rise up against me set me on high.
3a.  Deliver me from evil-doers,
 b.  and from blood-thirsty men save me.

4a.  For, look! They lie in ambush for my life.
 b.  Strong men are hostile against me,
 c.  for no rebellion of mine and no sin of mine, O Yahweh.
5a.  For no iniquity (of mine) they run and get ready.
 b.  Rouse yourself to meet me and examine.

6a.  You, O Yahweh-God of Hosts,
 b.  the God of Israel,
 c.  awake to punish all the nations;
 d.  do not be gracious to any who treacherously plot evil. SELAH

### REFRAIN A

7a.  *They return in the evening; they growl like dogs;*
 b.  *and they prowl about the city.*

8a.  Look! They foam forth from their mouth—
 b.  swords from their lips:
 c.  'For who hears?'
9a.  But you, Yahweh, laugh at them.
 b.  You mock all (the) nations.

### REFRAIN B

10a.  *O my strength, for you will I watch.*
 b.  *For you, God, are my fortress,*
11a.  *my loving God.*

11b. May God go before me.
  c. May he let me look down upon my foes.
12a. Do not kill them lest my people forget.
  b. Shake them by your power and bring them down,
  c. O Lord our shield.

13a. For the sin of their mouth, for the word of their lips,
  b. let them be caught in their pride.
  c. And for the curse and for the deceit which they utter,
14a. consume (them) in wrath; consume (them) that they be no more.
  b. Then they will know that God—
  c. rules in Jacob—
  d. to the ends of the earth. SELAH

## REFRAIN A

15a. *They return in the evening; they growl like dogs;*
  b. *and they prowl about the city.*

16a. As for them, they roam to devour.
  b. If they are not satisfied, they remain through the night.
17a. But as for me, I will sing of your strength;
  b. and I will sing aloud of your steadfast love in the morning.
  c. For you have become a fortress for me,
  d. and a refuge in the day of my distress.

## REFRAIN B

18a. *O my strength, to you I hymn.*
  b. *For you, God, are my fortress,*
  c. *my loving God.*

### 2.6.3 *Translation Notes*

v. 1. אל־תשחת לדוד מכתם—'According to "Do not Destroy". Of David. A Miktam'
See under Notes for Pss. 56.1; 57.1.

v. 1. בשלח שאול וישמרו את־הבית להמיתו—'When Saul sent (men) and they watched the house in order to kill him'
The historical note refers to 1 Sam. 19.11ff.

v. 2b. ממתקוממי תשגבני—'From those who rise up against me set me on high'
The prefixing verb תשגבני is optative here since it is in the context of imperatives (Williams 184). The piel of שגב means 'to set on high, exalt'

(Pss. 20.2; 69.30; 91.14; 107.41; Isa. 9.10). The prayer is that God would be a lofty tower for the psalmist far out of the reach of the self-exalted enemies. The root שגב forms an inclusion with משגבי in v. 18b.

**v. 3b. ומאנשי דמים**—'and from blood-thirsty men'
On the figurative sense of this phrase in the Psalms, see van Uchelen (1969).

**v. 4b. יגורו עלי עזים**—'Strong men are hostile against me'
On יגורו, see under Notes for Ps. 56.7. We read *'azzîm* with the other manuscripts instead of *'azîm* (cf. Ezek. 7.24).

**v. 5a. בלי־עון**—'For no iniquity (of mine)'
The first person singular suffix from פשעי and חטאתי in v. 4c is gapped.

**v. 6a. ואתה יהוה־אלהים צבאות**—'You, O Yahweh-God of Hosts'
Dahood (1968a: 68) attaches ואתה to v. 5b, 'and see for yourself'. However, v. 9a—ואתה יהוה—argues against splitting up ואתה and יהוה.
The phrase יהוה־אלהים צבאות is difficult. It occurs three other times (Pss. 80.5, 20; 84.9) and אלהים צבאות occurs twice (Ps. 80.8, 15). Hummel (1957: 97) takes the final *mēm* of אלהים in these cases as an enclitic *mēm*. Although this is possible, Tsevat (1965: 50) persuasively argues that 'opposed to it is the formulaic nature of יהוה אלהי צבאות, 18 times, that should have protected the wording, and also that in two of the verses (59.6; 84.9) the construct אלהי is unchanged in other compounds'. Therefore, we prefer an old explanation offered by Delitzsch (1871: 188) that אלהים became a proper name like יהוה and that צבאות is a genitive dependent upon the compound name 'Yahweh-Elohim'.
The refrains in Psalm 80 reveal how this phrase developed. The sequence is אלהים (v. 4) to אלהים צבאות (vv. 8, 15) to יהוה אלהים צבאות (v. 20). This sequence indicates that אלהים was considered a personal name and יהוה אלהים a compound name.
One might also understand יהוה...צבאות as a broken construct chain with אלהים as a displaced nominative absolute, 'You, O Yahweh of Hosts, God, the God of Israel'. However, we feel that the two occurrences of אלהים צבאות (Ps. 80.8, 15) weigh against this option.
For the sequence יהוה אלהים צבאות־אלהי ישראל, compare Pss. 69.7 and 84.9. On the analogy of v. 9a and Pss. 69.7; 84.9, we take v. 6a-b as an extended vocative with v. 6c-d serving as the main clauses. Verse 6a-d is an example of what O'Connor calls 'mixing' (1980: 421-22).

**v. 7a. יהמו ככלב**—'they growl like dogs'
The verb המה is used of dogs only here. Since נבח denotes a dog's 'barking' (Isa. 56.10) and המה is applied to the 'growling' or 'groaning' of bears (Isa. 59.11), we translate יהמו 'they growl'. We take the singular כלב as a collective.

v.7b. עיר ויסובבו—'and they prowl about the city'
The phrase סבב עיר is equivalent to the phrase סבב בעיר, 'to roam through the city', in Cant. 3.2-4; 5.7. The preposition is omitted as often happens in poetry. The image is that of scavenger dogs which are sleepy and harmless by day but active and dangerous by night.

v.8a-b. בפיהם יביעון—'They foam forth from their mouth—'
חרבות בשפתותיהם—'swords from their lips'
The root נבע, 'to gush forth', is used once in the qal to designate a 'flowing wadi' (נחל נבע, Prov. 18.4). The other ten occurrences including this verse are in the hiphil, all of them with a direct object. In Eccl. 10.1 the object is perfume: 'deadly flies cause to stink, *they cause to bubble/ferment* the oil of the perfumer' (שמן רוקח). In Prov. 1.23 the object is Lady Wisdom's spirit: '*I will pour out* to you my spirit' (רוחי). Elsewhere the object is some form of speech: 'foolishness' (אולת, Prov. 15.2), 'evil words' (רעות, Prov. 15.28), 'arrogance' (עתק, Ps. 94.4), 'riddles' (חידות, Ps. 78.2), 'speech' (אמר, Ps. 19.3), 'praise' (תהלה, Ps. 119.171) and God's 'fame' (זכר, Ps. 145.7).

In light of this evidence, we take חרבות as the object of יביעון (so also Dahood 1968a: 69; *contra* Kraus 1978: 579-80). Thus cola A and B illustrate enjambement (Watson 1984: 335). Instead of pouring forth praises to God, the enemies pour forth 'swords', deadly words, arrogant pride (vv.8c, 13b), 'curses and lies' (v. 13c). Possibly *ḥărābôt*, 'swords', is a sound-play on *ḥărāpôt*, 'reproaches'. In light of Prov. 15.2 and 15.28 where פה is the subject and Ps. 119.171 where שפה is the subject of the verb נבע, we take the preposition ב in בפיהם and בשפתותיהם to mean 'from'.

Verse 8a-b has a structure of AC/BC′: verb–prepositional phrase/object–prepositional phrase. But when one reads v. 8a alone in light of v. 7, one gets the feeling that this colon still relates to the image of dogs growling. The enemies 'foam at their mouth' like dogs. Possibly the preposition ב is used instead of מן to maintain the ambiguity of 'pouring out from their mouth' and 'foaming at their mouth'. (For the comparative Northwest Semitic evidence which has been used to argue for the מ/ב interchange, see Zevit 1975.) To capture this ambiguity we translate, 'They foam forth from their mouth—swords from their lips'.

v.8c. שמע כי-מי—'"For who hears?"'
This colon is a quote without introduction (cf. Ps. 41.9; Prov. 23.35). The connection with the preceding is that the enemies utter lies and curses and then deny that God even hears them. The quote might also play on the homophonous word *ḥărāpôt*, 'reproaches', and thus represent the kind of reproach which they speak.

**v.9b. לכל־גוים**—'all (the) nations'
The definite article is ellipsed, as often happens in poetry. The noun is to be considered definite, however, on the analogy of הגוים in v.6c (Freedman p.c.).

**v.10a. עזי אליך אשמרה**—'O my strength, for you will I watch'
One might keep the MT עזו and consider this a vocative liturgical title, 'His Power', similar to English, 'His Royal Highness'. However, on the analogy of v.18a, we follow several Hebrew manuscripts, the LXX, Targums, and most commentators in reading עזי instead of MT עזו. The cohortative אשמרה expresses strong resolution (GKC 108a-b). There is no need to harmonize v.10a with v.18a and read אזמרה in both (*contra* Briggs 1907: 56). On the contrary, there is a movement between v.10 and v.18. Verse 10 expresses the hope; v.18 expresses the fulfillment. On the phrase, compare 1 Sam. 26.15; Ps. 130.6.

**v.10b. כי־אלהים משגבי**—'For you, God, are my fortress'
We take אלהים as a vocative in keeping with v.10a.

**v.11a. אלהי חסדי**—'my loving God'
The Kethib reads אלהי חסדו but the Qere reads אלהי חסדי. The Kethib agrees with the LXX (ὁ θεός μου, τὸ ἔλεος αὐτοῦ προφθάσει με) but the Qere agrees with v.18c and other manuscripts. We prefer the latter. In light of v.18c, אלהי חסדי is to be construed with v.10. On the translation of the phrase חסדי אלהי, see Weingreen 1954: 55-56.

**v.11b. יקדמני אלהים**—'May God go before me'
We take the verb יקדמני and the following יראני as optatives in light of the following imperatives. The verb קדם in the piel can mean either 'to come before' or 'to go before, precede' (BDB). We take it in the latter sense (cf. Ps. 68.26).

**v.12a. אל־תהרגם פן־ישכחו עמי**—'Do not kill them lest my people forget'
Verse 12a has disturbed commentators because of the apparent contradiction with v.14. Suggested solutions include the following: read אל־תרחם, 'do not have compassion' (Briggs 1907: 56; Weiser 1962: 433-34); read אל־תשכחם פן־יהרגו עמי, do not forget them lest they kill my people' (Jacquet 1977: 257); read אל־תהרגנעם, 'let them not have peace' (Kissane 1953: 255); understand אל as an asseverative, 'surely you shall slay them' (Dahood 1963: 293-94); and repoint *'al* to *'ēl*, 'O El, slay them' (Dahood 1968a: 71). The last two suggestions keep the consonantal text and therefore, are the most attractive. However, against the last suggestion is the fact that nowhere in the poem does *'ēl* occur nor does the divine name ever occur in initial position. Against taking *'al* as an asseverative is the related phrase אל־תחן of v.6d where אל is the negative particle. (Muraoka 1985: 123-25 disputes the existence of an asseverative *'al* in Biblical Hebrew.)

In our opinion, the text as it stands makes good sense. Often in Hebrew poetry two opposite statements are juxtaposed where we would use a modifying clause (Kidner 1973: 213). The psalmist is praying that God will not kill them *immediately* but rather 'make them shake/wander' and 'bring them down from their exalted state'. The desperate state of these enemies is to be an object lession and a visible warning lest Israel forget what are the consequences of human wickedness (v. 13) and who is the sole ruler in Jacob (v. 14). 'If they were completely destroyed, the nation would forget the triumph of God' (Oesterley 1962: 296). Only after they 'shake/wander' (v. 12b) and are 'caught in their pride' (v. 13) so that Israel can see it, should God consume them (v. 14) (so also Kraus 1978: 583-84; McKay 1979: 241; Kirkpatrick 1902: 336; *et al.*). With this understanding of the text, compare Exod. 9.14-16.

v. 12b. הניעמו בחילך והורידמו—'Shake them by your power and bring them down'
The verb נוע is polysemous; in the qal it is translated 'to shake/tremble'. and 'to wander/roam' (*TWAT* V.315-18). The hiphil, which always takes an object, retains this polysemy: 'to wag one's head' (2 Kgs 19.21 = Isa. 37.22; Pss. 22.8; 109.25; Lam. 2.15; Job 16.4, 'to shake with [במו] the head'); 'to shake one's hand' (Zeph. 2.15); 'to disturb bones' (2 Kgs 23.18); 'to make one tremble' (Dan. 10.10); and 'to make persons wander' (Num. 32.13; 2 Sam. 15.20). Thus the verb here could be translated 'shake them/make them tremble' or 'make them wander'.
The following prepositional phrase is also ambiguous. (On חיל, see *TWAT* II.902-11.) It could be translated 'by your power' (cf. Ezek. 28.5) or 'by your army' (cf. Ezek. 27.10).
Thus the phrase הניעמו בחילך is ambiguous and, in our opinion, deliberately so. It reads well both ways.

1. 'Make them totter/tremble by your power'. In this reading, the petition is that God should make these 'strong men' (v. 4b) who have proudly risen up against the psalmist (v. 2b) shake and tremble before God's 'power' (cf. Exod. 20.18).
2. 'Make them wander/roam by your (heavenly) army'. In this reading the petition is that God make these enemies who have 'stationed themselves' against the psalmist (v. 5a) roam like vagabonds from before the heavenly armies of Yahweh (v. 6a).

The first reading is developed by the following imperative, 'and bring them down', i.e. shake them and bring them down from their self-exalted position and pride (v. 13b). The second reading is developed in v. 16a—'They roam (יעוון) like dogs in order to eat'. (A similar ambiguity occurs in Amos 9.9, 'I will make the house of Israel wander

among all the nations' or 'I will shake the house of Israel... as one
shakes with a sieve'.)

v. 12c. מגנו אדני—'O Lord our shield'
The first person plural suffix of מגנו indicates that the psalmist here
identifies himself with 'Israel' (v. 6) and speaks on behalf of his
'people' (v. 12a). We prefer to keep the traditional translation of *māgēn*,
'shield', because the protective image conforms with the other divine
epithets in the psalm, 'my strength' and 'my refuge'. As God defeats
the enemies, he also acts as the people's defensive shield. (In favor of
translating מגנו 'our Suzerain', see Dahood 1968a: 72, but in opposition
see Loretz 1974b: 177-83. On the possibility of reading *mōgēn*,
'Geber/Schenker', see *TWAT* IV.658-59.)

v. 13a. חטאת־פימו דבר־שפתימו—'For the sin of their mouth, for the word of
their lips'
The preposition מן of ומאלה ומכחש in v. 13c serves double-duty for חטאת and
דבר. (For another example of an element gapped in the first colon but
written in the second, see Ps. 9.16, זו).

v. 14a. כלה בחמה כלה ואינמו—'consume (them) in wrath; consume (them)
that they be no more'
On the relationship between v. 14a and v. 12a, see above under v. 12a.
On the phrase כלה בחמה compare Ezek. 43.8 and Num. 25.11. On the
repetition of כלה, compare Ps. 37.20.

v. 14b-d. וידעו כי־אלהים—'Then they will know that God—
משל ביעקב rules in Jacob—
לאפסי הארץ to the ends of the earth'
This sentence can be understood two ways.

1. 'They (the enemies) will know that God rules in/from Jacob to the
   ends of the earth'. Here the phrase לאפסי הארץ is construed with
   משל ביעקב, indicating that God's rule extends to the ends of the
   earth (cf. 1 Sam. 2.10; Mic. 5.3; and especially Zech. 9.10 and Ps.
   72.8). The preposition ב indicates either location 'in' or source
   'from' (cf. Ps. 76.2; Mic. 5.1; 1 Kgs 18.36).
2. 'They will know to the ends of the earth that God rules in Jacob'.
   Here the phrase לאפסי הארץ is construed with וידעו, indicating that
   all people to the ends of the earth will recognize God's rule
   in/from Jacob (cf. 1 Sam. 17.46; Pss. 67.8; 98.3).

In our opinion, the phrase לאפסי הארץ is placed at the end of the sentence precisely to promote both understandings. All the nations are to
know that God rules in Jacob and also from Jacob over all the nations.
Since the last phrase goes with both וידעו כי־אלהים and משל ביעקב, we consider v. 14b-d a tricolon.

v. 16a. המה—'As for them'
Patton (1944: 37), followed by Dahood (1964: 404), suggested that המה is
an emphasizing particle 'lo, behold', on the basis the supposed meaning of Ugaritic *hm*. But de Moor (1969) demonstrated that Ugaritic *hm*
always means 'if'. Dahood later (1968a: 73) repointed *hēmmâ* to the
infinitive absolute *hāmōh*—'growling'. Such an emendation is unnec-
essary. The personal pronoun *hēmmâ* makes acceptable sense in this
context, since it contrasts with אני in v. 17a—'As for them … But as for
me'.

v. 16a. יעון—'they roam to devour'
We follow the Kethib יעון. The Qere יניעון apparently was influenced by
the parallel יביעון in v. 8a. Here the verb נע picks up on the second meaning of הניעמו in v. 12b, 'to wander/roam' (see above). The phrase as it
applies to the simile of v. 15 refers to scavenger dogs roaming the
streets in search of grub. (Contrast v. 8 which develops the image of the
dog's growling.) As it applies to the enemies, it refers to their desire to
devour the psalmist (cf. Ps. 109.10; Amos 4.8; Job 15.23, נדד).

v. 16b. וילינו—'they remain through the night'
We folllow the MT *wayyālînû* from לין—'to stay through the night'. The
MT fits appropriately in the context. Verse 15 compares the enemies to
scavenger dogs that return in the evening to hunt for food. But unlike
normal scavenger dogs that leave before the morning and then return
the next evening, these 'dogs' stay the night if they do not find enough
food. In v. 17 the psalmist picks up on this evening–morning image. In
spite of the threat of the dogs/enemies spending the night, the psalmist
is confident he will rejoice 'in the morning'.

The LXX has καὶ γογγύσουσιν, which is based on the Hebrew
*wĕyallînû*, the hiphil of לין, 'and they murmur'. The LXX probably represents a hearing mistake. Nevertheless, the MT *wayyālînû* might
form a sound play with the homophonous *w ĕyallînû*. The
dogs/enemies not only 'spend the night' but they also 'murmur and
grumble' if they are not satisfied. In contrast to their grumbling, the
psalmist praises God (v. 17).

v. 17b. לבקר—'in the morning'
On the 'morning' as the time of God's help and the psalmist's
response of praise, see Ziegler (1950).

### 2.6.4 *Structure*

2.6.4.1 *Versification.* Psalm 59 is based on a 'non-alphabetic'
acrostic structure with 46 cola (= 23 × 2). (On 23-unit acrostics, compare Psalms 25 and 34. See also Skehan 1951: 160 n.
13; Freedman 1972d: 385; 1986.) It has two halves each of
which has 23 cola (vv. 2-11a, 11b-18). There are 20 verses (17

according to the MT) consisting of 14 bicola and 6 tricola. Each
half has 3 tricola, two of which are located internally (vv. 4 and
8 in the first half, vv. 12 and 14b-d in the second half) and one
in the final position serving as refrain B (vv. 10-11a, 18). The
tricola in vv. 10-11a and 18 are matched. The tricola in vv. 4
and 12 are similar in that the C colon of each contains a second person address to God. The tricola in vv. 8 and 14b-d are
also related in that each consists of one long sentence with
three phrases.

| | |
|---|---|
| v. 2 | Bicolon—This bicolon exhibits a chiastic 'pivot pattern'—ABC/B'A' (Watson 1984: 214-21). The vocative אלהי is the pivotal word (C). The initial imperative with suffix and the final optative with suffix are paired; likewise the two prepositional phrases with suffixes. |
| v. 3 | Bicolon—The two cola match syntactically and are arranged chiastically—AB//B'A': hiphil imperative with suffix plus prepositional phrase beginning with *min*//prepositional phrase beginning with *min* plus hiphil imperative with suffix. |
| v. 4 | Tricolon—The suffixing verb in A and the prefixing verb in B are paired; likewise the two prepositional phrases—לנפשׁי in A and עלי in B. The C colon is a concessive clause dependent on the preceding. The first person suffixes in C connect it with the first person suffixes in A and B. |
| v. 5 | Bicolon—The two cola are semantically related. The B colon petitions God to examine the situation expressed in the A colon. |
| v. 6a-b | Bicolon—אלהים in A and אלהי in B are paired. Both cola together form an extended vocative addressed to God with B in apposition to A. One could divide the bicolon after אלהים on the basis of a 3″3 stress pattern—8 + 9 syllable pattern. In that case, it would be an example of enjambement with a split construct chain. We prefer to divide after צבאית on the basis of grammar. |
| v. 6c-d | Bicolon—The initial imperative in A and the initial vetitive in B are paired. כל is repeated and הגוים in A is paired with בגדי און in B. |

| | |
|---|---|
| v. 7 | Bicolon—The plural prefixing verb in B parallels the two prefixing verbs in A. ישׁובו לערב in A and ויסובבו עיר in B form a sound pair. One could divide the bicolon after יהמו to produce a regular stress pattern of 3″3. Then it would be an example of enjambement. We prefer to divide after ככלב on the basis of grammar with *waw* beginning the B colon. |
| v. 8 | Tricolon—Cola A and B are an example of enjambement (see under Notes). The two suffixed prepositional phrases in A and B are paired. The C colon is the direct quotation which comes 'from their mouth/lips'. |
| v. 9 | Bicolon—אתה יהוה in A is gapped in B. The qal prefixing verbs in A and B are paired and so are the prepositional phrases beginning with ל. Because the syllable count is 15, we take the stress count as 3″2 rather than 4″3. |
| v. 10-11a | Tricolon—(on this tricolon, see under Notes). Cola A and B are joined by the vocatives עזי and אלהים. אילך in A and אלהים in B form a sound pair. The pair of אלהים and אלהי and the final rhyme (-*î*) in B and C connect those two cola. Because the syllable count is 8 + 7 + 5 = 20, we count כי in B as one stress for a 3″3″2 stress pattern. |
| v. 11b-c | Bicolon—The two prefixing verbs with suffixes are paired. אלהים in A is gapped in B. |
| v. 12 | Tricolon—The vetitive in A and the two imperatives in B, all of which have a third person plural suffix, connect these two cola. The vocative מגננו אדני names the one addressed by the preceding verbs and thus forms the C colon. |
| v. 13a-b | Bicolon—The two cola are joined by syntax with the first colon forming a causal clause and the second colon the main clause (see under Notes). The third person plural pronominal suffixes also serve to unite the cola. The *waw* begins the B colon. |
| v. 13c-14a | Bicolon—This bicolon operates the same way as the previous one, i.e. causal clause in A and main clause in B. Also, the third person plural verb in A (יספרו) and the third person plural suffix in B (ואינמו) serve to connect the two cola. |

| v. 14b-d | Tricolon—We consider this a tricolon because C is to be syntactically construed with both A and B (see under Notes). Because the syllable count is 8 + 5 + 5, we count כי as one stress for a corresponding stress count of 3"2"2 (cf. vv. 10b, 18b). |
|---|---|
| v. 15 | Bicolon—This bicolon is the same as v. 7. |
| v. 16 | Bicolon—Both cola use third person plural prefixing verbs. The second colon follows the first in sequence: 'They roam to eat//If they are not satisfied...' |
| v. 17a-b | Bicolon—The two first person singular prefixing verbs (אשיר and וארנן) and the two suffixed direct objects (עזך and חסדך) are parallel. Also, the initial ואני in A and the initial וארנן in B form a sound pair. |
| v. 17c-d | Bicolon—The verb היית is gapped in B. משגב in A and מנוס in B are a word pair. לי in final position is repeated. |
| v. 18 | Tricolon—This verse is the same as vv.10-11a. |

## 2.6.4.2 *Stress and Syllable Count*

| Verse | Syllables | | Totals | Stresses | | Totals |
|---|---|---|---|---|---|---|
| 2 | 11 + 10 | = | 21 | 3 + 2 | = | 5 |
| 3 | 9 + 10 | = | 19 | 3 + 3 | = | 6 |
| 4 | 9 + 7 + 10 | = | 26 | 3 + 3 + 4 | = | 10 |
| 5 | 12 + 8 | = | 20 | 4 + 3 | = | 7 |
| 6a-b | 11 + 6 | = | 17 | 4 + 2 | = | 6 |
| 6c-d | 9 + 8 | = | 17 | 3 + 3 | = | 6 |
| 7 | 9 + 5 | = | 14 | 4 + 2 | = | 6 |
| 8 | 8 + 8 + 4 | = | 20 | 3 + 2 + 2 | = | 7 |
| 9 | 9 + 6 | = | 15 | 3 + 2 | = | 5 |
| 10a-11a | 8 + 7 + 5 | = | 20 | 3 + 3 + 2 | = | 8 |
| 11b-c | 8 + 7 | = | 15 | 2 + 2 | = | 4 |
| 12 | 10 + 13 + 7 | = | 30 | 4 + 3 + 2 | = | 9 |
| 13a-b | 10 + 8 | = | 18 | 4 + 2 | = | 6 |
| 13c-14a | 11 + 11 | = | 22 | 3 + 4 | = | 7 |
| 14b-d | 8 + 5 + 5 | = | 18 | 3 + 2 + 2 | = | 7 |
| 15 | 10 + 5 | = | 15 | 4 + 2 | = | 6 |
| 16 | 7 + 9 | = | 16 | 3 + 3 | = | 6 |
| 17a-b | 8 + 9 | = | 17 | 3 + 3 | = | 6 |
| 17c-d | 7 + 7 | = | 14 | 3 + 3 | = | 6 |
| 18 | 9 + 7 + 5 | = | 21 | 3 + 3 + 2 | = | 8 |
| TOTALS: | 20 verses/46 cola | | 375 | | | 131 |

### Distribution of Stresses

| Cola | Bicola | Tricola |
|------|--------|---------|
| 2″ - 15 | 2″2 - 1 | 3″2″2 - 2 |
| 3″ - 23 | 2″3 - 0 | 3″3″2 - 2 |
| 4″ - 8 | 3″2 - 2 | 3″3″4 - 1 |
|  | 3″3 - 5 | 4″3″2 - 1 |
|  | 4″2 - 4 |  |
|  | 3″4 - 1 |  |
|  | 4″3 - 1 |  |

The dominant stress pattern is 3″3. Of the poem's 14 bicola, 9 exhibit this pattern (64%), including the variant 4″2. Four of the six tricola have a similar pattern, two with 3″3″2, one with 3″3″4 and one with 4″3″2. Thus, 13 of the poem's 20 verses (65%) represent a 3″3 pattern. Matching the poem's acrostic structure of 23 × 2 cola, one half of the 46 cola are 3-stress, and the other 23 cola are distributed among 2-stress and 4-stress cola although somewhat unevenly, 15 to 8. The average per colon is 2.85 stresses (131 divided by 46). These figures confirm that overall the poem corresponds to a 3″3 stress pattern even though there is deviation among the verses.

### Distribution of Syllables

| Syllables | | Cola | | Total Syllables |
|-----------|---|------|---|-----------------|
| 4 | × | 1 | = | 4 |
| 5 | × | 6 | = | 30 |
| 6 | × | 2 | = | 12 |
| 7 | × | 8 | = | 56 |
| 8 | × | 9 | = | 72 |
| 9 | × | 8 | = | 72 |
| 10 | × | 6 | = | 60 |
| 11 | × | 4 | = | 44 |
| 12 | × | 1 | = | 12 |
| 13 | × | 1 | = | 13 |
| TOTALS | | 46 | | 375 |

No colon is less than 4 or more than 13 syllables. Most of the cola congregate in the middle: 31 are 7–10 syllables (67%). The most frequent lengths are 8-syllable cola with 9 and 7-syllable and 9-syllable cola with 8 each. The short and long cola balance each other: 9 cola are 4–6 syllables in length, and 12 cola are 10–13 syllables. The total of 375 syllables for 46 cola yields a mean of 8.15 syllables per colon (368 syllables would produce a perfect 8 syllables per colon). These figures also indicate that this psalm is based on a 3″3 stress/8 + 8 syllable pattern.

**2.6.4.3** *Strophes.* The poem consists of seven strophes plus two pairs of refrains: vv. 2-3, 4-5, 6 (7 = refrain A), 8-9 (10-11a = refrain B), 11b-12, 13-14 (15 = refrain A), 16-17 (18 = refrain B).

| | |
|---|---|
| vv. 2-3 | These two bicola are an example of 'alternating parallelism' (Willis 1987). They consist of four petitions, three hiphil imperatives and one piel precative. All four verbs have a first person singular suffix and are connected with a prepositional (מן) phrase. The verb הצילני is repeated in v. 2a and 3a. The reference to the deity (אלהי) is a vocative. |
| vv. 4-5 | This unit begins with כי plus the interjection הנה. It contains the motives for the previous petitions. They consist of complaints against the enemies and declaratives of the psalmist's innocence. The latter use a common set of nouns for 'sin': פשעי, חטאתי, עון. The four verbs are third person plural, one suffixing and three prefixing. The reference to the deity in v. 4c is second person and is picked up again by the imperatives in v. 5b. The petition in v. 5b is that God examine the situation described in vv. 4-5a. Verse 5b also anticipates the petitions in v. 6 and thus acts as a transition. |
| v. 6 | This strophe is introduced by an extended address to God (v. 6a-b). Then follow two petitions that God punish the enemies, an imperative in v. 6c and a vetitive in v. 6d. |
| vv. 8-9 | The interjection הנה introduces the strophe. It is preceded by refrain A and followed by refrain B. It begins with complaints against the enemies' slander and deadly words. Verse 9 is the psalmist's response to the previous speech of the enemies, ' "For who hears?" But you, Yahweh, laugh at them'. The suffix of למו in v. 9 ties v. 9 to the preceding. (On the 'antithetic structure' of vv. 8-9, see Krašovec 1984: 71-72.) |

| vv. 11b-12c | This strophe is demarcated by its distinction from the previous refrain (אלהים is in third person in v. 11b in contrast to second person in the refrain) and from the following strophe. It consists of petitions: two jussives with first person singular suffixes in v. 11b-c, a vetitive with third person plural suffix in v. 12a, and two hiphil imperatives with third person plural suffixes in v. 12b. אלהים (third person) in v. 11b and אדני (second person) in v. 12c form an inclusion. |
|---|---|
| vv. 13-14 | The two bicola (vv. 13a-b, 13c-14a) are in 'alternating parallelism' (Willis 1987). Both bicola begin with causal clauses which describe the enemies' cursing, and both end with petitions (a jussive in v. 13b and imperatives in v. 14a). Thus, these two bicola are really a combination of complaints and petitions. The tricolon (v. 14b-d) is a purpose clause syntactically joined to v. 14a. 'God' is in the second person in v. 14a but switches to third person in v. 14b, possibly to mark the end of the unit. |
| vv. 16-17 | This unit is introduced by the pronoun המה. It is preceded by refrain A and followed by refrain B. Verse 16 consists of complaints against the enemies. Verse 17a-b expresses the psalmist's contrasting response of a vow to praise God. The contrasts between המה and אני and between וילינו and לבקר serve to connect v. 17 with v. 16. (On the antithetic structure of vv. 16-17, see Krašovec 1984: 71-72.) Verse 17c-d gives the basis for the vow of praise in 17a-b. The reference to the deity is in second person. |

### Length of Strophes

|  | verses | cola | syllables | stresses |
|---|---|---|---|---|
| vv. 2-3 | 2 | 4 | 40 | 11 |
| 4-5 | 2 | 5 | 46 | 17 |
| 6 | 2 | 4 | 34 | 12 |
| 8-9 | 2 | 5 | 35 | 12 |
| 11b-12 | 2 | 5 | 45 | 13 |
| 13-14 | 3 | 7 | 58 | 20 |
| 16-17 | 3 | 6 | 47 | 18 |

The strophes vary in length. They range from 4 to 7 cola, from 34 to 58 syllables, and from 11 to 20 stresses.

2.6.4.4 *Refrains*. Psalm 59 contains two pairs of refrains: refrain A—vv. 7, 15; refrain B—vv. 10-11a, 18. Each refrain A is preceded by *selāh*. Refrain A, a bicolon, consists of complaints against the enemies. Verse 7 is preceded by petitions and v. 15 by petitions plus a purpose clause. Verse 7 is followed by the interjection הנה and v. 15 by the pronoun המה. This indicates that there is a pause both before and after each. They are identical except for the addition of initial *waw* with v. 15.

The two refrains B (vv. 10-11a, 18), both tricola, consist of addresses to God. The first expresses the psalmist's confidence and hope, and the second expresses his praise. They too are structurally distinct from the stanzas. They both begin with the vocative divine epithet עזי followed by a first person singular verb: 'O my strength, for you will I watch (v. 10a) and 'O my strength, to you I hymn' (v. 18a). Nowhere else in the psalm does a vocative divine name or epithet begin a verse. The switch in suffix from second person to first person in v. 17a and v. 18a (עזי–עזך) and in v. 17b and v. 18c (חסדי–חסדך) indicates a pause between v. 17 and v. 18. In v. 17 עזך and חסדך are the objects of the verbs, but in v. 18 עזי and חסדי are vocatives. In other words, v. 17 is a promise to praise addressed to God whereas v. 18 is the hymn itself. Also, refrain B in v. 10-11a is distinguished from what follows, since אלהי חסדי (v. 11a) is second person but אלהים in v. 11b is third person.

There is one notable difference between these two refrains. The first has אשמרה (v. 10a) and the second has אזמרה (v. 18a). This difference reflects the change in the psalmist's attitude. In the middle of the psalm the poet still awaits God's future intervention ('for you will I watch'). But by the end of the psalm the poet has in effect already received God's intervention, or at least is more confident of it, and thus he begins to praise God ('O my strength, to you I hymn').

2.6.4.5 *Stanzas*. The structure of Psalm 59 consists of four stanzas which are delimited by the four refrains (so also Oesterley 1962: 294).

|  |  |  |
|---|---|---|
| vv. 2-6 | — | Stanza I + *selāh* |
| v. 7 | — | Refrain A |
| vv. 8-9 | — | Stanza II |
| vv. 10-11a | — | Refrain B |

| vv. 11b-14 | — | Stanza III + *selāh* |
| v. 15 | — | Refrain A |
| vv. 16-17 | — | Stanza IV |
| v. 18 | — | Refrain B |

Repetitions and word pairs serve to unify stanza I: אלהים (vv. 2a, 6a, b) and יהוה (vv. 4c, 6a); פעלי און (v. 3a) and בגדי און (v. 6d). The references to the deity are in second person. Repetitions and word pairs also serve to unify Stanza III: אלהים (vv. 11b, 14b) and אדני (v. 12c); עמי (v. 12a) and יעקב (v. 14c); חטאת־פימו דבר־שפתימו (v. 13a) and ומאלה ומכחש (v. 13c). The third person usages of אלהים (vv. 11b, 14b) form an inclusion. In vv. 12-13 the deity is in second person. For discussion of Stanzas II and IV, see above under 2.6.4.3 *Strophes*.

*Length of Stanzas*

| | strophes | vv. | bicola | tricola | cola | syllables | stresses |
| --- | --- | --- | --- | --- | --- | --- | --- |
| vv. 2-6 | 3 | 6 | 5 | 1 | 13 | 120 | 40 |
| 8-9 | 1 | 2 | 1 | 1 | 5 | 35 | 12 |
| 11b-14 | 2 | 5 | 3 | 2 | 12 | 103 | 33 |
| 16-17 | 1 | 3 | 3 | 0 | 6 | 47 | 18 |

The stanzas vary in length. However, Stanzas I and III are somewhat similar—13 to 12 cola, 120 to 103 syllables, and 40 to 33 stresses. Stanzas II and IV (each one strophe) are also somewhat alike—5 to 6 cola, 35 to 47 syllables, 12 to 18 stresses. More significant is the fact that the first two stanzas together and the last two stanzas together are almost identical to each other in length: 8 verses, 6 bicola, 2 tricola, 18 cola, 155 syllables, 52 stresses to 8 verses, 6 bicola, 2 tricola, 18 cola, 150 syllables, 51 stresses.

2.6.4.6 *Sections*. Psalm 59 is bipartite with refrain B completing each section: vv. 2-11a, 11b-18. The major break in the psalm occurs between v. 11a and v. 11b. In the former, 'my loving God' is in second person wheras in the latter 'God' is in third person. Also, vv. 10-11a are a statement of confidence addressed to God whereas v. 11b begins a series of petitions. On the other hand there is less of a break between the preceding and refrain B. Verse 9 leads into vv. 10-11a by addressing God with a vocative. Although there is a functional distinction between v. 17 and v. 18 (see above under 2.6.4.4 *Refrains*), v. 17

anticipates v. 18. Both verses refer to God in the second person. אשיר ...וארנן and עזך in v. 17a-b anticipate אזמרה and עזי in v. 18a. Verse 18b-c gives the basis for the praise, thereby echoing v. 17c-d—משגב לי ... כי in v. 17c and כי ...משגבי in v. 18b. Also חסדך in v. 17b anticipates חסדי in v. 18c.

Whereas refrain B completes each half and is thus in final position, refrain A is internal in each half. Because the description of the enemies with plural verbs in vv. 7 and 15 is continued in vv. 8 and 16, refrain A serves more as an introduction to the stanza following it than as a completion of the stanza preceding it.

*Length of Sections*

|          | verses | bicola | tricola | cola | syllables | stresses |
|----------|--------|--------|---------|------|-----------|----------|
| vv. 2-11a | 10    | 7      | 3       | 23   | 189       | 66       |
| 11b-18    | 10    | 7      | 3       | 23   | 186       | 65       |

The two sections are virtually identical in length. Each section is based on a 'non-alphabetic' acrostic structure with 23 cola. The second section is only 3 syllables and 1 stress shorter than the first section.

2.6.4.7 *Views of Structure.* Many scholars divide the poem into two halves after the first occurrence of refrain B: vv. 2-11a/11b-18 (Wahl 1977: 264-72); 2-10/11-18 (Briggs 1907: 49-57; Weiser 1962: 435-37; and Kissane 1953: 253, although Kissane treats vv. 2-3 as an introduction); 2-11/12-18 (Trublet–Aletti 1983: 35). Beaucamp (1976: 248-51) divides after v. 11 but treats vv. 2-3 as an introduction and v. 18 as a conclusion (vv. 2-3/4-11/12-17/18).

Baumann, Jacquet, van der Lugt, Alden and Gerstenberger go their own ways. Baumann (1950: 115-20) divides it into four strophes and considers v. 6 and v. 14 (rather than the refrains) to be responses by the congregation; his strophes are vv. 2-5, (6), 7 and 16 and 9 and 10, 11-13, (14), 15-18. Jacquet (1977: 253-62) splits it after v. 9 (before the first refrain B) and considers the other refrain B to be a later liturgical addition (2-9/10-17). Van der Lugt (1980: 474) divides it after v. 8 and v. 16 (vv. 2-8/9-16/17-18), thereby splitting up vv. 7-9 and 15-17 and including the refrain of v. 10 in the second section. Alden (1976: 193) tries to force the psalm into a chiastic structure

(vv. 2-3 = A, 4-9 = B, 10 = C, 11 = C, 12-16 = B', 17-18 = A').
That the first refrain B (v. 10) should be C but the other refrain
B (v. 18) should be A' is odd. Finally, Gerstenberger (1988: 235-
39) structures the psalm on the basis of refrain A: vv. 2-6/7-8 =
refrain/9-14/15-16 = refrain/17-18. He fails to take note of
refrain B and its greater structural significance.

With respect to strophic divisions, the following are fairly
similar to each other: Beaucamp (vv. 2-3, 4-5, 6, 7-8, 9-11, 12-
13b, 13c-14, 15-16, 17, 18); Wahl (vv. 2-3, 4-5a, 5b-6, 7-8, 9-
11a, 11b-12, 13, 14, 15-16, 17-18); Kraus (1978: 581— vv. 2-3,
4-5a, 5b-6, 7-8, 9-11, 12-14, 15-16, 17-18); Trublet–Aletti
(vv. 2-3, 4-5a, 5b-6, 7-8, 9-11, 12, 13a, 13b-14, 15-16, 17-18);
and Gerstenberger (vv. 2-3, 4-5a, 5b-6, 7-8, 9-10, 11-14, 15-16,
17-18). Our analysis (vv. 2-3, 4-5, 6, 7, 8-9, 10-11a, 11b-12, 13-
14, 15, 16-17, 18) resembles these, except that we consider
vv. 7, 10-11a, 15, and 18 to be the refrains. Van der Lugt (vv. 2-
4a, 4b-5, 6, 7-8, 9-11, 12-13, 14, 15-16, 17-18), Jacquet (vv. 2-3,
4-5a, 5b-6, 7 and 16, 8-9, 10-11, 12-13b, 13c-14, 15-16, 17), and
Briggs (vv. 2-3, 4-5a, 5b-6, 7 and 10, 11-12b, 12c-13b, 13c-14,
15 and 18) are also fairly similar. However, van der Lugt connects v. 4a with the first strophe; Jacquet inserts v. 16 after v. 7
and omits v. 18; and Briggs omits vv. 8-9 and vv. 16-17. Finally,
Weiser divides both halves into two strophes, apparently on
the basis of *selāh*: vv. 2-6, 7-10/11-14, 15-18.

### 2.6.5 *Repetition*

Psalm 59 exhibits two repeated elements that we want to
mention. First, there are fourteen divine appellatives: אלהים
four times (vv. 10b, 11b, 14b, 18b); the suffixed אלהי once (v. 2a);
the construct אלהי three times (vv. 6b, 11a, 18c); the compound
name יהוה־אלהים once (v. 6a); יהוה twice (vv. 4c, 9a); the title אדני
once (v. 12c); and the appellative עזי twice (vv. 10a, 18a). Second, the psalmist refers to God as his protection seven times:
'my strength' (עזי, vv. 10a, 18a), 'my fortress' (משגבי, vv. 10b,
18b; משגב לי, v. 17c), 'a refuge (מנוס, v. 17d), and 'our shield' (מגננו,
v. 12c). These two repeated elements highlight a dominant
motif in the psalm, that *God* is the psalmist's *protection* in the
midst of the enemies' assaults.

### 2.6.6 *Thought Progression*

Psalm 59 is generally recognized as an individual lament or complaint (Sabourin 1974: 249; Gerstenberger 1988: 238). All the elements of an individual lament are found here: invocation, complaint about the enemies, assertion of innocence, petition, expression of trust, and vow of praise. Yet this poem exhibits these features in its own unique way. Its dominant tone is one of confidence and praise, as expressed in the major refrains. We will focus on the stanza level first and then summarize the movement of the whole poem.

2.6.6.1 *Stanzas.* Stanza I (vv. 2-6) contains all the above elements of an individual lament except the expression of trust and the vow of praise. It begins with four petitions to God to save the psalmist from the enemies. This is followed by complaints against the enemies and his assertion of innocence (vv. 4-5a). Four third person plural verbs describe the enemies' activites: 'they lie in ambush... they are hostile... they run and get ready'. There are three assertions of innocence: 'For no rebellion of mine and no sin of mine... for no iniquity'. Verses 5b-6d contain two petitions calling on God to help the psalmist, two appellations of God ('you, Yahweh-God of hosts, the God of Israel'), and two petitions that God punish not only these particular enemies but all the wicked. Thus vv. 5b-6d have four petitions to match those of vv. 2-3. The arrangement of Stanza I is as follows:

A    —    four petitions (vv. 2-3)
B    —    four verbs of complaint and three assertions
          of innocence (vv. 4-5a)
A′   —    four petitions and two appellations (vv. 5b-6)

Stanza II (vv. 8-9) begins with more complaints against the enemies (v. 8). But instead of following this complaint with an assertion of innocence, the psalmist in v. 9 expresses confidence in Yahweh, 'But you, Yahweh, laugh at them...' Verse 9 echoes v. 6—ואתה יהוה.

Stanza III (vv. 11b-14) also consists of petitions and complaints against the enemies. It begins with two wishes that God (third person) should intervene and cause the psalmist to triumph over the enemies (v. 11b-c). It continues with a vetitive

plus negative purpose clause and two imperatives of impreca-
tion against the enemies (v. 12). Verses 13-14 continue the
imprecations but intersperse them with complaints against
the enemies: two noun clauses of complaint followed by a jussive (v. 13a-b) and two nouns of complaint followed by two
imperatives plus a purpose clause (vv. 13c-14d). Altogether
this section has two positive wishes for the psalmist and six
petitions against the enemies. The two purpose clauses are
related semantically. The psalmist begins, 'Don't kill them
(immediately) lest my people forget'. But after God 'shakes
them', 'brings them down' and lets them be 'caught in their
pride', then he prays 'consume (them)... so that they may
know to the ends of the earth that God rules in Jacob to the
ends of the earth'.

Stanza IV (vv. 16-17) continues the complaints. But v. 17
contrasts the psalmist's activities with those of the enemies,
'As for them (v. 16)... But as for me (v. 17)...' Whereas the
enemies have insatiable desires and even spend the night
waiting for the psalmist, he confidently vows that he will
praise God in the morning. Finally the vow of praise appears.
A contrast is also made on the basis of the homophonous word
*yallînû*—'they grumble... but I will sing'. The basis for this
confidence is that God has been a fortress and refuge (v. 17c-
d).

2.6.6.2 *Poem*. The poem exhibits two movements corresponding to its bipartite structure. The first movement (vv. 2-11a)
begins with introductory petitions for deliverance from the
enemies (vv. 2-3). Verses 4-5a give the reason why God should
save the psalmist, i.e. because the enemies seek the psalmist's
life in spite of his innocence. The first section continues with
petitions for help and against the enemies (vv. 5b-6). Complaints which liken the enemies to scavenger dogs follow
(vv. 7-8). While the enemies utter deadly words thinking that
God does not hear (v. 8), the poet believes that Yahweh not only
hears but even 'laughs at them' (v. 9). Refrain B (v. 10-11a)
concludes the first movement with an expression of hopeful
confidence, 'O my strength, for you will I watch'.

The second movement (vv. 11b-18) begins by picking up on
the petitions of vv. 5b-6. The first two wishes of v. 11b-c that

God intervene for the psalmist (יראני... יקדמי) echo the petitions
of v. 5b (עורה לקראתי וראה). The next three prayers against the
enemies of v. 12 echo the two of v. 6c-d: the vetitive of v. 12a
(אל תחרגם) and the hiphil imperatives of v. 12b (הניעמו... והורידמו)
echo in reverse order the vetitive (אל תחן) and hiphil imperative (הקיצה לפקד) of v. 6d and 6c. The complaints of vv. 13-14
recall the complaints and assertion of innocence of v. 4-5a.
Note especially the repetition of חטאת (vv. 4c, 13a). The complaint against the enemies' slanderous speech in v. 13 also
echoes that of v. 8 (בפיהם... בשפתותיהם v. 8//שפתימו... פימו, v. 13).
Verses 15-17 relate to vv. 7-9. Verses 15 and 7 (= refrain A) are
identical. The beginning of v. 16 forms a sound pair with the
beginning of v. 8: (הנה יביעון v. 8)//המה ינועון (v. 16). And the beginning of v. 17 echoes the beginning of v. 9: ואתה (v. 9)//ואני (v. 17).
Verses 15-16 liken the enemies to insatiable dogs that seek to
devour. Yet the psalmist is certain he will praise God in the
morning (v. 17a-b). This confidence is based on the fact that
God has already become (היית) a fortress and a refuge for him
(v. 17c-d). The second movement concludes with the refrain in
v. 18. However, in contrast to his hopeful watching for God's
future help expressed in the refrain of vv. 10-11a, now the
psalmist already begins to praise God in v. 18.

The two parts of the psalm exhibit the following outline:

|   |   |   |   |
|---|---|---|---|
| | vv. 2-3 | — | Introductory petitions; |
| A | vv. 4-5a | — | Complaint against the enemies and assertion of innocence; |
| B | vv. 5b-6 | — | Petitions for the psalmist and against the enemies; |
| C | vv. 7-9 | — | Complaints against the enemies (including refrain A) and confidence in God; |
| D | vv. 10-11a | — | Refrain B—hope in God's future help. |
| B | vv. 11b-12 | — | Petitions for the psalmist and against the enemies; |
| A | vv. 13-14 | — | Complaints and petitions against the enemies; |
| C | vv. 15-17 | — | Complaints against the enemies (including refrain A) and vow to praise; |
| D | v. 18 | — | Refrain B—praise based on God's past help. |

In summary, the first half moves from petitions and complaints to an expression of hope; the second half moves from petitions and complaints to the beginning of a hymn of praise. Refrain B climaxes each half.

In addition to the climaxing refrains, there is a high point in the middle of each stanza. Verse 6a-b, 'you, Yahweh-God of hosts, the God of Israel', serves as the mid-peak for section I (9 cola preceding—vv. 2-5, 12 cola following—vv. 6c-11a). Verse 14b-d, 'Then they will know that God rules in Jacob to the ends of the earth', serves as the mid-peak for section II (9 cola preceding—vv. 11b-14a, 11 cola following—vv. 15-18). The phrases אלהי ישראל (v. 6b) and אלהים משל ביעקב (v. 14b-c) parallel each other.

The poem's petitions exhibit a shift of emphasis which corresponds to its bipartite structure. Each half has 8 petitions: vv. 2a, 2b, 3a, 3b, 5bα, 5bβ, 6c, 6d//11b, 11c, 12a, 12bα, 12bβ, 13b, 14aα, 14aβ. In the first half, 6 petitions call for divine help for the psalmist (vv. 2a, 2b, 3a, 3b, 5bα, 5bβ) and 2 petitions are directed against the enemies (v. 6c, 6d). In the second half, the ratio is reversed—2 for the psalmist (v. 11b, 11c) and 6 against the enemies (vv. 12a, 12bα, 12bβ, 13b, 14aα, 14aβ). Thus the first half is a prayer oriented primarily *for* the psalmist whereas the second half is oriented primarily *against* the enemies. In the first half, the prayer is that God intervene for the sake of the psalmist, i.e. because he is being unjustly attacked. In the second half, the purpose of the divine intervention is for the sake of others, i.e. that all the world might know that 'God rules in Jacob' (v. 14).

# Chapter 3

## CONCLUSIONS

### 3.1 *Introduction*

Our goal is to describe the 'building blocks' that Hebrew lyric poets use to construct a psalm. We have focused on psalms with refrains since these psalms have clear stanzaic structures. We do not maintain that all the psalms in the Psalter correspond to or possess all of the 'building blocks' that we have isolated. We do believe, however, that our corpus of 7 psalms (= 6 poems), 88 masoretic verses, and 247 cola is representative. Only further research can determine the universality of these 'building blocks' for the Psalter. In this section we will summarize the results.

### 3.2 *Stress Patterns*

Here we will compile the results of sections 2.x.4.2. In no psalm is there a stress pattern which is *consistent* and *predictable* from verse to verse. (On the question of 'meter', see 1.4.) But usually there is a *dominant* stress pattern. The 3″3 stress pattern is most often the dominant pattern, being dominant for Psalms 49, 56, and 59. The 3″2 stress pattern dominates Psalms 42–43. Psalm 46 has a mixed pattern of 4″4 plus 3″3 in a ratio of two to one. Psalm 57 also has a mixed pattern of 3″3 and 3″2. In order to determine the dominant stress pattern, we observe the means and modes (= most frequent lengths) of both stress and syllable counts. The stress count and the syllable count serve as a check on each other. Here we will compile the results of the three psalms with a dominant stress of 3″3— Psalms 49, 56, 59. (See under Psalms 42–43, 46, and 57 for an analysis of their stress-syllable patterns.)

### Psalms with Dominant 3″3 Stress Pattern
#### (Pss. 49, 56, 59)

##### Stress Distribution on Colon Level

| Stresses | | Cola | | Total Stresses |
|---|---|---|---|---|
| 2″ | × | 27 (22%) | = | 54 |
| 3″ | × | 79 (64%) | = | 237 |
| 4″ | × | 17 (14%) | = | 68 |
| TOTALS | | 123 | | 359 |

On the colon level, 64% of the cola have 3-stresses. The other 36% of the cola are divided between 2-stress (22%) and 4-stress (14%) cola. The average number of stresses per colon is 2.92 which is only 0.08 short of the expected 3.0.

##### Syllable Length of Cola (Pss. 49, 56, 59)

| Syllables | | Cola | | Total Syllables |
|---|---|---|---|---|
| 3 | × | 1 | = | 3 |
| 4 | × | 2 | = | 8 |
| 5 | × | 11 | = | 55 |
| 6 | × | 14 | = | 84 |
| 7 | × | 22 | = | 154 |
| 8 | × | 26 | = | 208 |
| 9 | × | 30 | = | 270 |
| 10 | × | 9 | = | 90 |
| 11 | × | 5 | = | 55 |
| 12 | × | 2 | = | 24 |
| 13 | × | 1 | = | 13 |
| TOTALS | | 123 | | 964 |

The expected length for a psalm dominated by a 3″3 stress pattern is 8 syllables per colon. The mean score is 7.84 syllables per colon. The mode is 9 syllables with 30 cola (24%). If we increase the length, then 56 cola are 8–9 syllables (46%); 78 cola are 7–9 syllables (63%); 101 cola are 6–10 syllables (82%); and 112 cola are 5–10 cola (91%). These results correspond with the stress distribution above and confirm that for these three psalms the norm is 3 stresses/8 syllables per colon.

##### Stress Distribution on Verse Level

| Strs | mono cola | Total Strs | Strs | | bic. | | Total Strs | Strs | | tric. | | Total Strs |
|---|---|---|---|---|---|---|---|---|---|---|---|---|
| 2 × 1 | | = 2 | 2 + 2 = 4 | × | 2 | = | 8 | 3 + 2 + 2 | = | 7 × 2 | = | 14 |
| | | | 2 + 3 = 5 | × | 2 | = | 10 | 3 + 2 + 3 | = | 8 × 1 | = | 8 |
| | | | 3 + 2 = 5 | × | 6 | = | 30 | 3 + 3 + 2 | = | 8 × 2 | = | 16 |

| | | | | | | | | | | |
|---|---|---|---|---|---|---|---|---|---|---|
| 3 + 3 = 6 | × | 23 | = | 138 | 3 + 3 + 3 | = | 9 × 1 | = | 9 |
| 2 + 4 = 6 | × | 2 | = | 12 | 4 + 3 + 2 | = | 9 × 1 | = | 9 |
| 4 + 2 = 6 | × | 4 | = | 24 | 3 + 3 + 4 | = | 10 × 2 | = | 20 |
| 3 + 4 = 7 | × | 4 | = | 28 | 3 + 4 + 3 | = | 10 × 1 | = | 10 |
| 4 + 3 = 7 | × | 3 | = | 21 | | | | | |
| TOTAL 1    2 | | 46 | | 271 | | | | | 10    86 |

Psalms 49, 56, and 59 have a total of 57 verses of which 46 (81%) are bicola and 10 (18%) are tricola. The other verse is a monocolon. The averages are: 2 stresses per monocolon; 5.9 stresses per bicolon; and 8.6 stresses per tricolon. The latter two correspond closely to the expected mean scores of 6 per bicolon and 9 per tricolon.

The 3"3 bicolon is the most common bicolon (23 = 50%). If we include its variants of 2"4 and 4"2, then 29 of the 46 bicola have 6 stresses (63%). The eight 5-stress bicola and the seven 7-stress bicola balance each other. The remaining two bicola have 4 stresses each. Only two of the ten tricola have 9 stresses (20%). The three 8-stress tricola and the three 10-stress tricola balance each other. These eight tricola (80%) yield an average of 9 stresses per tricolon.

*Syllable Length of Verses*
(Pss. 49, 56, 59)

| Syll. | mono cola | | Total Syll. | Syll. | | bic. | | Total Syll. | Syll | | tric. | | Total Syll. |
|---|---|---|---|---|---|---|---|---|---|---|---|---|---|
| 6 | × 1 | = | 6 | 9 | × | 1 | = | 9 | 18 | × | 1 | = | 18 |
| | | | | 10 | × | 2 | = | 20 | 19 | × | 0 | = | 0 |
| | | | | 11 | × | 0 | = | 0 | 20 | × | 2 | = | 40 |
| | | | | 12 | × | 0 | = | 0 | 21 | × | 2 | = | 42 |
| | | | | 13 | × | 3 | = | 39 | 22 | × | 0 | = | 0 |
| | | | | 14 | × | 5 | = | 70 | 23 | × | 0 | = | 0 |
| | | | | 15 | × | 12 | = | 180 | 24 | × | 1 | = | 24 |
| | | | | 16 | × | 9 | = | 144 | 25 | × | 0 | = | 0 |
| | | | | 17 | × | 6 | = | 102 | 26 | × | 1 | = | 26 |
| | | | | 18 | × | 2 | = | 36 | 27 | × | 1 | = | 27 |
| | | | | 19 | × | 2 | = | 38 | 28 | × | 1 | = | 28 |
| | | | | 20 | × | 1 | = | 20 | 29 | × | 0 | = | 0 |
| | | | | 21 | × | 1 | = | 21 | 30 | × | 1 | = | 30 |
| | | | | 22 | × | 2 | = | 44 | | | | | |
| TOTAL | 1 | | 6 | | | 46 | | 723 | | | 10 | | 235 |

The mean scores are 6 syllables per monocolon; 15.7 syllables per bicolon; and 23.5 syllables per tricolon. The latter two closely approximate the expected lengths of 16 and 24. The mode of the bicola is 15 syllables with 12 bicola (26%). If we add the next most frequent length (16 syllables), then 21 bicola are 15-16 syllables (46%). If we add one on each side, then 32 bicola are 14-17 syllables (70%). There is no significant mode for the tricola.

*Conclusion*

Our results correspond to the results of Freedman's work on the acrostic poems (1972d; 1986). On the one hand there is considerable diversity of colon/verse length within a poem or a group of similar poems. One should not expect absolute and consistent equivalence of colon/verse length. In that sense, Hebrew psalms are not written in a rigid 'meter' (so also Pardee 1981). And certainly one should not emend the text *metri causa*. On the other hand, it is not the case that there is no regularity at all. There is usually an overarching regularity and a dominant colon/verse length in a given poem. For Psalms 49, 56, and 59 the norm is a 3 stress/8 syllable colon and a 6 stress/16 syllable bicolon. For Psalms 42–43 the norm is a 2.55 stress/6.7 syllable colon and a 5.09 stress/13.4 syllable bicolon (= $3''2$ stress pattern; see 2.1.4.2). Only Psalm 46 and Psalm 57 do not exhibit an overall norm. But even there one finds a pattern (see 2.2.4.2, 2.5.4.2). One needs to focus attention on the means and modes of length. It is precisely the combination of overall regularity and internal variation that is an integral feature of Hebrew poetry (Freedman 1986).

Finally one should note that all of the cola in our corpus are 2 to 4 stresses. Although we believe that this is usually the case in the Psalter, we do not doubt that there is an occasional 5-stress colon (e.g. Pss. 38.12a; 119.43a; 145.15b). Most of the cola in our corpus have 3-stresses—136 of 247 = 55%. The next most common length is the 2-stress colon—74 of 247 = 30%. The least frequent is the 4-stress colon—37 of 247 = 15%.

### 3.3 *Strophes*

Most scholars recognize that the verses of a psalm tend to congregate into larger groups which they term 'strophes'. (For surveys of the scholarly discussion, see Kraft 1938; 1956; Wahl 1977; van der Lugt 1980.) We have followed this conventional terminology in using the term 'strophe' (so also Kraft 1938; 1956; Wahl 1977; van der Lugt 1980; Watson 1984; Korpel–de Moor 1986; O'Connor 1980 prefers the term 'batch'). We define a 'strophe' as one or more verses (usually two to four verses) which exhibit a unity of structure and content. Thus, the term is used in an extended sense and not in the technical sense as denoting the initial division of a Greek choral interlude in classical Greek drama (cf. Preminger 1974: 811). The following will summarize our results.

### 3.3.1 *Length of Strophes*

| Strophe | vv. | mono cola | bic. | tric. | cola | Syllables | Stresses |
|---------|-----|-----------|------|-------|------|-----------|----------|
| 42.2 | 1 | | 1 | | 2 | 21 | 8 |
| 42.3 | 2 | | 2 | | 4 | 23 | 10 |
| 42.4 | 2 | | 2 | | 4 | 27 | 10 |
| 42.5 | 3 | | 3 | | 6 | 37 | 15 |
| 42.7 | 2 | | 2 | | 4 | 24 | 10 |
| 42.8 | 2 | | 2 | | 4 | 27 | 10 |
| 42.9 | 1 | | | 1 | 3 | 24 | 10 |
| 42.10 | 2 | | 2 | | 4 | 23 | 10 |
| 42.11 | 2 | | 2 | | 4 | 27 | 9 |
| 43.1 | 2 | | 2 | | 4 | 28 | 10 |
| 43.2 | 2 | | 2 | | 4 | 26 | 10 |
| 43.3 | 2 | | 2 | | 4 | 31 | 10 |
| 43.4 | 2 | | 2 | | 4 | 29 | 10 |
| 46.2-4b | 3 | | 3 | | 6 | 52 | 22 |
| 46.5-7 | 3 | | 3 | | 6 | 56 | 22 |
| 46.9-11 | 3 | | 2 | 1 | 7 | 63 | 26 |
| 49.2-5 | 4 | | 4 | | 8 | 59 | 24 |
| 49.6-9 | 4 | | 4 | | 8 | 60 | 24 |
| 49.10-12 | 3 | | 1 | 2 | 8 | 65 | 24 |
| 49.14-16 | 4 | | 4 | | 8 | 63 | 24 |
| 49.17-20 | 4 | | 4 | | 8 | 61 | 24 |
| 56.2-4 | 4 | 1 | 3 | | 7 | 50 | 19 |

| | | | | | | |
|---|---|---|---|---|---|---|
| 56.6-8 | 3 | | 2 | 1 | 7 | 55 | 21 |
| 56.9-10 | 3 | | 3 | | 6 | 45 | 18 |
| 56.13-14 | 3 | | 3 | | 6 | 44 | 17 |
| 57.2 | 2 | 1 | | 1 | 4 | 31 | 11 |
| 57.3-4 | 3 | | 3 | | 6 | 39 | 15 |
| 57.5 | 2 | | 1 | 1 | 5 | 32 | 13 |
| 57.7 | 2 | | 2 | | 4 | 24 | 10 |
| 57.8-9 | 2 | | | 2 | 6 | 35 | 14 |
| 57.10-11 | 2 | | 2 | | 4 | 35 | 11 |
| 59.2-3 | 2 | | 2 | | 4 | 40 | 11 |
| 59.4-5 | 2 | | 1 | 1 | 5 | 46 | 17 |
| 59.6 | 2 | | 2 | | 4 | 34 | 12 |
| 59.8-9 | 2 | | 1 | 1 | 5 | 35 | 12 |
| 59.11b-12 | 2 | | 1 | 1 | 5 | 45 | 13 |
| 59.13-14 | 3 | | 2 | 1 | 7 | 58 | 20 |
| 59.16-17 | 3 | | 3 | | 6 | 47 | 18 |

(38 strophes)

Our corpus of 7 psalms (= 6 poems) has a total of 38 strophes. The ranges in length are: 1–4 verses; 2–8 cola; 21–65 syllables; 8-26 stresses. The following are the frequency counts.

| No. of vv. in strophe | No. of Strophes | No. of Cola in strophe | No. of Strophes |
|---|---|---|---|
| 1 | 2 (5%) | 2 | 1 (3%) |
| 2 | 20 (53%) | 3 | 1 (3%) |
| 3 | 11 (29%) | 4 | 15 (39%) |
| 4 | 5 (13%) | 5 | 4 (11%) |
| | | 6 | 8 (21%) |
| | | 7 | 4 (11%) |
| | | 8 | 5 (13%) |
| TOTALS | 38 | | 38 |

In terms of verses, strophes of 2 verses are the most frequent (53%) followed by 3 verses (29%), 4 verses (13%) and 1 verse (5%). Only 2 of the 38 strophes are single verses, one a bicolon and one a tricolon. The vast majority are 2–4 verse strophes.

In terms of cola, strophes of 4 cola are the most frequent (39%) followed by 6 cola (21%), 8 cola (13%), 5 and 7 cola (11% each), and 2 and 3 cola (3%) each. Again, only 6% of the strophes are 2–3 cola. The vast majority are 4–8 cola.

These results correspond well with the strophes—clearly delineated by their acrostic format—of Lamentations 1–4. In Lamentations 1–3 each strophe has 3 verses and 6 cola (with occasional variation). In Lam. 4 each strophe has 2 verses and 4 cola. Also compare the similar results obtained by Krahmalkov's study of two Neo-Punic poems (1975).

The lengths of the strophes in a psalm usually vary. In Psalms 42–43 the 13 strophes range in length from 1 to 3 verses, 2 to 6 cola, 21 to 37 syllables, and 8 to 15 stresses. In Psalm 56 the 4 strophes range from 3 to 4 verses, 6 to 7 cola, 44 to 55 syllables, and 17 to 21 stresses. In Psalm 57 five of the six strophes are each 2 verses, but this is misleading since they vary in cola length (4 to 6), in syllable length (24 to 35), and in stress length (10 to 14). In Psalm 59 the 7 strophes range in length from 2 to 3 verses, 4 to 7 cola, 34 to 58 syllables, and 11 to 20 stresses. These data indicate that one should not expect to find equivalence or symmetry in strophe length in a psalm. Rather, as we shall see, the equivalence or symmetry in length is to be found on the stanza level.

However, equivalence or near equivalence in strophe length does occur occasionally. In our corpus this is true for Psalms 46 and 49. The 3 strophes in Psalm 46 are close in size: 3 verses, 6 + 6 + 7 cola, 52 + 56 + 63 syllables, and 22 + 22 + 26 stresses. The first two strophes are the same, but the third has one extra colon. One should recognize, though, that these 3 strophes are the same as the 3 stanzas of the psalm (see below). The 5 strophes of Psalm 49 are practically identical in size: 4 + 4 + 3 + 4 + 4 verses; 8 cola each; 59 + 60 + 65 + 63 + 61 syllables; and 24 stresses each.

### 3.3.2 *Criteria for Strophic Divisions*
The criteria we have followed for determining strophic divisions have been rhetorical and formal in nature. Basically, our criteria have been similar to those of Wahl (1977). The most important criteria are: the reference to the deity—usually second or third person; repetition and word pairs; inclusion; syntax; congeries of similar verbal moods such as imperatives/jussives or third person plural 'indicatives'; in the first colon there is an initial question, imperative or jussive, vocative, pronoun, interjection, or particle; and alternating parallelism. The following chart identifies the devices which serve to unite each of the 38 strophes in our corpus. Except for the bicolon of Ps. 42.2 and the tricolon of Ps. 42.9, we only note the devices which

help to unify two or more verses but not those which unify cola into a bicolon or tricolon. Under 'syntax' we include the instances of 'syntactic dependency', i.e. when two verses together form one sentence, and the instances when the antecedent of a pronominal suffix appears in the previous verse(s). Under 'repetition' we include both verbatim repetition and root repetition. 'Alternating parallelism' refers to verses which semantically and/or syntactically are parallel.

| Strophe | Person of Deity | S | impv. | ind. | R/WP | I | AP | IPn, IV, IPt, II, IImv, IQ |
|---------|-----------------|---|-------|------|------|---|----|-----------------------------|
| 42.2 | 2nd | S | | | R | | | |
| 42.3 | 3rd | | | | R | | | |
| 42.4 | 3rd | S | | | R | | | |
| 42.5 | 3rd | S | | | | | | IPn |
| 42.7 | 2nd | | | | | | | |
| 42.8 | 2nd | | | | WP | | | |
| 42.9 | 3rd | | | | WP | | | |
| 42.10 | 3rd–2nd | S | | | R | | | |
| 42.11 | 3rd | S | | | | | | |
| 43.1 | 2nd | | impv. | | WP | | | IImv, IV |
| 43.2 | 2nd | S | | | R | | | IPn, IPt |
| 43.3 | 2nd | | impv. | | WP | | | IImv |
| 43.4 | 3rd–2nd | | | | R, WP | | | |
| 46.2-4b | 3rd | S | | | R, WP | | | |
| 46.5-7 | 3rd | S | | | R | | | |
| 46.9-11 | 3rd–1st | | | | R | I | | IImv |
| 49.2-5 | | S | | | WP | I | | IImv, IV |
| 49.6-9 | 3rd | S | | | R | | | IQ |
| 49.10-12 | | S | | | R | | | IImv |
| 49.14-16 | 3rd | S | | | R, WP | | | IPn |
| 49.17-20 | | S | | | R, WP | | | IImv |
| 56.2-4 | 2nd | | | | R | I | AP | IImv, IV |
| 56.6-8 | 2nd | | | ind. | | | | |
| 56.9-10 | 2nd–3rd | | | | R | | | IPn |
| 56.13-14 | 2nd–3rd | S | | | R, WP | I | | IV |
| 57.2 | 2nd | S | | | R | | | IImv, IV |
| 57.3-4 | 3rd | | | | R | | | |
| 57.5 | | S | | | | | | |
| 57.7 | | | | ind. | WP | | | |
| 57.8-9 | 2nd | | | | R, WP | | AP | IV |
| 57.10-11 | 2nd | S | | | | | | IV |
| 59.2-3 | 2nd | | impv. | | R, WP | | AP | IImv, IV |
| 59.4-5 | 2nd | | | ind. | WP | | | II, IPt |
| 59.6 | 2nd | S | impv. | | | | | IPn, IV |

| | | | | | | | |
|---|---|---|---|---|---|---|---|
| 59.8-9 | 2nd | S | | | | | II |
| 59.11b-12 | 3rd-2nd | | impv. | WP | I | | IImv |
| 59.13-14 | 2nd-3rd | S | impv. | WP | | AP | |
| 59.16-17 | 2nd | | | WP | | | IP |

| | | | | | | | |
|---|---|---|---|---|---|---|---|
| SUMMARY | 3rd = 10 | 20 | 6 | 3 | R = 20 | 5 | 4 | IPn = 6/IV = 9 |
| | 2nd = 16 | | | | WP = 17 | | | IPt = 2/II = 2 |
| | 3rd-2nd = 3 | | | | | | | IImv = 10/IQ = 1 |
| | 2nd-3rd = 3 | | | | | | | |
| | 3rd-1st = 1 | | | | | | | |

| | |
|---|---|
| impv./ind. = dominant mood | IPn = Initial Pronoun |
| S = Syntax | IV = Initial Vocative |
| R = Repetitions | II = Initial Interjection |
| WP = Word Pairs | IPt = Initial Particle |
| I = Inclusion | IImv = Initial Imperative |
| AP = Alternating Parallelism | IQ = Initial Interrogative |

Of the various criteria used for determining strophic divisions, the most frequent are the person of the deity, syntax, word pairs and repetition. In 26 of the 33 strophes which mention God, the references are exclusively either second or third person (79%). Only 7 of those 33 exhibit a shift of person within the strophe (21%). This indicates that this criterion is usually reliable, though not always. In 30 of the 38 strophes repetition and/or word pairs are evident (79%). In 19 strophes (56%) syntax holds two or more verses together (20 strophes if we include the bicolon of Ps. 42.2). Ten strophes (26%) have an imperative or jussive and nine strophes (24%) have a vocative in their initial colon. The other features, although important, are far less frequent.

We have indicated the criteria we prefer in determining strophic divisions. However, the wide variety in strophic divisions, which scholars give for each psalm, indicates the uncertainties and difficulties involved. The differences are due to varying criteria (see 1.5.2). We believe further research is needed to determine which critieria are most reliable. However, the question is not of prime importance, since the stanza and section divisions are primary in a psalm's structure (see 3.5; 3.6).

### 3.4 *Refrains*

Our corpus consists of six poems in the Psalter that have refrains. A 'refrain' is a verse that is repeated at regular intervals in a poem (Preminger 1974: 686-87; Watson 1984: 295-99). It should be distinguished from a 'repetend', a recurring phrase which occurs irregularly in a poem and which carries less weight in determining a poem's formal structure (Preminger 1974: 699; Fox 1985: 209-15). The following will summarize the results of our study. We include in our discussion other psalms with refrains which are not part of our corpus (Pss. 39, 67, 80, 99; see Appendix II). (On the refrains in 2 Sam. 1, see Freedman 1972a; O'Connor 1980: 468-71; on those in Ps. 107, see O'Connor 1980: 475-81. On the repetends in Canticles, see Fox 1985: 209-15.)

#### 3.4.1 *Refrain Locations*
There is disagreement among scholars as to the relationship between refrain and stanza. Some scholars consider a refrain to be integral to a stanza (usually Kissane 1953; Weiser 1962; Kraus 1978; van der Lugt 1980). Others consider it extrinsic to a stanza (usually Briggs 1906; 1907; Segal 1935; Beaucamp 1976; Wahl 1977). Our results agree with the latter position (2.x.4.4). Each refrain—in Psalms 42–43 each major refrain—is structurally distinguished from the surrounding material. (By contrast, the minor refrains of Pss. 42–43 are intrastanzaic [see 2.1.4.4].)

In our corpus there are two basic refrain-stanza structures. Type I is a psalm structure that has one or more internal refrains plus a final refrain. Type II is a psalm structure with internal refrains but no final refrain. Type I has four subdivisions: two refrains (Pss. 49.13, 21; 57.6, 12; 99.5, 9); three refrains (Pss. 42.6, 12; 43.5; 46.4c-d [reconstructed], 8, 12); and four refrains (Pss. 59.7 = A, 10-11a = B, 15 = A, 18 = B; 80.4, 8, 15-16a, 20). All of the psalms in Type II have two refrains (Pss. 39.6c, 12d; 56.5, 11-12; 67.4, 6). One might also posit two additional types: type III with an initial and final refrain bracketing the body of the psalm (e.g. Pss. 8.2a-b, 10; 118.1, 29) and type IV with the refrain completing each verse (Ps. 136). The following displays Types I and II.

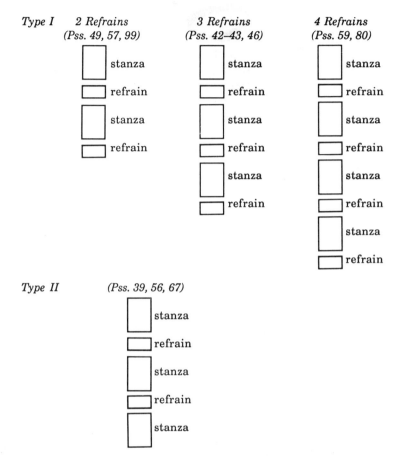

Type I    2 Refrains          3 Refrains          4 Refrains
          (Pss. 49, 57, 99)   (Pss. 42–43, 46)    (Pss. 59, 80)

          stanza              stanza              stanza
          refrain             refrain             refrain
          stanza              stanza              stanza
          refrain             refrain             refrain
                              stanza              stanza
                              refrain             refrain
                                                  stanza
                                                  refrain

Type II    (Pss. 39, 56, 67)

           stanza
           refrain
           stanza
           refrain
           stanza

These refrain-structures indicate that the Hebrew psalmists had a highly developed sense of symmetry. At least for this corpus of refrain-psalms, they divided each psalm into two, three, or four parts. These psalms also reveal equivalence or symmetry in length among the parts (see 3.5).

Another question that arises is whether one should consider a refrain to precede or follow a stanza. We designate stanza-plus-refrain a 'section' (see 2.x.4.6). Again there is scholarly disagreement (see 2.x.4.7). We have found that usually the refrain follows the stanza and thus concludes the section (Pss. 42–43, 46, 49, 56, 57). In Psalm 59 refrain A precedes its stanza but refrain B follows its stanza. However, refrain B is the structurally significant refrain. In the other refrain-

psalms that are not part of our corpus, Psalms 80 and 99 seem
to have section-final refrains. Pss 39 and 67 are more debatable. Pss. 39.12d and 67.6 appear to be section-final, but one
could argue that 39.6c and 67.4 are section-initial. At any rate,
in the vast majority of cases the refrain follows the stanza and
concludes the section.

### 3.4.2 *Refrain Length*

| *Refrain* | *1 colon* | *2 cola* | *3 cola* | *4 cola* | *5 cola* |
|---|---|---|---|---|---|
| 39.6c | X | | | | |
| 39.12d | X | | | | |
| 42.6 | | | | | X |
| 42.12 | | | | | X |
| 43.5 | | | | | X |
| 46.4c-d | | X | | | |
| 46.8 | | X | | | |
| 46.12 | | X | | | |
| 49.13 | | X | | | |
| 49.21 | | X | | | |
| 56.5 | | | X | | |
| 56.11-12 | | | | X | |
| 57.6 | | X | | | |
| 57.12 | | X | | | |
| 59.7 | | X | | | |
| 59.10-11a | | | X | | |
| 59.15 | | X | | | |
| 59.18 | | | X | | |
| 67.4 | | X | | | |
| 67.6 | | X | | | |
| 80.4 | | X | | | |
| 80.8 | X | | | | |
| 80.15-16a | | | | X | |
| 80.20 | | X | | | |
| 99.5 | | | X | | |
| 99.9 | | | X | | |
| 26 | 2 (8%) | 14 (54%) | 5 (19%) | 2 (8%) | 3 (11%) |

The length of a refrain is one to five cola. Most refrains are bicola (54%) followed by tricola (19%). This is as expected since most verses in our corpus are bicola and tricola. Usually each refrain in a given psalm has the same length. However, occasionally one finds variation. In Psalm 56 the first refrain (v. 5) is a tricolon but the second is a tetracolon (vv. 11-12). In Ps. 59 refrain A (vv. 7, 15) is a bicolon but refrain B (vv. 10-11a, 18) is a tricolon. In Psalm 80 three refrains are each a bicolon (vv. 4, 8, 20) but one has two bicola (vv. 15-16a; we follow most scholars in taking v. 16b as a scribal dittograph of v. 18b). These occasional variations argue against emending the text to make each refrain equivalent in length (*contra* Segal 1935: 132).

### 3.4.3 *Variation in Refrains*

It is surprising how often the spelling and wording of a refrain vary in a given psalm (so also Goldingay 1978). One can arrange the refrains into three categories: fixed composition, minor variations, major variations (see 2.x.4.4).

Refrains with fixed composition occur in Psalms 8, 46, 67, 118, and 136. Here the spelling and wording in each psalm's refrains are identical.

Refrains with minor variations occur in Psalms 39, 42–43, 49, 57, and 59. In Psalm 39 the second refrain (v. 12d) omits two words from the first refrain of v. 6c—כל and נצב. In Psalms 42–43 the second and third major refrains (42.12; 43.5) add a word (מה) and spell ישועות—written *plene* in 42.6—defectively (ישעת). In Psalm 49 the A colon of the second refrain (v. 21) alters the A colon of the first refrain (v. 13). The initial *waw* of v. 13 is placed internally in v. 21a and the words בל-ילין of v. 13 are replaced by לא יבין in v. 21. In Ps. 57 the second refrain (v. 12) deletes the article ה of השמים in v. 6. In Psalm 59 an initial *waw* is added in the second refrain A (v. 15; cf. v. 7). Also, the second refrain B (v. 18) replaces the verb אשמרה in v. 10 with the verb אזמרה.

Refrains with major variations occur in Psalms 56, 80, and 99. In Psalm 56 the second refrain adds a colon (v. 11b). It also omits the suffix of דברו (v. 5a) in v. 11 and replaces the noun בשר of v. 5c with the noun אדם in v. 12b. In Psalm 80 the third refrain (v. 15-16a) begins the same as v. 8 with אלהים צבאות, but it changes the following hiphil imperative (השיבנו) to the Qal imperative of the same root (שוב־נא). The b–d cola in the third refrain are entirely different. Also, the initial vocative of three of the four refrains varies—אלהים (v. 4)... אלהים צבאות (v. 8)... אלהים צבאות (v. 15)... יהוה אלהים צבאות (v. 20). In Psalm 99 the second refrain (v. 9) replaces להדם רגליו of the first refrain (v. 5) with להר קדשו. The third colon of each refrain is very different—קדוש הוא (v. 5c)... כי קדוש יהוה אלהינו (v. 9c).

The frequency with which the psalmists vary the spelling and wording of refrains carries with it two implications. First, it calls into question the tendency to eliminate the variations by emendation, which appears among some scholars (e.g. Briggs 1906; 1907; Segal 1935; Kissane 1953). Second, when variation is evident, it probably indicates that the audience or congregation did not join in (Watson 1984: 298). However, when the refrains are identical, there is a strong possibility that the congregation did participate. This is supported by the fact that the refrains of Psalms 8 and 46 use the first person plural. The fact that the refrains of Psalm 67 are calls for all the peoples to praise supports a communal participation for that psalm. The parallel in 2 Chron. 7.3 shows the probability of communal participation in the refrains of Pss. 118 and 136.

### 3.5 *Stanzas*

Some scholars tend to recognize only the 'strophe' level while others frequently distinguish between 'strophes' and 'stanzas' (see 1.5.2). Our results confirm the latter view. Our corpus of psalms with refrains indicates that there is clearly a unit larger than the strophe. We define a 'stanza' as 'a major subdivision of a poem... which comprises one or more strophes' (Watson 1984: 161; cf. Häublein 1978: 1-17). The following will summarize the results of our study (see 2.x.4.5). We include in our discussion other psalms with refrains which are not part of our corpus (Pss. 39; 67; 80; 99; see Appendix II).

### 3.5.1 *Length of Stanzas*

| Stanza | Strophes | vv. | mono- | bic. | tric. | cola | Sylls. | Strs. |
|--------|----------|-----|-------|------|-------|------|--------|-------|
| 39.2-6b | 2 | 5 | 0 | 1 | 4 | 14 | 103 | 40 |
| 39.7-12c | 2 | 6 | 0 | 7 | 2 | 14 | 107 | 40 |

| | | | | | | | | |
|---|---|---|---|---|---|---|---|---|
| 39.13-14 | 1 | 3 | 0 | 2 | 1 | 7 | 53 | 20 |
| 42.2-5 | 4 | 8 | 0 | 8 | 0 | 16 | 108 | 43 |
| 42.7-11 | 5 | 9 | 0 | 8 | 1 | 19 | 125 | 49 |
| 43.1-4 | 4 | 8 | 0 | 8 | 0 | 16 | 114 | 40 |
| 46.2-4b | 1 | 3 | 0 | 3 | 0 | 6 | 52 | 22 |
| 46.5-7 | 1 | 3 | 0 | 3 | 0 | 6 | 56 | 22 |
| 46.9-11 | 1 | 3 | 0 | 2 | 1 | 7 | 63 | 26 |
| 49.2-5 | 1 | 4 | 0 | 4 | 0 | 8 | 59 | 24 |
| 49.6-12 | 2 | 7 | 0 | 5 | 2 | 16 | 125 | 48 |
| 49.14-20 | 2 | 8 | 0 | 8 | 0 | 16 | 124 | 48 |
| 56.2-4 | 1 | 4 | 1 | 3 | 0 | 7 | 50 | 19 |
| 56.6-10 | 2 | 6 | 0 | 5 | 1 | 13 | 100 | 39 |
| 56.13-14 | 1 | 3 | 0 | 3 | 0 | 6 | 44 | 17 |
| 57.2-5 | 3 | 7 | 1 | 4 | 2 | 15 | 102 | 39 |
| 57.7-11 | 3 | 6 | 0 | 4 | 2 | 14 | 94 | 35 |
| 59.2-6 | 3 | 6 | 0 | 5 | 1 | 13 | 120 | 40 |
| 59.8-9 | 1 | 2 | 0 | 1 | 1 | 5 | 35 | 12 |
| 59.11b-14 | 2 | 5 | 0 | 3 | 2 | 12 | 103 | 33 |
| 59.16-17 | 1 | 3 | 0 | 3 | 0 | 6 | 47 | 18 |
| 67.2-3 | 1 | 2 | 0 | 2 | 0 | 4 | 35 | 12 |
| 67.5 | 1 | 1 | 0 | 0 | 1 | 3 | 25 | 9 |
| 67.7-8 | 1 | 2 | 0 | 2 | 0 | 4 | 37 | 12 |
| 80.2-3 | 1 | 2 | 0 | 0 | 2 | 6 | 53 | 18 |
| 80.5-7 | 1 | 3 | 0 | 3 | 0 | 6 | 55 | 19 |
| 80.9-14 | 2 | 6 | 0 | 6 | 0 | 12 | 101 | 36 |
| 80.17-19 | 1 | 3 | 0 | 3 | 0 | 6 | 53 | 19 |
| 99.1-4 | 2 | 5 | 0 | 5 | 0 | 10 | 74 | 32 |
| 99.6-8 | 2 | 4 | 0 | 2 | 2 | 10 | 79 | 29 |

30 Stanzas

The 10 poems (= 11 psalms) surveyed here have a total of 30 stanzas. The ranges in stanza length are: 1–5 strophes; 1–9 verses; 3–19 cola; 25–125 syllables; 9–49 stresses. The following gives the frequency of the different stanza sizes.

| strophes in stanza | | no. of stanzas | cola in stanza | | no. of stanzas |
|---|---|---|---|---|---|
| 1 | — | 15 (50%) | 3 | — | 1 (3%) |
| 2 | — | 9 (30%) | 4 | — | 2 (7%) |
| 3 | — | 3 (10%) | 5 | — | 1 (3%) |
| 4 | — | 2 (7%) | 6 | — | 7 (23%) |

| verses in stanzas | | no. of stanzas | | | |
|---|---|---|---|---|---|
| 5 | — | 1 (3%) | 7 | — | 3 (10%) |
| | | 30 stanzas | 8 | — | 1 (3%) |
| | | | 9 | — | 0 |
| | | | 10 | — | 2 (7%) |
| | | | 11 | — | 0 |
| | | | 12 | — | 2 (7%) |
| 1 | | 1 (3%) | 13 | — | 2 (7%) |
| 2 | — | 4 (13%) | 14 | — | 3 (10%) |
| 3 | — | 8 (27%) | 15 | — | 1 (3%) |
| 4 | — | 3 (10%) | 16 | — | 4 (13%) |
| 5 | — | 3 (10%) | 17 | — | 0 |
| 6 | — | 5 (17%) | 18 | — | 0 |
| 7 | — | 2 (7%) | 19 | — | 1 (3%) |
| 8 | — | 3 (10%) | | | 30 stanzas |
| 9 | — | 1 (3%) | | | |
| | | 30 stanzas | | | |

The wide variety of lengths indicates that there is no one standard stanza size. One half of the stanzas consist of one strophe. The other half have two to five strophes in descending order—stanzas of two strophes (30%), of three strophes (10%), of four strophes (7%), of five strophes (3%). This confirms the conclusion that one should distinguish between strophes and stanzas. Two psalms have only single-strophes for their stanzas, Psalms 46 and 67. These two psalms are also the shortest psalms of the corpus—Psalm 46 has 25 cola and Psalm 67 has 15 cola (or 16?—see Appendix II). This suggests that the length of the psalm is a factor. Our tentative hypothesis is that short psalms have single-strophe stanzas while longer psalms can have stanzas of more than one strophe. Obviously, further research is necessary.

In terms of verses, stanzas of 3 verses are the most frequent (27%). The next most frequent size is stanzas of 6 verses (17%) followed by 2-verse stanzas (13%), and 4-, 5-, and 8-verse stanzas (10% each). In terms of cola, stanzas of 6 cola are the most frequent (23%) followed by stanzas of 16 cola (13%) and 7 and 14 cola (10% each). However, these statistics are misleading because they do not distinguish between single-strophe stanzas and multiple-strophe stanzas. Therefore, the following will separate out the multiple-strophe stanzas. (On strophe length, see 3.3.1.)

*Multiple-strophe Stanzas*

| verses in stanza | | no. of stanzas | cola in stanza | | no. of stanzas |
|---|---|---|---|---|---|
| 4 | — | 1 (7%) | 10 | — | 2 (13%) |
| 5 | — | 3 (20%) | 11 | — | 0 |
| 6 | — | 5 (33%) | 12 | — | 2 (13%) |
| 7 | — | 2 (13%) | 13 | — | 2 (13%) |
| 8 | — | 3 (20%) | 14 | — | 3 (20%) |
| 9 | — | 1 (7%) | 15 | — | 1 (7%) |
| | | 15 stanzas | 16 | — | 4 (27%) |
| | | | 17 | — | 0 |
| | | | 18 | — | 0 |
| | | | 19 | — | 1 (7%) |
| | | | | | 15 stanzas |

The range of multiple-strophe stanzas is 4–9 verses and 10–19 cola. Most of them have 5–8 verses (86%) and 12–16 cola (80%). In terms of verses, the most frequent size is the 6-verse stanza (33%) followed by 5 and 8-verse stanzas (20% each). In terms of cola, the most frequent length is the 16-cola stanza (27%) followed by 14-cola stanzas (20%) and 10-, 12- and 13-cola stanzas (13% each). These results correspond well with the clearly delineated stanzas of the acrostic Psalm 119. There each stanza has 8 verses and 16 cola. (On the relationship between the stanza lengths within a psalm, see 3.5.2.)

### 3.5.2 *Stanzaic Structures*
The refrains mark the stanza divisions of these 10 poems. (In Ps. 49 the first stanza (vv. 2-5) is clearly the introduction even though it is not followed by a refrain.) Consequently, the types of stanzaic structures correspond to the types of refrain placement observed in 3.4.1. Basically there are refrain-psalms with two stanzas (Type I), three stanzas (Type II), and four stanzas (Type III). Psalms with two stanzas have stanzas of equal size (Pss. 57; 99). The latter two types can be sub-divided. Psalms with three stanzas can have stanzas of equal size (A—Pss. 42–43; 46; 67), or two half-stanzas plus one full stanza B—Ps. 56), or one half-stanza plus two full-stanzas (C—Pss. 39; 49). Psalms with four stanzas can have two half-stanzas plus two full-stanzas (A—Ps. 59) or three half-stanzas and one full-stanza (B—Ps. 80).

The following displays these structural types.

### Type 1—2 Stanzas—Equal Size

Ps. 57

I–15 cola

refrain

II–14 cola

refrain

Ps. 99

I–10 cola

refrain

II–10 cola

refrain

### Type 2—3 Stanzas

### A—Equal Size

Pss. 42–43

I–16 cola

refrain

II–19 cola

refrain

III–16 cola

refrain

Ps. 46

I–16 cola

refrain

II–6 cola

refrain

III–7 cola

refrain

Ps. 67

I–4 cola

refrain

II–3(4?) cola

refrain

III–4 cola

*B—2 Half-stanzas + 1 Full-stanza*

*Ps. 56*

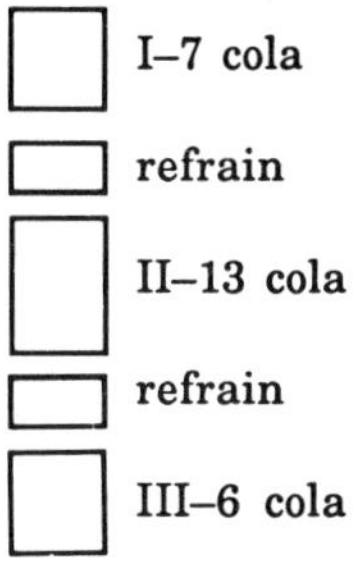

I–7 cola

refrain

II–13 cola

refrain

III–6 cola

*C—1 Half-stanza + 2 Full-stanzas*

*Ps. 39*

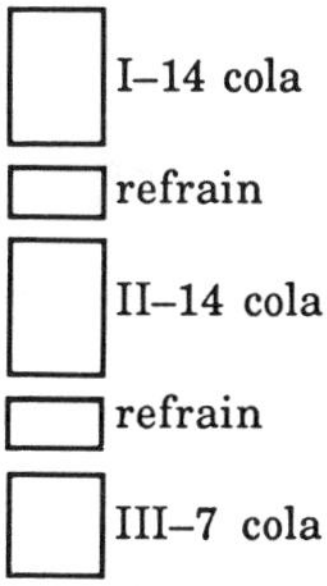

I–14 cola

refrain

II–14 cola

refrain

III–7 cola

*Ps. 49*

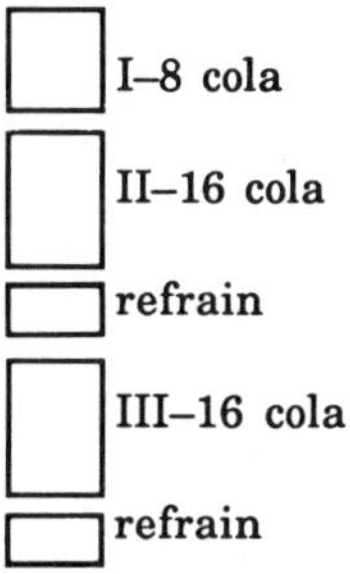

I–8 cola

II–16 cola

refrain

III–16 cola

refrain

*Type 3—4 Stanzas*

*A—2 Half-stanzas + 2 Full-stanzas*

*Ps. 59*

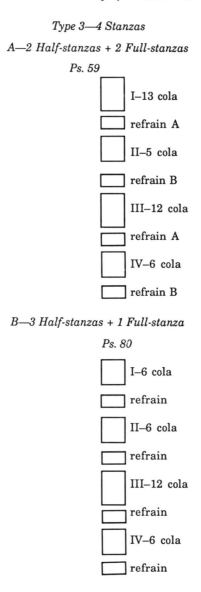

*B—3 Half-stanzas + 1 Full-stanza*

*Ps. 80*

### Conclusions

There are several conclusions that derive from this evidence.
First, the psalmists seem to prefer to divide a poem that has

15–66 cola (all ten are within this range) into two, three, or four stanzas. Yet, it is not the case that short psalms always have two stanzas and long psalms always have four stanzas. The shortest psalm, Psalm 67, has three stanzas and the longest poem, Psalms 42–43, has three stanzas. Also, one cannot conclude that every psalm must have more than one stanza. But at least this should be one's expectation.

Second, the psalmists exhibit a strong sense of symmetry. They work with stanzas of equal size or with half-stanzas plus full-stanzas in a given psalm. The half-stanzas in Psalms 39, 49, and 80 are exactly one half of their respective full-stanzas. In Psalm 56 the two half-stanzas together equal the size of the full-stanza (7 + 6 = 13 cola). Psalm 59 is unique. There the first full-stanza is one colon longer and the first half-stanza is one colon shorter than the other full-stanza and half-stanza. However, the sum of the first two is equal to the sum of the second two—13 + 5 = 18 cola and 12 + 6 = 18 cola.

Although the psalmists exhibit a sense of symmetry, they also have freedom for variation. Of the five psalms with stanzas of equal size, four show variation. In Psalms 42–43 the middle stanza is 3 cola longer than the other two. In Psalm 46 the last stanza is 1 colon longer than each of the other two. The middle stanza of Psalm 67 has one colon less than the other two. (However, the textual variant of Ps. 67.5 produces a stanza equal in size with the other two stanzas—see Appendix II.)

Third, this symmetry in length operates on the stanza level rather than the strophe level (so also van der Lugt 1980). The strophic lengths vary considerably in Psalms 49, 42–43, 56, 57, 59, 80, and 99. Only in Psalms 46, 49, and 67 is there equivalence or near equivalence in strophe size (see 3.3.1; Appendix II). However, the strophes of Psalms 46 and 67 are the same as their stanzas.

Finally, one should count cola rather than verses to determine stanza size (*contra* van der Lugt 1980). Counting only verses can be misleading. The following chart compares our versification and the MT versification with the cola count.

| Stanza | Our Verses | MT Verses | Cola |
|---|---|---|---|
| 39.2-6b | 5 | 5 | 14 |
| 39.7-12c | 6 | 6 | 14 |
| 39.13-14 | 3 | 2 | 7 |
| | | | |
| 42.2-5 | 8 | 4 | 16 |
| 42.7-11 | 9 | 5 | 19 |
| 43.1-4 | 8 | 4 | 16 |
| | | | |
| 46.2-4b | 3 | 3 | 6 |
| 46.5-7 | 3 | 3 | 6 |
| 46.9-11 | 3 | 3 | 7 |
| | | | |
| 49.2-5 | 4 | 4 | 8 |
| 49.6-12 | 7 | 7 | 16 |
| 49.14-20 | 8 | 7 | 16 |
| | | | |
| 56.2-4 | 4 | 3 | 7 |
| 56.6-10 | 6 | 5 | 13 |
| 56.13-14 | 3 | 2 | 6 |
| | | | |
| 57.2-5 | 7 | 4 | 15 |
| 57.7-11 | 6 | 5 | 14 |
| | | | |
| 59.2-6 | 6 | 5 | 13 |
| 59.8-9 | 2 | 2 | 5 |
| 59.11b-14 | 5 | 4 | 12 |
| 59.16-17 | 3 | 2 | 6 |
| | | | |
| 67.2-3 | 2 | 2 | 4 |
| 67.5 | 1 | 1 | 3 |
| 67.7-8 | 2 | 2 | 4 |
| | | | |
| 80.2-3 | 2 | 2 | 6 |
| 80.5-7 | 3 | 3 | 6 |
| 80.9-14 | 6 | 6 | 12 |
| 80.17-19 | 3 | 3 | 6 |
| | | | |
| 99.1-4 | 5 | 4 | 10 |
| 99.6-8 | 4 | 3 | 10 |

The symmetry of length on the colon level is lost by our versification in Psalms 39, 49, 56, 80, and 99. In Psalm 39 each of the first two stanzas is twice the length of the last stanza in cola, but only the second stanza is twice the length of the last stanza in verses. The middle stanza of Psalm 49 is one verse shorter than the last stanza but both have the same colonic length. The sum of the first and last stanzas in Psalm 56 is equivalent to the middle stanza's length in cola, but the former sum is one verse longer than the latter. The first half-stanza of Psalm 80 is one verse shorter than the other half-stanzas but it has the same number of cola. Finally, the first stanza of Psalm 99 is one verse longer than the second although both stanzas have 10 cola.

The MT versification loses the symmetry of colonic length in Psalms 39, 49, 57, 59, 80, and 99. The first stanza in Psalm 39 is one verse shorter than the second stanza although the two have the same number of cola. Also, the third stanza which is one-half the length of the other two in cola is one-half the length of neither in verse-length. In Psalm 49 the first stanza, which is one half the size of each of the other two stanzas in cola, is not one half their length in verses. The first stanza of Psalm 57 is one verse shorter than the second but one colon longer than the second. In Psalm 59 the sum of the first two stanzas is equivalent to the sum of the last two stanzas in number of cola, but their sums are not equivalent in number of verses. The first half-stanza of Psalm 80 is one verse shorter than the other half-stanzas though each half-stanza has 6 cola. Finally, the first stanza of Psalm 99 is one verse longer than the second, but both stanzas have the same number of cola.

These discrepancies indicate that stanza-length operates on the colon level rather than the verse level (see 1.5.2). For example, the two tricola of Ps. 80.2-3 are equivalent to the three bicola of 80.5-7 and 80.17-19. Counting cola captures the symmetry involved more consistently than counting verses. Also, counting stresses and syllables serves as a check on the colonic divisions. In our corpus, the symmetries that we detected in stanza length are confirmed by the stress and syllable counts.

### 3.5.3 *Criteria for Stanzaic Divisions*

In the ten poems surveyed here, the stanza divisions are clearly marked by the use of the refrain. The stanzas consist of the material before and/or after each refrain. (The refrain is extrinsic to the 'stanza' and it usually concludes the 'section'; see 3.4.1.) Here we will discuss some of the devices which in addition to the refrains serve to unify and demarcate each stanza (see 2.x.4.5; Appendix II; cf. 3.3.2). These devices include: the reference to the deity—usually second or third person; whether imperatives/jussives or 'indicatives' (perfects and imperfects) are predominant in the stanza; repetition (verbatim repetition and root repetition) and word pairs which occur across two or more verses (not included are the repetitions and word pairs that unite cola into one verse); inclusion; and when the stanza's initial colon has a pronoun, vocative, interjection, particle, imperative, jussive, or interrogative.

| *Stanza* | *Person of Deity* | *impv./juss.* | *ind.* | *R/WP* | *I* | *IPn/IV* | *IPt/IV* | *I Imv./IJ/IQ* |
|---|---|---|---|---|---|---|---|---|
| 39.2-6b | 2nd | | X | R, WP | | | | |
| 39.7-12c | 2nd | X | | | I | | IPt | |
| 39.13-14 | 2nd | X | | | | I V | | I Imv. |
| | | | | | | | | |
| 42.2-5 | 2nd-3rd | | X | R | | | | |
| 42.7-11 | 2nd-3rd | | X | | | | | |
| 43.1-4 | 2nd | X | | | I | I V | | I Imv. |
| | | | | | | | | |
| 46.2-4b | 3rd | | X | R | | | | |
| 46.5-7 | 3rd | | X | R | | | | |
| 46.9-11 | 3rd-1st | X | | R | I | | | I Imv. |
| | | | | | | | | |
| 49.2-5 | | | | | I | I V, IPn | | I Imv. |
| 49.6-12 | 3rd | | X | R, WP | | | | IQ |
| 49.14-20 | 3rd | | X | R, WP | | IPn | | |
| | | | | | | | | |
| 56.2-4 | 2nd | | X | R | I | I V | | I Imv. |
| 56.6-10 | 2nd-3rd | | | R | I | | | |
| 56.13-14 | 2nd-3rd | | X | R, WP | I | I V | | |
| | | | | | | | | |
| 57.2-5 | 2nd-3rd | | X | R | | I V | | I Imv. |
| 57.7-11 | 2nd | | | R, WP | | | | |
| | | | | | | | | |
| 59.2-6 | 2nd | X | | R, WP | | I V | | I Imv. |
| 59.8-9 | 2nd | X | | | | | I I | |
| 59.11b-14 | 3rd-2nd-3rd | X | | R, WP | I | | | IJ |
| 59.16-17 | 2nd | X | | WP | | IPn | | |
| | | | | | | | | |
| 67.2-3 | 3rd-2nd | X | | | | | | IJ |
| 67.5 | 2nd | X | | R, WP | I | | | IJ |
| 67.7-8 | 3rd | | X | R | I | | | |
| | | | | | | | | |
| 80.2-3 | 2nd | X | | | | I V | | I Imv. |
| 80.5-7 | 2nd | | X | | | I V | | IQ |
| 80.9-14 | 2nd | | X | WP | | | | |
| 80.17-19 | 2nd | X | | | | | | |

| 99.1-4 | 3rd-2nd | X | R | | | | IJ |
| 99.6-8 | 3rd-2nd | X | R, WP | | | | |

| SUMMARY | 3rd = 5 | 10 | 17 | R = 18 | 10 | IPn = 3 | I I = 1 | I Imv. = 8 |
| | 2nd = 14 | | | WP = 11 | | I V = 9 | IPt = 1 | IJ = 4 |
| | 3rd - 2nd = 3 | | | | | | IQ = 2 | |
| | 2nd - 3rd = 5 | | | | | | | |
| | 3rd - 1st = 1 | | | | | | | |
| | 3rd - 2nd - 3rd = 1 | | | | | | | |

| | |
| impv./juss. = dominant mood | I V = Initial Vocative |
| ind. = dominant mood | I I = Initial Interjection |
| R = Repetitions | IPt = Initial Particle |
| WP = Word Pairs | I Imv. = Initial imperative |
| I = Inclusion | IJ = Initial Jussive |
| IPn = Initial Pronoun | IQ = Initial Interrogative |

The most frequently attested devices that serve to unify and demarcate a stanza are repetition, word pairs, inclusion, dominant imperative/jussive or indicative mood, and an initial colon with an imperative/jussive or vocative. Eighteen stanzas exhibit repetition (60%) and eleven stanzas have word pairs (37%). Usually both occur in the same stanza. Only in two stanzas are there word pairs without repetition. Ten stanzas exhibit inclusion (33%). 'Indicative' verbs dominate 17 stanzas (57%) and imperatives and/or jussives dominate 10 stanzas (33%). There are only three stanzas that are equally divided between imperatives and indicatives (Pss. 49.2-5; 56.6-10; 57.7-11). Twelve stanzas open with an imperative or jussive in the initial colon (40%). Nine stanzas open with a vocative in the initial colon (30%). The last two devices correlate with the fact that usually a new stanza opens with a turn or change in the poem's thought progression (see 3.7.1). These devices should help the reader the most in determining a psalm's stanzaic structure.

The other devices are less helpful. Initial interrogatives, pronouns, interjections and particles occur rarely. In 19 stanzas the reference to the deity is either second or third person (63%), but in 10 stanzas the reference changes in the middle of the stanza (33%). Consistency in the person of the deity seems to be a criterion which is more beneficial for strophic determination than for stanzaic determination (see 3.3.2).

### 3.5.4 *Selāh*

Some scholars believe that the enigmatic term *selāh* functions to demarcate strophes or stanzas (Weiser 1962; van der Lugt 1980; *et al.*). They generally assume that it comes at the end of a strophe or stanza. Unfortunately, the meaning of the term is uncertain and therefore cannot resolve the question. (For helpful discussions, see Kraus 1978: 22-24; Casetti 1982: 40-42; Craigie 1983: 76-77.) However, this corpus of Psalms with clearly delineated stanzas allows one to test this hypothesis.

*Selāh*, no doubt a technical liturgical term, occurs 74 times in the Hebrew Bible, 71 times in 39 psalms and 3 times in Habakkuk 3. Usually it occurs at the end of a masoretic verse, but three times it appears in mid-verse (Hab. 3.9; Pss. 55.20; 57.4). It occurs once in 16 psalms (Pss. 7; 20; 21; 44; 47; 48; 50; 54; 60; 61; 75; 81; 82; 83; 85; 143); twice in 15 psalms (Pss. 4; 9; 24; 39; 49; 52; 55; 57; 59; 62; 67; 76; 84; 87; 88); three times in 8 psalms including the Psalm of Habakkuk (Hab. 3; Pss. 3; 32; 46; 66; 68; 77; 140); and four times in Psalm 89.

In our corpus, *selāh* occurs 13 times. In five of those it appears after the refrain—Pss. 39.6, 12; 46.4 (the refrain has been reconstructed here; see 2.2.3 Notes), 8, 12. It appears at the end of a stanza three times—Pss. 59.6, 14; 67.5.

Three times it appears after a stanza's *initial* verse—Pss. 49.14; 57.7; 67.2. To this we should also add Habakkuk 3.3, since v. 2 is clearly the introduction with v. 3 opening the first stanza. (On the structure of Hab. 3, see Hiebert 1986: 59-80.) The remaining two occurrences are not so clear, but in both *selāh* seems to be located in the middle of a stanza. In Ps. 49.16 it appears in the exact center of the second full-stanza, after v. 16. In that stanza 8 cola precede (vv. 14-16) and 8 cola follow (vv. 17-20) *selāh*. In Psalm 57 it appears in the near-center of stanza I, after v. 4b. In that stanza 8 cola precede (vv. 2-4b) and 7 cola follow (vv. 4c-5) *selāh*. Possibly this explains why it appears in mid-verse in Ps. 57.4. If it were located after v. 4d, then 10 cola would precede and only 5 cola would follow.

In summary, *selāh* occurs after a refrain, after the initial or final verse of a stanza, and in the middle of a stanza. In other words, it seems to mark the beginning, middle or end of a stanza. Only further research can determine whether or not *selāh* functions this way in the rest of the Psalter. One should

note, however, that the number of occurrences of *selāh* in a
psalm does not indicate the number of stanzas in that psalm. It
occurs twice in psalms of two stanzas (Ps. 57), three stanzas
(Pss. 39, 49, 67), and four stanzas (Ps. 59).

### 3.6 *Sections*

We designate stanza-plus-refrain a 'section' (see 2.x.4.6).
Usually the refrain follows the stanza and thus concludes the
section. In Psalm 59 refrain A (vv. 7, 15) precedes its stanza.
However, refrain B (vv. 10-11a, 18) carries the weight structurally and it closes each section. The refrains of Pss. 39.6c and
67.4 are debatable. One could argue that each is section-initial.
Ps. 39.7 expands on the theme of the refrain of v. 6c and both
employ the particle אך. Ps. 67.5 continues the plural jussives of
the refrain of v. 4. However, in view of the fact that the other
refrains in those psalms are section-final (Pss. 39.12d; 67.6)
and that the Masoretes treated 39.6c as a conclusion rather
than an introduction, we consider 39.6c and 67.4 to be section-
final. Here we will examine the lengths of these sections. We
include Psalms 39, 67, 80, and 99 (see Appendix II). For the
sake of comparison we include the stanzas which precede a
section or follow a refrain even though technically they are not
sections (Pss. 39.13-14; 49.2-5; 56.13-14; 67.7-8).

| Sections | vv. | mono-cola | bic. | tric. | cola | Sylls. | Strs. |
|----------|-----|-----------|------|-------|------|--------|-------|
| 39.2-6c | 6 | 1 | 1 | 4 | 15 | 111 | 43 |
| 39.7-12d | 7 | 1 | 4 | 2 | 15 | 112 | 42 |
| 39.13-14 | 3 | 0 | 2 | 1 | 7 | 53 | 20 |
| 42.2-6 | 10 | 0 | 9 | 1 | 21 | 139 | 55 |
| 42.7-12 | 11 | 0 | 9 | 2 | 24 | 157 | 61 |
| 43.1-5 | 10 | 0 | 9 | 1 | 21 | 146 | 52 |
| 46.2-4d | 4 | 0 | 4 | 0 | 8 | 69 | 29 |
| 46.5-8 | 4 | 0 | 4 | 0 | 8 | 73 | 29 |
| 46.9-12 | 4 | 0 | 3 | 1 | 9 | 80 | 33 |
| 49.2-5 | 4 | 0 | 4 | 0 | 8 | 59 | 24 |
| 49.6-13 | 8 | 0 | 6 | 2 | 18 | 141 | 54 |
| 49.14-21 | 9 | 0 | 9 | 0 | 18 | 140 | 54 |
| 56.2-5 | 5 | 1 | 3 | 1 | 10 | 74 | 28 |

| | | | | | | |
|---|---|---|---|---|---|---|
| 56.6-12 | 8 | 0 | 7 | 1 | 17 | 131 | 51 |
| 56.13-14 | 3 | 0 | 3 | 0 | 6 | 44 | 17 |
| 57.2-6 | 8 | 1 | 5 | 2 | 17 | 119 | 45 |
| 57.7-12 | 7 | 0 | 5 | 2 | 16 | 109 | 41 |
| 59.2-11a | 10 | 0 | 7 | 3 | 23 | 189 | 66 |
| 59.11b-18 | 10 | 0 | 7 | 3 | 23 | 186 | 65 |
| 67.2-4 | 3 | 0 | 3 | 0 | 6 | 50 | 18 |
| 67.5-6 | 2 | 0 | 1 | 1 | 5 | 40 | 15 |
| 67.7-8 | 2 | 0 | 2 | 0 | 4 | 37 | 12 |
| 80.2-4 | 3 | 0 | 1 | 2 | 8 | 71 | 23 |
| 80.5-8 | 4 | 0 | 4 | 0 | 8 | 76 | 25 |
| 80.9-16a | 8 | 0 | 8 | 0 | 16 | 134 | 49 |
| 80.17-20 | 4 | 0 | 4 | 0 | 8 | 75 | 26 |
| 99.1-5 | 6 | 0 | 5 | 1 | 13 | 95 | 40 |
| 99.6-9 | 5 | 0 | 2 | 3 | 13 | 105 | 38 |

Two observations are noteworthy. First, except when a psalm has no final refrain, one can see the same symmetries involved in a psalm's sections as in its stanzas (see 3.5.2). The sections in Psalms 59 and 99 are equivalent in length and those in Psalms 42–43, 46, and 57 are virtually equivalent. The two sections of Psalm 49, excluding the opening half-stanza which has no refrain, are also equivalent. In Psalm 80 the first, second, and fourth sections are half the size of the third. In Psalm 56 the sum of the first section and the final stanza is one colon shorter than the middle section. This is due to the fact that the second refrain has one extra colon. In Psalms 39 and 67 the absence of a final refrain explains the asymmetry of their sectional lengths. In Psalm 67 it is possible that a colon was omitted by haplography in the MT (see Appendix II). If that is the case, then the two sections are identical in size with 6 cola each (vv. 2-4, 5-6).

Second, five of these ten poems are based on a 'non-alpha-betic' acrostic structure. Psalms 42–43 has 66 cola (22 × 2); Psalms 56 and 57 have 33 cola each (22 + 11); and Psalm 59 has 46 cola (23 × 2; on 23-unit acrostics, compare Pss. 25 and 34. (See also Skehan 1951: 160n. 13; Freedman 1972d: 385; 1986. On 'non-alphabetic acrostics', see Freedman 1986.) In Psalms 42–43 and 59, the sections follow this 'acrostic' pattern. In Psalms 42–43 the base pattern is 22 + 22 + 22 cola.

This underlying pattern has been varied by omitting one colon from the first and last sections and adding these two cola to the middle section (21 + 24 + 21). This was probably due to the desire to add an extra verse to the middle section. Appropriately, this verse, a tricolon, occurs in the middle of the poem and is the only place where the name *Yahweh* appears (42.9). In Psalm 59 each of the sections has 23 cola.

## 3.7 *Thought Progression*

Recognizing the stanzas of a psalm is essential for understanding the meaning of a psalm. Surface structure and semantic content belong together. These two can never be totally divorced from each other (so Häublein 1978 on English poetry). Yet, such a divorce is precisely what happens in many of the contemporary structural and form-critical studies of the psalms. Structural analyses often deal with a psalm's surface structure without—or at least only superficially—relating its content to that structure (Alden 1974; 1976; 1978; Auffret 1977; 1981; 1982; Girard 1984; Trublet–Aletti 1983; van der Lugt 1980). Form-critical studies often commit the opposite error. They study the elements of a psalm's genre, such as the petitions, complaints, expressions of confidence, and vows of praise in a lament, without examining how these elements are shaped by and developed in a psalm's stanzaic structure (Kraus 1978; Gerstenberger 1988). In contrast, we have attempted to maintain a balance between these two concerns in our study of six poems (= seven psalms). Therefore, we have studied the stanzaic/sectional structure of each poem (2.x.4.5; 2.x.4.6) and have examined how the poem's content is integrated into its structure (2.x.6.1; 2.x.6.2). Here we will make some general observations about the latter in the hope of encouraging future studies to integrate the two concerns of structure and content. Also, we will make some comments concerning the importance that studying a psalm's *Leitwörter* has for interpretation.

### 3.7.1 *A Psalm's Turning Points*
In our corpus of refrain-psalms, the major turning points come between the sections, i.e. after the refrains. (We assume

that in other non-refrain-psalms the turning points come between the stanzas.) Each section closes with a climactic refrain. The refrain functions as a completion or resolution of the preceding material. It resolves the tension that the previous material developed. Then the following section begins with a shift in theme, image, or mood. Sometimes the sectional opening reintroduces the tension only to be resolved again in the next refrain. A few times a section begins with a thetical statement which the following sectional material develops or defends. Here we will note the turning points of the psalms studied in Chapter 2.

In the first stanza of Psalms 42–43, the psalmist expresses his longing for God. This longing is intensified by the memory of past pilgrimages to the temple (42.5). Then in the first major refrain the psalmist admonishes himself: 'Why are you cast down, O my soul, and so groan within me? Wait for God, for again I will praise him, the salvation of my countenance and my God.' The second section begins by reintroducing the tension. The psalmist acknowledges his despair, but now the addressee is God and not himself, 'Within me my soul is cast down because I remember you...' (42.7). The rest of the second section intensifies the distress. God is the problem (42.8, 10). Again the tension is resolved when the psalmist encourages himself in the major refrain (42.12). The third section begins with a change to petitions addressed to God (43.1). These petitions together with those of 43.3 are the only ones in the poem. The section concludes with the major refrain that also serves as the climax to the whole poem.

In Psalm 46 the first stanza concludes with the psalmist's defiant taunt against the waters of chaos, 'Let its waters roar and foam! Let the mountains shake at its haughtiness!' In spite of their threatening terror, the community will not fear, 'Yahweh of hosts is with us; the God of Jacob is a fortress for us' (refrain reconstructed, v. 4c-d). The second section begins by continuing this water imagery, but with a contrast, 'There is a river whose streams make glad the city of God...' (v. 5). In contrast to the terrifying waters of chaos, a gentle, paradisiacal and eschatological river gladdens the city of God. Also, note the change in the reference to the community. In the first stanza and refrain the community is spoken of in the first person plural but the second stanza switches to a third person singular designation, 'city of God'. At the end of the second stanza mention is made of the 'nations' and 'kingdoms' of the earth (v. 7). After the refrain of v. 8, these nations and kingdoms are addressed with plural imperatives, 'Come, see the deeds of Yahweh...' (v. 9). Thus, the beginning of the third section recalls the end of the second stanza just as the beginning of the second section recalls the end of the first stanza. Yet the switch between the sections is marked.

In Psalm 49 each of the major sections begins with an introductory statement that is developed in the following sectional material. After the prelude (vv. 2-5), the first section begins with a rhetorical question, 'Why should I fear...?' The following explains why there is no need to fear the arrogant rich—they perish and leave their wealth to others. The second section also begins with an introductory statement, 'This (the following) is the destiny of those who have foolish self-confidence, and that of their followers who are pleased with their words'. The section then continues by defining their destiny—Sheol.

After beseeching God to 'be gracious' because of the psalmist's enemies, the psalmist of Psalm 56 expresses his confidence in God in the first refrain, 'In God whose word I will praise, in God I trust, I will not fear. What can flesh do to me?' (v. 5). The second section then begins by reintroducing the stressful situation of the attacking enemies, 'All day long they find fault...' (v. 6). The section ends again with an expression of confidence as the refrain (vv. 11-12). Then the third stanza begins with the palmist's promise to fulfill his vows (v. 13). Whereas the first two stanzas contained petitions, the third stanza responds to the *answered* petitions, 'For you *have* delivered my life from death...' (v. 14). Also note the switch from speaking of God in the third person (vv. 11-12) to addressing God in the second person (v. 13).

The first stanza of Psalm 57 ends with the psalmist still being threatened by his enemies, 'My life is in the midst of lions...' (v. 5). In this context the first refrain is to be understood as a petition, 'Be exalted over the heavens, O God. Let your glory be exalted over all the earth' (v. 6). The petition is answered in the beginning of the second section, 'A net they set for my feet. They bent down my life. They dug before me a pit—they fell into it' (v. 7). In the rest of the second section the psalmist responds to this answered prayer by expressing his desire to praise God. The second refrain now functions as such a doxology (v. 12).

Finally, in Psalm 59 the first section describes the psalmist's plight under the attack of enemies. It concludes with an expression of confidence in refrain B, 'O my strength, for you will I watch. For you, God, are my fortress, my loving God' (vv. 10-11a). The second section begins by reintroducing the tension, this time with petitions, 'May God go before me. May he let me look down upon my foes' (v. 11b-c). The petitions and complaints continue until at the section's end we encounter refrain B again, but with one notable change. This time the refrain is a doxology, 'O my strength, to you I *hymn...*' (v. 18).

It can be seen from our corpus of psalms that some type of turning point always occurs between a psalm's sections. Sometimes there is a crescendo–decrescendo effect at the psalm's junctures (Pss. 42.6-7; 56.5-6; 59.10-11). Sometimes the new section begins with imperatives or jussives (Pss. 43.1; 46.9; 59.11b-c). Or it begins with an introductory statement which is then developed (Ps. 49.6, 14). A section can also begin with a changed situation (Ps. 57.7) or the psalmist's response to a changed situation (Ps. 56.13). Sometimes there is a change in mood (Pss. 42.7; 46.5; 56.6). In all cases the content matches the sectional divisions.

### 3.7.2 *Reading a Psalm by Stanzas/Sections*

Psalms that are structured into stanzas and sections, as the ones studied here are, need to be read in accordance with their structures. As Robert Alter states:

> Nevertheless, given form does tend to invite a particular orientation in the poetic ordering of the world. The Shakespearean sonnet can lend itself to love poetry, reflections on life's transience, celebrations of the power of art, and a good deal else, but whatever the topic or mood, a writer using this form can scarcely avoid organizing his statement in a sequence of three equal and balanced blocks, usually with an implied progression from one to the next, and concluding in the pithy summary or witty antithesis embodied in the couplet that follows the three quatrains. The artifice of form, in other words, becomes a particular way of conceiving relations and defining linkages, sequence,

and hierarchies in the reality to which the poet addresses himself (Alter 1985: 62).

Alter's observation holds not only for one's perception of the
external reality designated by the literary work but also for
one's perception of the literary work itself. Here we wish to
focus on the latter.

Each psalm studied here exhibits a progression, a development, an increase of intensity until it reaches its resolution (so
also Alter 1985: 27-81, 111-36). A psalm has, in other words, a
beginning and an ending. Psalms 42–43 begins with the
psalmist's longing for God from a distance and ends with his
confidence that he will praise God at the temple (43.4-5).
Psalm 46 begins with the thesis that God is our refuge and
ends with God himself addressing the nations followed by the
reassertion of the thesis (vv. 2-12). Psalms 56, 57, and 59 all
begin with a petition that God save the psalmist and they all
conclude with the psalmist's doxological response to God's
intervention. Psalm 49 develops its theme differently. This
psalm is a meditation on the refrains that answer the implied
riddle, 'How are the arrogant rich like cattle?' The refrains
answer that they are dumb and slaughtered like cattle. The
rest of the psalm expands on this observation. Yet even here
there is a progression, a stepping-up of assertion from verse to
verse. These psalms do not contain simply a series of 'one-lin-
ers'. There is movement here (cf. Alter 1985).

Yet they move from start to finish in stages corresponding to
their sections. Their stanzaic/sectional structures dictate a
'reading' that follows these stages. First the reader should
focus on each stanza with its own integrity (2.x.6.1) and then
investigate the relationship of the stanzas, or in our case sections, within the poem as a whole (2.x.6.2). If the poem has two
sections (Pss. 49, 57, 59), it should be read as a bipartite poem.
If it has three sections (Pss. 42–43, 46, 56), it should be treated
accordingly, and not as if it had five parts.

However, it is precisely here where many of the form-critical studies are inadequate. First, they are usually content to
divide a psalm according to the various elements of its genre
without examining its stanzaic structure (so Kraus 1978;
Gerstenberger 1988).

Second and more importantly, they often simply identify
and label each genre-element without examining its specific
function within the particular stanza. For example, Gerstenberger labels 42.10 and 43.2 'complaints' and notes their similar wording (1988: 178, 181). But he ignores their different
functions. The complaint in 42.10, 'Why have you forgotten
me?', expresses the psalmist's deep agony and perplexity over
the present absence of God. Whereas formerly 'Yahweh used
to commission his steadfast love' (v. 9), now God has seemingly
forgotten him. The similar complaint in 43.2 in the third
stanza has a different function. In this context, surrounded by
petitions, the complaint is designed to motivate God to intervene and bring the psalmist to the temple. They are similar
complaints but their different stanzaic contexts give them different functions.

Another example comes from Psalm 56, where one finds
complaints against the enemies in the first two stanzas (vv. 2b-
3, 6-7). Here again Gerstenberger simply identifies them as
complaints (1988: 226-28). Yet here too they function differently. In the first stanza the complaint is introduced with כי
and preceded by a petition, 'be gracious to me, O God. For man
hounds me...' (vv. 2-3). The complaint expresses the reason
why the psalmist needs divine assistance. In the second stanza
the complaint precedes the petitions. Here the first petition is
for divine wrath against the enemies. In this stanza the poet
uses the description of the enemies to argue that they deserve
to be punished and overcome by God. They are both complaints
against the enemies but their different stanzaic contexts cause
the reader to understand them differently.

Our final example comes from Psalm 57. Form-critics such
as Kraus (1978: 570-73) and Gerstenberger (1988: 229-32)
miss the internal logic of the poem because they fail to inter-
pret it in light of its bipartite structure. They both struggle over
the joining of lament (vv. 2-7) and hymnic (vv. 8-12) elements.
Gerstenberger is troubled by the interruption of the complaint
against the enemies (vv. 5, 7) by the refrain of v. 6. Yet there is
a logic to its progression. At the end of the first stanza the
psalmist lies down to sleep in the midst of his threatening
enemies (v. 5). In this context the first refrain functions as a
petition (v. 6). The second section begins with the enemies'

defeat, 'They dug before me a pit—they fell into it' (v. 7c-d). The psalmist responds to this divine intervention by expressing his earnest desire to praise God. In fact, so eager is he to praise God in public that he wants to hasten the dawn when he can sing praises publicly (vv. 8-11). In this context the second refrain functions as a doxology (v. 12). It is irrelevant whether or not this sequence of events corresponds to external historical reality. The point is that in the literary world created by the poem this is the sequence of events. The first section ends with the petition of the psalmist under attack by his enemies. The second section begins with the defeat of the enemies to which the psalmist responds with hymns in the following verses. The complaints against the enemies of vv. 5 and 7 and the refrains of vv. 6 and 12 function differently because each verse occurs in a different section. Only by reading the content of a psalm in connection with its stanzaic/sectional structure, can its inner logic and thought progression be perceived.

### 3.7.3 *Leitwörter*

Scholars are increasingly examining the *Leitwörter*, the thematic key-words, of a psalm (see Muilenburg 1953; Ridderbos 1963; 1972: 19-47; Watson 1984: 287-95 and the bibliographies cited there). By repeating a significant word—verbatim repetition or root repetition—or by using a series of near-synonyms, a psalmist reinforces the principal theme of the poem. Often these key-words are repeated seven or a multiple of seven times. Studying the *Leitwörter* of a psalm can aid the reader not only in determining the psalm's structure but also in identifying its dominant emphasis.

In our corpus of six poems, these *Leitwörter* reinforce the dominant emphasis of each psalm (see. 2.x.5 for details). The *Leitwörter* of Psalms 42–43, 'my soul' and some form of 'God', correspond to that poem's theme, 'My soul longs for God'. In Psalm 46 the repeated references to 'God', 'refuge' or its near-synonym, and 'earth' reinforce the two-fold theme, 'God is our refuge and the lord over the earth'. In Psalm 49 the repeated nouns that denote 'wealth' and 'death' highlight its theme, 'The arrogant rich perish in the grave'. The repeated divine appellatives and references to the 'enemies' of Psalm 56 focus attention on its two-fold concern, the psalmist's relationship with God and with the enemies. The dominant mood of Psalm 57 is the psalmist's faith in and praise of God. Its repeated diving appellatives and its frequent use of first person singular verbs expressing confidence or praise reinforce this mood. Finally, the divine appellatives and nouns denoting 'protection' highlight the theme of Psalm 59, 'God is my protection'.

Many of these *Leitwörter* are repeated seven or a multiple of seven times. There are fourteen divine appellatives in Psalm 46 (including the reconstructed refrain of v. 4c-d) and Psalm 59. Seven divine appellatives in Psalm 57 and twenty-one in Psalms 42–43 are glossed 'God' (אל, אלהים plus suffixed forms). Nouns denoting 'wealth' and 'death' occur seven times each in Psalm 49. Nouns denoting 'protection' occur seven times in Psalm 59. The suffixed form נפשי, 'my soul', is found seven times in Psalms 42–43. The 'enemies' are mentioned seven times in nominal form in Psalm 56. Finally, Psalm 57 uses a first person singular verb to express confidence or praise seven times.

### 3.8 *Summation*

This study has examined ten poems in the Psalter (including those of Appendix II) in an effort to describe the various 'building blocks' of a psalm. Here the major conclusions will be given.

Every colon in our corpus has 2–4 stresses. Most common are cola of 3 stresses (55%) followed by 2 stresses (30%) and 4 stresses (15%). While no psalm has a consistent and predictable stress pattern and therefore no 'meter' in any traditional sense, a psalm does exhibit an overall regularity and a dominant stress pattern, albeit with internal variations from the norm. This can be observed by counting syllables along with stresses.

Of the units larger than the verse, most strophes have 4–6 cola (60%) and most multiple-strophe stanzas have 12–16 cola (80%). One should count cola rather than verses to determine the size of these units, since counting verses is often misleading. All ten poems have 2–4 stanzas. Six have 3 stanzas; two have 2 stanzas; and two have 4 stanzas. Symmetry in length is evident among the larger units of a psalm, but it is located on the stanza level rather than the strophe level. The psalmists work with stanzas of equal size or with a combination of half-stanzas plus full-stanzas in a given psalm. In addition to the refrains, the devices that most frequently serve to unify and demarcate a stanza are repetition, word pairs, inclusion, dominant imperative/jussive or indicative verbal mood, and an initial colon with an imperative/jussive or vocative. The enigmatic word *selāh* occurs at the beginning, middle, or end of a stanza/section in our corpus. The refrains are stanza-external and section-final. A surprising discovery is that five of the ten poems are based on a 'non-alphabetic' acrostic structure. Finally, a major turning point in a psalm's thought progression occurs between the psalm's sections. Only by integrating a psalm's semantic content with its stanzaic-sectional structure can one sensitively read a psalm. It is hoped that these conclusions will contribute toward a better understanding of how to read a psalm.

## APPENDIX I

*Prose Particle Counts*

| | אשר | את | ה | No. of Words | Frequency |
|---|---|---|---|---|---|
| Ps. 42–43 | 0 | 0 | 1 (v. 4)<br>1 (v. 11) | 187 | 1.1% |
| Title | 0 | 0 | 0 | 4 | 0% |
| Ps. 46 | 1 (v. 9) | 0 | 1 (v. 10) | 91 | 2.2% |
| Title | 0 | 0 | 0 | 6 | 0% |
| Ps. 49 | 0 | 0 | 1 (v. 2)<br>1 (v. 7)<br>1 (v. 10)<br>1 (v. 18) | 161 | 2.5% |
| Title | 0 | 0 | 0 | 4 | |
| Ps. 56 | 1 (v. 7) | 0 | 1 (v. 2)<br>1 (v. 3)<br>1 (v. 6)<br>1 (v. 14) | 109 | 4.6% |
| Title | 0 | 1 | 0 | 11 | 9.1% |
| Ps. 57 | 0 | 0 | 2 (v. 6)<br>1 (v. 9)<br>1 (v. 12) | 95 | 4.2% |
| Title | 0 | 0 | 0 | 9 | 0% |
| Ps. 59 | 0 | 0 | 1 (v. 6)<br>1 (v. 14) | 143 | 1.4% |
| Title | 0 | 1 | 1 | 11 | 18.2% |
| TOTAL PSALMS | 2 | 0 | 17 | 786 | 2.4% |
| TOTAL TITLES | 0 | 2 | 1 | 45 | 6.7% |

It is generally recognized that the relative אשר, the nota accusativi את, and the definite article written with ה are typical of Hebrew prose and atypical of Hebrew poetry. Statistical analysis has confirmed this (Andersen–Freedman 1980: 60-66; Andersen–Forbes 1983). The frequency of prose particles in standard prose is high (15% or more of all words) whereas in poetry it is low (5% or less).

We based our count on the MT. We obtained the particle frequency by dividing the number of prose particles by the number of words. For our purposes, a 'word' is what is written between the spaces in the MT. We did not count *selāh*. We also distinguished between the psalms proper and the psalm titles.

The results for our corpus of seven psalms (six poems since Psalms 42–43 are one poem) confirm that these psalms are poetry as expected. The particle frequency for the entire corpus is 2.4%. The range is from 1.1% to 4.6%. It is remarkable that there are no occurrences of את and only two occurrences of אשר. (The כאשר in Ps. 56.7 and the אשר in Ps. 46.9 are used as conjunctions introducing an object clause, and therefore perhaps they should not be counted. If this is the case, the particle frequency becomes 2.2%.) What does occur with some frequency (17 times) is the definite article ה. This too is normal in Hebrew poetry, since very often it introduces a vocative, is attached to a participle or is part of a stereotypical phrase.

In our corpus, ה is attached once to a participle (Ps. 49.7) and once to a vocative (Ps. 57.9). In nine of the remaining fifteen occurrences ה is part of a stereotyped phrase. Eight of these cases have ה attached to the noun following כל. According to a concordance (Even-Shoshan 1984), the statistics for the Hebrew Bible are as follows:

| In Our Corpus | | In Hebrew Bible |
|---|---|---|
| כל־היום (Pss. 42.4, 11; 56.2, 3, 6) | — | 49 occurrences |
| כל־יום (none) | — | 4 occurrences, 3 of which are בכל יום |
| כל־העמים (Ps. 49.2) | — | 39 occurrences |
| כל־עמים (none) | — | 0 occurrences |
| כל־הארץ (Ps. 57.6, 12) | — | 86 occurrences |
| כל־ארץ (none) | — | 0 occurrences |
| עד־קצה הארץ (Ps. 46.10) | — | 9 occurrences |
| עד־קצה ארץ (none) | — | 0 occurrences |

It can be seen on the basis of these statistics that the poets had very little freedom to omit the definite article ה for eleven of the total seventeen cases.

If we omit these eleven instances of ה (one participle + one vocative + nine stereotypical phrases), and the one אשר and one כאשר which act as conjunctions, then our corpus contains only six prose particles that the poet had freedom to omit, all of which are definite articles: Pss. 49.10, 18; 56.14; 57.6 (cf. v. 12); 59.6 (cf. v. 9), 14. This yields a prose particle frequency of 0.76% for our corpus (6 particles out of 786 words). In this case the particle frequency for each psalm would be as follows: Psalms 42–43 = 0%; Psalm 46 = 0%; Psalm 49 = 1.2%; Psalm 56 = 0.9%; Psalm 57 = 1.1%; Psalm 59 = 1.4%. Thus, it is certain that these seven psalms represent poetry with a very infrequent use of prose particles.

The psalm titles are a different story. The prose particle frequency for the total of these is 6.7%. However, this figure is misleading, since the titles consist mostly of names and musical notations rather than sentences. If we isolate the brief historical narratives in the titles, the prose particle frequency is considerably higher. These brief narratives are:

| Ps. 56.1 | — | באחז אתו פלשתים בגת |
| Ps. 57.1 | — | בברחו מפני־שאול במערה |
| Ps. 59.1 | — | בשלח שאול וישמרו את־הבית להמיתו |

Of these 14 words there are 3 prose particles (2 direct object markers and 1 definite article ה) which yields a prose particle frequency of 21.4%. Although this is a small sample and therefore one cannot make too much out of it, it is well within the prose category and in stark contrast to the poems.

APPENDIX II

## Other Refrain-Psalms (Psalms 39, 67, 80, 99)

Here we will give the text, syllable count, stress count, versification, and strophic divisions of the four other psalms with internal refrains (Pss. 39; 67; 80; 99; Pss. 80 and 99 also have final refrains). Space prohibits us from giving a detailed analysis of each psalm and a defense of our stress count, versification, and strophic divisions. However, the colonic divisions are usually clear and the stanzaic structures are certain due to the refrains. The data from these four psalms are included in sections 3.4, 3.5, and 3.6.

### Psalm 39

|        | Text | Syllables | | Total | Stresses |
|--------|------|-----------|---|-------|----------|
| v. 2a. | אמרתי | (3) | = | (3) | (1) |
|        | אשמרה דרכי מחטוא בלשוני | 3+3+3+3 | = | 12 | 4 |
| b.     | אשמרה לפי מחסום | 3+2+2 | = | 7 | 3 |
| c.     | בעד רשע לנגדי | 2+2+3 | = | 7 | 3 |
| 3a.    | נאלמתי דומיה | 3+3 | = | 6 | 2 |
| b.     | החשיתי מטוב | 3+2 | = | 5 | 2 |
| c.     | וכאבי נעכר | 4+2 | = | 6 | 2 |
| 4a.    | חם־לבי בקרבי | 1+2+3 | = | 6 | 3 |
| b.     | בהגיגי תבער־אש | 4+2+1 | = | 7 | 3 |
| c.     | דברתי בלשוני | 3+3 | = | 6 | 2 |
| 5a.    | הודיעני יהוה קצי | 4+2+2 | = | 8 | 3 |
| b.     | ומדת ימי מה־היא | 3+2+1+1 | = | 7 | 3 |
| c.     | אדעה מה־חדל אני | 3+1+2+2 | = | 8 | 3 |
| 6a.    | הנה טפחות נתתה ימי | 2+3+3+2 | = | 10 | 4 |
| b.     | וחלדי כאין נגדך | 3+2+3 | = | 8 | 3 |
| c.     | אך כל־הבל כל־אדם נצב סלה | 1+1+1+1+2+2 | = | 8 | 4 |
| 7a.    | אך־בצלם יתהלך־איש | 1+2+3+1 | = | 7 | 3 |
| b.     | אך־הבל יהמיון יצבר | 1+1+3+2 | = | 7 | 3 |
| c.     | ולא־ידע מי־אספם | 2+2+1+3 | = | 8 | 3 |

| | | | | | |
|---|---|---|---|---|---|
| 8a. | ותהה מה־קויתי אדני | 3+1+3+3 | = | 10 | 3 |
| b. | תוחלתי לך היא | 3+2+1 | = | 6 | 3 |
| 9a. | מכל־פשעי הצילני | 2+3+4 | = | 9 | 3 |
| b. | חרפת נבל אל־תשימני | 2+2+1+4 | = | 9 | 3 |
| 10a. | נאלמתי לא אפתח־פי | 3+1+2+1 | = | 7 | 3 |
| b. | כי אתה עשית | 1+2+3 | = | 6 | 2 |
| 11a. | הסר מעלי נגעך | 2+3+3 | = | 8 | 3 |
| b. | מתגרת ידך אני כליתי | 3+3+2+3 | = | 11 | 4 |
| 12a. | בתוכחות על־עון | 4+1+2 | = | 7 | 2 |
| b. | יסרת איש | 3+1 | = | 4 | 2 |
| c. | ותמס כעש חמודו | 3+2+3 | = | 8 | 3 |
| d. | אך הבל כל־אדם סלה | 1+1+1+2 | = | 5 | 2 |
| 13a. | שמעה־תפלתי יהוה | 2+4+2 | = | 8 | 3 |
| b. | ושועתי האזינה | 4+3 | = | 7 | 2 |
| c. | אל־דמעתי אל־תחרש | 1+3+1+2 | = | 7 | 3 |
| d. | כי גר אנכי עמך | 1+1+3+2 | = | 7 | 3 |
| e. | תושב ככל־אבותי | 2+2+3 | = | 7 | 3 |
| 14a. | השע ממני ואבלינה | 2+3+4 | = | 9 | 3 |
| b. | בטרם אלך ואיני | 2+2+4 | = | 8 | 3 |

### Length of Strophes

| Strophe | vv. | bic. | tric. | cola | Sylls. | Stresses |
|---|---|---|---|---|---|---|
| vv. 2-4 | 3 | 0 | 3 | 9 | 62 | 24 |
| 5-6b | 2 | 1 | 1 | 5 | 41 | 16 |
| 7 | 1 | 0 | 1 | 3 | 22 | 9 |
| 8-12c | 5 | 4 | 1 | 11 | 85 | 31 |
| 13-14 | 3 | 2 | 1 | 7 | 53 | 20 |

### Length of Stanza

| Stanza | Strophes | vv. | bic. | tric. | cola | Sylls. | Stresses |
|---|---|---|---|---|---|---|---|
| vv. 2-6b | 2 | 5 | 1 | 4 | 14 | 103 | 40 |
| 7-12c | 2 | 6 | 4 | 2 | 14 | 107 | 40 |
| 13-14 | 1 | 3 | 2 | 1 | 7 | 53 | 20 |

## Comments

We take the opening word אמרתי as an example of anacrusis, an 'extra-metrical word' (cf. Watson 1984: 110-11). Therefore, both v. 2a and 2b begin with אשמרה. In contrast, one might consider אמרתי integral, in which case v. 2a is either an exceptionally long colon (15 syllables/5 stresses) or else a bicolon— אמרתי אשמרה דרכי // מחטוא בלשוני (9 + 6 syllables/3 + 2 stresses). If we choose the latter, then stanza I has 15 cola, 106 syllables,

and 41 stresses. At any rate, the first two stanzas are virtually
equivalent in length and the third stanza is half that length.
The refrains, which are monocola, occur in v. 6c and v. 12d.
The second, fourth, and fifth strophes consist of direct address
to God.

## Psalm 67

| | Text | Syllables | | Total | Stresses |
|---|---|---|---|---|---|
| v. 2a. | אלהים יחננו ויברכנו | 3+4+5= | | 12 | 3 |
| b. | יאר פניו אתנו סלה | 2+2+3 | = | 7 | 3 |
| 3a. | לדעת בארץ דרכך | 2+2+3 | = | 7 | 3 |
| b. | בכל־גוים ישועתך | 2+2+5 | = | 9 | 3 |
| 4a. | יודוך עמים אלהים | 3+2+3 | = | 8 | 3 |
| b. | יודוך עמים כלם | 3+2+2 | = | 7 | 3 |
| 5a. | ישמחו וירננו לאמים | 3+4+3 | = | 10 | 3 |
| b. | כי־תשפט עמים מישור | 1+2+2+2 | = | 7 | 3 |
| c. | ולאמים בארץ תנחם סלה | 4+2+2 | = | 8 | 3 |
| 6a. | יודוך עמים אלהים | 3+2+3 | = | 8 | 3 |
| b. | יודוך עמים כלם | 3+2+2 | = | 7 | 3 |
| 7a. | ארץ נתנה יבולה | 1+3+3 | = | 7 | 3 |
| b. | יברכנו אלהים אלהינו | 5+3+4 | = | 12 | 3 |
| 8a. | יברכנו אלהים | 5+3 | = | 8 | 2 |
| b. | וייראו אתו כל־אפסי־ארץ | 4+2+1+2+1 | = | 10 | 4 |

### Length of Stanzas

| Stanza | vv. | bic. | tric. | cola | Sylls. | Stresses |
|---|---|---|---|---|---|---|
| vv. 2-3 | 2 | 2 | 0 | 4 | 35 | 12 |
| 5 | 1 | 0 | 1 | 3 | 25 | 9 |
| 7-8 | 2 | 2 | 0 | 4 | 37 | 12 |

## Comments

The refrains, which are bicola, occur in v. 4 and v. 6. The strophes are identical with the stanzas in this psalm. The reading
of the codex Sinaiticus—κρινεῖ τὴν οἰκουμένην ἐν δικαιοσύνῃ—
suggests the strong possibility that the masoretic scribe
omitted a colon by haplography of תשפט (so Kraus 1978: 621). If
that is the case, then one should read v. 5:

| a. | ישמחו וירננו לאמים | 3+4+3 | = | 10 | 3 |
|---|---|---|---|---|---|
| b. | כי־תשפט [תבל בצדק] | 1+2+2+2 | = | 7 | 3 |

| | Text | Syllables | | Total | Stresses |
|---|---|---|---|---|---|
| c. | עמים מישור [השפט] | 2+2+2 | = | 6 | 3 |
| d. | ולאמים בארץ תנחם סלה | 4+2+2 | = | 8 | 3 |

With this one can compare Pss. 9.9; 96.13; 98.9. In this case, the middle stanza is nearly identical in length with the other two stanzas—4 cola, 31 syllables, 12 stresses. In favor of this reading is also the fact that with it there are ten references to the inhabited world: בכל־גוים ...לאמים (v. 3b), עמים (v. 4), עמים...עמים ...עמים (v. 5), עמים...עמים (v. 6), כל־אפסי־ארץ (v. 8b).

According to the MT, the first and third stanzas are identical in length but the middle stanza is one colon less. In its favor are the seven references to 'the peoples' in vv. 4-6 with the symmetrical sequence: לאמים ...עמים...עמים לאמים (v. 5), עמים ...עמים (v. 4), עמים ...עמים (v. 6). We prefer the MT but we recognize the uncertainty involved.

*Psalm 80*

| | Text | Syllables | | Total | Stresses |
|---|---|---|---|---|---|
| v.2a. | רעה ישראל האזינה | 2+3+3 | = | 8 | 3 |
| b. | נהג כצאן יוסף | 2+2+2 | = | 6 | 3 |
| c. | ישב הכרובים הופיעה | 2+4+3 | = | 9 | 3 |
| 3a. | לפני אפרים ובנימן ומנשה | 2+2+4+4 | = | 12 | 4 |
| b. | עוררה את־גבורתך | 3+1+5 | = | 9 | 2 |
| c. | ולכה לישעתה לנו | 3+4+2 | = | 9 | 3 |
| 4a. | אלהים השיבנו | 3+4 | = | 7 | 2 |
| b. | והאר פניך ונושעה | 3+3+5 | = | 11 | 3 |
| 5a. | יהוה אלהים צבאות | 2+3+3 | = | 8 | 3 |
| b. | עד־מתי עשנת בתפלת עמך | 1+2+3+3+3 | = | 12 | 4 |
| 6a. | האכלתם לחם דמעה | 3+1+2 | = | 6 | 3 |
| b. | ותשקמו בדמעות שליש | 4+3+2 | = | 9 | 3 |
| 7a. | תשימנו מדון לשכנינו | 4+2+4 | = | 10 | 3 |
| b. | ואיבינו ילעגו־למו | 5+3+2 | = | 10 | 3 |
| 8a. | אלהים צבאות השיבנו | 3+3+4 | = | 10 | 3 |
| b. | והאר פניך ונושעה | 3+3+5 | = | 11 | 3 |
| 9a. | גפן ממצרים תסיע | 1+3+2 | = | 6 | 3 |
| b. | תגרש גוים ותטעה | 3+2+5 | = | 10 | 3 |
| 10a. | פנית לפניה | 3+4 | = | 7 | 2 |
| b. | ותשרש שרשיה ותמלא־ארץ | 3+4+4+1 | = | 12 | 4 |
| 11a. | כסו הרים צלה | 2+2+2 | = | 6 | 3 |
| b. | וענפיה ארזי־אל | 5+2+1 | = | 8 | 3 |
| 12a. | תשלח קצירה עד־ים | 3+4+1+1 | = | 9 | 3 |
| b. | ואל־נהר יונקותיה | 2+2+5 | = | 9 | 3 |

| | | | | | |
|---|---|---|---|---|---|
| 13a. | למה פרצת גדריה | 2+3+4 | = | 9 | 3 |
| b. | וארוה כל־עברי דרך | 4+1+3+1 | = | 9 | 3 |
| 14a. | יכרסמנה חזיר מיער | 5+2+2 | = | 9 | 3 |
| b. | חיו שדי ירענה | 2+2+3 | = | 7 | 3 |
| 15a. | אלהים צבאות שוב־נא | 3+3+2 | = | 8 | 3 |
| b. | הבם משמים וראה | 2+3+3 | = | 8 | 3 |
| c. | ופקד גפן זאת | 3+1+1 | = | 5 | 3 |
| 16a. | וכנה אשר־נטעה ימינך | 3+2+3+4 | = | 12 | 4 |
| 17a. | שרפה באש כסוחה | 3+2+3 | = | 8 | 3 |
| b. | מגערת פניך יאבדו | 3+3+3 | = | 9 | 3 |
| 18a. | תהי־ידך על־איש | 2+3+1+1 | = | 7 | 3 |
| b. | ימינך על־בן־אדם אמצת לך | 4+1+1+2+3+1 | = | 12 | 4 |
| 19a. | ולא־נסוג ממך | 2+2+3 | = | 7 | 3 |
| b. | תחינו ובשמך נקרא | 4+4+2 | = | 10 | 3 |
| 20a. | יהוה אלהים צבאות השיבנו | 2+3+3+4 | = | 12 | 4 |
| b. | האר פניך ונושעה | 2+3+5 | = | 10 | 3 |

### Length of Strophes

| Strophe | vv. | bic. | tric. | cola | Sylls. | Stresses |
|---|---|---|---|---|---|---|
| vv. 2-3 | 2 | 0 | 2 | 6 | 53 | 18 |
| 5-7 | 3 | 3 | 0 | 6 | 55 | 19 |
| 9-12 | 4 | 4 | 0 | 8 | 67 | 24 |
| 13-14 | 2 | 2 | 0 | 4 | 34 | 12 |
| 17-19 | 3 | 3 | 0 | 6 | 53 | 19 |

### Length of Stanzas

| Stanza | Strophes | vv. | bic. | tric. | cola | Sylls. | Stresses |
|---|---|---|---|---|---|---|---|
| vv. 2-3 | 1 | 2 | 0 | 2 | 6 | 53 | 18 |
| 5-7 | 1 | 3 | 3 | 0 | 6 | 55 | 19 |
| 9-14 | 2 | 6 | 6 | 0 | 12 | 100 | 36 |
| 17-19 | 1 | 3 | 3 | 0 | 6 | 53 | 19 |

## Comments

The refrains occur in vv. 4, 8, 15-16a, and 20. The third refrain has two bicola; the others have one each. We follow most commentators in omitting v. 16b as a dittograph of v. 18b. The first, second, and fourth stanzas—one strophe each—are virtually identical in length down to the syllable count. If we count the particle זאת as stressed in v. 3b, then the first stanza also has 19 stresses like the other two. One should note that the two tricola of the first stanza are equivalent to the three bicola

of each of the other two stanzas (6 cola each). The third stanza
is twice the length of the other three. Appropriately, the third
refrain is twice the length of the other refrains (4 cola compared to 2 cola). The interrogative למה in v. 13a begins the second strophe of the third stanza. Thus the third stanza consists
of two strophes whereas each of the other stanzas consists of
one.

## Psalm 99

| | Text | Syll. Count | | | Total | Stresses |
|---|---|---|---|---|---|---|
| v. 1a. | יהוה מלך ירגזו עמים | 2+2+3+2 | = | | 9 | 4 |
| b. | ישב כרובים תנוט הארץ | 2+3+2+2 | = | | 9 | 4 |
| 2a. | יהוה בציון גדול | 2+3+2 | = | | 7 | 3 |
| b. | ורם הוא על־כל־העמים | 2+1+1+1+3 | = | | 8 | 3 |
| 3a. | יודו שמך גדול ונורא | 2+2+2+3 | = | | 9 | 4 |
| b. | קדוש הוא | 2+1 | = | | 3 | 2 |
| 4a. | ועז מלך משפט אהב | 2+1+2+2 | = | | 7 | 4 |
| b. | אתה כוננת מישרים | 2+3+3 | = | | 8 | 3 |
| c. | משפט וצדקה ביעקב | 2+4+3 | = | | 9 | 3 |
| d. | אתה עשית | 2+3 | = | | 5 | 2 |
| 5a. | רוממו יהוה אלהינו | 3+2+4 | = | | 9 | 3 |
| b. | והשתחוו להדם רגליו | 4+3+2 | = | | 9 | 3 |
| c. | קדוש הוא | 2+1 | = | | 3 | 2 |
| 6a. | משה ואהרן בכהניו | 2+3+4 | = | | 9 | 3 |
| b. | ושמואל בקראי שמו | 4+4+2 | = | | 10 | 3 |
| c. | קראים אל־יהוה | 3+1+2 | = | | 6 | 2 |
| d. | והוא יענם | 2+2 | = | | 4 | 2 |
| 7a. | בעמוד ענן ידבר אליהם | 3+2+3+3 | = | | 11 | 4 |
| b. | שמרו עדתיו | 3+3 | = | | 6 | 2 |
| c. | וחק נתן למו | 2+2+2 | = | | 6 | 3 |
| 8a. | יהוה אלהינו אתה עניתם | 2+4+2+3 | = | | 11 | 4 |
| b. | אל נשא היית לדם | 1+2+3+2 | = | | 8 | 4 |
| c. | ונקם על־עלילותם | 3+1+4 | = | | 8 | 2 |
| 9a. | רוממו יהוה אלהינו | 3+2+4 | = | | 9 | 3 |
| b. | והשתחוו להר קדשו | 4+2+2 | = | | 8 | 3 |
| c. | כי־קדוש יהוה אלהינו | 1+2+2+4 | = | | 9 | 3 |

### Length of Strophes

| Strophes | vv. | bic. | tric. | cola | Sylls. | Stresses |
|---|---|---|---|---|---|---|
| vv. 1-3 | 3 | 3 | 0 | 6 | 45 | 20 |
| | 4 | 2 | 2 | 0 | 4 | 29 | 12 |

| 6-7 | 3 | 2 | 1 | 7 | 52 | 19 |
| 8 | 1 | 0 | 1 | 3 | 27 | 10 |

### Length of Stanzas

| Stanza | Strophes | vv. | bic. | tric. | cola | Sylls. | Stresses |
|--------|----------|-----|------|-------|------|--------|----------|
| vv. 1-4 | 2 | 5 | 5 | 0 | 10 | 74 | 32 |
| 6-8 | 2 | 4 | 2 | 2 | 10 | 79 | 29 |

## Comments

The refrains, which are tricola, occur in vv. 5 and 9. The strophes are distinguished by the switch in person. In the first (except v. 3a) and third strophes the divine name is in the third person but in the second and fourth strophes it is in the second person. The two stanzas are identical in length with 10 cola each. Note that the difference in number of verses—5 to 4—is deceptive. The first stanza is 5–6 syllables shorter but three stresses longer than the second. (If we count the preposition על as one stress in v. 8c, then the difference between the two stanzas is two stresses.)

# SELECTED BIBLIOGRAPHY

Aejmelaeus, A.
1986a   'Function and Interpretation of *ky* in Biblical Hebrew'. *Journal of Biblical Literature* 105: 193-209.
1986b   *The Traditional Prayer in the Psalms*. Berlin: de Gruyter.
Alden, R.L.
1974    'Chiastic Psalms: A Study in the Mechanics of Semitic Poetry in Psalms 1–50'. *Journal of the Evangelical Theological Society* 17: 11-28.
1976    'Chiastic Psalms (II): A Study in the Mechanics of Semitic Poetry in Psalms 51–100'. *Journal of the Evangelical Theological Society* 19: 191-200.
1978    'Chiastic Psalms (III): A Study in the Mechanics of Semitic Poetry in Psalms 101–150'. *Journal of the Evangelical Theological Society* 21: 199-210.
Alonso Schökel, L.
1963    *Estudios de poética hebrea*. Barcelona: Juan Flors. = *Das Alte Testament als literarisches Kunstwerk*. Trans. K. Bergner. Köln: Bachem, 1971.
1975    'Hermeneutical Problems of a Literary Study of the Bible'. *Supplements to Vetus Testamentum* 28: 1-15.
1976    'The Poetic Structure of Psalm 42–43'. *Journal for the Study of the Old Testament* 1: 4-11.
1977    'Psalm 42–43. A Response to Ridderbos and Kessler'. *Journal for the Study of the Old Testament* 3: 61-65.
1988    *A Manual of Hebrew Poetics*. Rome: Pontifical Biblical Institute.
Alter, R.
1985    *The Art of Biblical Poetry*. New York: Basic Books.
Andersen, F.I. and Forbes, A.D.
1983    ' "Prose Particle" Counts of the Hebrew Bible', in C.L. Meyers and M. O'Connor, eds., pp. 165-83.
Andersen, F.I. and Freedman, D.N.
1980    *Hosea*. Anchor Bible, 24. Garden City: Doubleday.
Auffret, P.
1977    'Note sur la structure littéraire du Psaume LVII'. *Semitica* 27: 59-73.
1978    'Pivot Pattern: nouveaux exemples'. *Vetus Testamentum* 28: 103-10.
1981    *Hymnes d'Égypte et d'Israël: études de structures littéraires*. Orbis biblicus et orientalis, 34. Göttingen: Vandenhoeck & Ruprecht.

1982     *La sagesse a bâti sa maison: études de structures littéraires dans l'Ancien Testament et spécialement dans les psaumes.* Fribourg: Editions Universitaires.

Avishur, Y.
1975     'Word Pairs Common to Phoenician and Biblical Hebrew'. *Ugarit-Forschungen* 7: 13-47.
1984     *Stylistic Studies of Word-Pairs in Biblical and Ancient Semitic Literatures.* Alter Orient und Altes Testament, 210. Neukirchen-Vluyn: Neukirchener Verlag.

Baumann, E.
1945/48  'Struktur-Untersuchungen im Psalter I'. *Zeitschrift für die alttestamentliche Wissenschaft* 61: 114-76.
1950     'Struktur-Untersuchungen im Psalter II'. *Zeitschrift für die alttestamentliche Wissenschaft* 62: 115-52.

Beaucamp, E.
1968     'Structure strophique des Psaumes'. *Recherches de Science Religieuse* 56: 199-224.
1976     *Le Psautier. Ps. 1–72.* Sources Bibliques, 7. Paris: Gabalda.

Bee, R.E.
1978a    'The Textual Analysis of Psalm 132: A Response to Cornelius B. Houk'. *Journal for the Study of the Old Testament* 6: 49-53.
1978b    'The Mode of Composition and Statistical Scansion'. *Journal for the Study of the Old Testament* 6: 58-68.

Begrich, J.H.
1934     'Das priesterliche Heilsorakel'. *Zeitschrift für die alttestamentliche Wissenschaft* 52: 81-92.

Berlin, A.
1979     "Grammatical Aspects of Biblical Parallelism'. *Hebrew Union College Annual* 50: 17-43.
1985     *The Dynamics of Biblical Parallelism.* Bloomington: Indiana University Press.

Beyerlin, W.
1970     *Die Rettung der Bedrängten in den Feindpsalmen der Einzelnen auf institutionelle Zusammenhänge untersucht.* Göttingen: Vandenhoeck & Ruprecht.

Blenkinsopp, J.
1963     'Stylistics of Old Testament Poetry'. *Biblica* 44: 352-58.

Boling, R.G.
1960     '"Synonymous" Parallelism in the Psalms'. *Journal of Semitic Studies* 5: 221-55.

Bowra, C.M.
1962     *Primitive Song.* New York: World.

Bream, H.N., Heim, R.D., and Moore, C.A., eds.
1974     *A Light Unto My Path: Old Testament Studies in Honor of Jacob M. Myers.* Gettysburg Theological Studies, 4. Pittsburgh: Temple University Press.

Briggs, C.A.
1906     *A Critical and Exegetical Commentary on the Book of the Psalms.* Vol. I. International Critical Commentary. Edinburgh: T. & T. Clark.

1907    *A Critical and Exegetical Commentary on the Book of the Psalms.*
        Vol. II. International Critical Commentary. Edinburgh: T. & T.
        Clark.

Brown, F., Driver, S.R., and Briggs, C.A.
1907    *A Hebrew and English Lexicon of the Old Testament.* Oxford:
        Clarendon.

Calès, J.
1936    *Le livre des Psaumes.* Vol. I. Paris: Beauchesne.

Casetti, P.
1982    *Gibt es ein Leben vor dem Tod? Eine Auslegung von Psalm 49.*
        Orbis biblicus et orientalis, 44. Göttingen: Vandenhoeck &
        Ruprecht.

Childs, B.S.
1971    'Psalm Titles and Midrashic Exegesis'. *Journal of Semitic Studies.*
        16: 137-50.

Christensen, D.L.
1983    'The Book of Jonah as a Narrative Poem'. Paper presented to the
        Institute of Advanced Studies of the Hebrew University of
        Jerusalem.
1984    'Two Stanzas of a Hymn in Deuteronomy 33'. *Biblica* 65: 382-89.
1985a   'The Song of Jonah: A Metrical Analysis'. *Journal of Biblical Lit-
        erature* 104: 217-31.
1985b   'Prose and Poetry in the Bible: The Narrative Poetics of Deuteron-
        omy 1.9-18'. *Zeitschrift für die alttestamentliche Wissenschaft* 97:
        179-89.

Clines, D.J.A.
1967    'Psalm Research since 1955: I. The Psalms and the Cult'. *Tyndale
        Bulletin* 18: 103-26.
1969    'Psalm Research since 1955: II. The Literary Genres'. *Tyndale
        Bulletin* 20: 105-26.

Collins, T.
1978    *Line-Forms in Hebrew Poetry.* Rome: Biblical Institute Press.

Cooper, A.
1976    *Biblical Poetics: A Linguistic Approach.* Ph.D. Dissertation, Yale
        University.

Craigie, P.C.
1971    'The Poetry of Ugarit and Israel'. *Tyndale Bulletin* 22: 3-31.
1972    'Psalm XXIX in the Hebrew Poetic Tradition'. *Vetus Testamen-
        tum* 22: 143-51.
1974    'The Comparison of Hebrew Poetry: Psalm 104 in the Light of
        Egyptian and Ugaritic Poetry'. *Semitics* 4: 10-21.
1977    'The Problem of Parallel Word Pairs in Ugaritic and Hebrew
        Poetry'. *Semitics* 5: 45-58.
1983    *Psalms 1-50.* Word Biblical Commentary, 19. Waco, TX: Word
        Books.

Crenshaw, J.L.
1970    'A Liturgy of Wasted Opportunity (Am. 4.6-12: Isa. 9.7-10.4, 5.25-
        29)'. *Semitics* 1: 27-37.

Cross, F.M.
1974    'Prose and Poetry in the Mythic and Epic Texts from Ugaritic'.
        *Harvard Theological Review* 67: 1-15.

1983    'Studies in the Structure of Hebrew Verse: The Prosody of Lamentations 1.1-22', in C.L. Meyers and M. O'Connor, eds., pp. 129-55.

Cross, F.M. and Freedman, D.N.

1948    'The Blessing of Moses'. *Journal of Biblical Literature* 67: 191-210.
1952    *Early Hebrew Orthography: A Study of the Epigraphic Evidence.* American Oriental Series, 36. New Haven: American Oriental Society.
1953    'A Royal Song of Thanksgiving: II Samuel 22 = Psalm 18'. *Journal of Biblical Literature* 72: 15-34.
1972    'Some Observations on Early Hebrew'. *Biblica* 53: 413-20.
1975    *Studies in Ancient Yahwistic Poetry.* Society of Biblical Literature Series, 21. Missoula: Scholars Press.

Culley, R.C.

1970    'Metrical Analysis of Classical Hebrew Poetry', in Wevers and Redford, eds., pp. 12-28.

Dahood, M.

1953a    'The Divine Name "Eli" in the Psalms'. *Theological Studies* 14: 452-57.
1953b    'Philological Notes on the Psalms'. *Theological Studies* 14: 85-88.
1953c    'The Root *GMR* in the Psalms'. *Theological Studies* 14: 595-97.
1954    'Ugaritic *DRKT* and Biblical *DEREK*'. *Theological Studies* 15: 627-31.
1959    'The Value of Ugaritic for Textual Criticism'. *Biblica* 40: 160-70.
1962    'Ugaritic Studies and the Bible'. *Gregorianum* 43: 55-79.
1963    'Hebrew–Ugaritic Lexicography I'. *Biblica* 44: 289-303.
1964    'Hebrew–Ugaritic Lexicography II'. *Biblica* 45: 393-412.
1965a    *Psalms I.* Anchor Bible, 16. Garden City, NY: Doubleday.
1965b    'Hebrew–Ugaritic Lexicography III'. *Biblica* 46: 311-32.
1966a    'Hebrew–Ugaritic Lexicography IV'. *Biblica* 47: 403-19.
1966b    'Vocative Lamedh in the Psalter'. *Vetus Testamentum* 16: 299-311.
1967a    'Hebrew–Ugaritic Lexicography V'. *Biblica* 48: 421-33.
1967b    'Congruity of Metaphors'. *Supplements to Vetus Testamentum* 16: 40-49.
1967c    'A New Metrical Pattern in Biblical Poetry'. *Catholic Biblical Quarterly* 29: 574-79.
1968a    *Psalms II.* Anchor Bible, 17. Garden City, NY: Doubleday.
1968b    'Hebrew–Ugaritic Lexicography VI'. *Biblica* 49: 355-69.
1969a    'Hebrew–Ugaritic Lexicography VII'. *Biblica* 50: 337-56.
1969b    'Ugaritic–Hebrew Syntax and Style'. *Ugarit-Forschungen* 1: 15-36.
1970a    *Psalms III.* Anchor Bible, 17a. Garden City, NY: Doubleday.
1970b    'Hebrew–Ugaritic Lexicography VIII'. *Biblica* 51: 391-404.
1971    'Hebrew–Ugaritic Lexicography IX'. *Biblica* 52: 337-56.
1972    'Hebrew–Ugaritic Lexicography X'. *Biblica* 53: 386-403.
1973    'Hebrew–Ugaritic Lexicography XI'. *Biblica* 54: 351-66.
1974    'Hebrew–Ugaritic Lexicography XII'. *Biblica* 55: 381-93.
1976    'Hebrew Poetry' in K. Crim, *et al.*, *The Interpreter's Dictionary of the Bible: Supplementary Volume* (Nashville: Abingdon), pp. 669-72.

Delitzsch, F.

1871    *Psalms.* Translated by J. Martin. Grand Rapids: Eerdmans. Reprinted 1976.

Driver, G.R.
  1931  'Studies in the Vocabulary of the Old Testament IV'. *Journal of Theological Studies* 33:38-47.
  1936  'Textual and Linguistic Problems of the Book of Psalms'. *Harvard Theological Review* 29: 171-95.
  1942  'Notes on the Psalms'. *Journal of Theological Studies* 43: 149-60.
  1943  'Notes on the Psalms'. *Journal of Theological Studies* 44: 12-23.
Eaton, J.H.
  1967  *Psalms*. Torch Bible Commentaries. London: SCM.
Even-Shoshan, A., ed.
  1984  *A New Concordance of the Old Testament*. Grand Rapids, MI: Baker Book House.
Fox, M.V.
  1985  *The Song of Songs and the Ancient Egyptian Love Songs*. Madison: University of Wisconsin Press.
Freedman, D.N.
  1960  'Archaic Forms in Early Hebrew Poetry'. *Zeitschrift für die alttestamentliche Wissenschaft* 72: 101-107.
  1963  'The Original Name of Jacob'. *Israel Exploration Journal* 13: 125-26.
  1968  'The Structure of Job 3'. *Biblica* 49: 503-508.
  1969  'The Burning Bush'. *Biblica* 50: 245-46.
  1970  ' "Mistress Forever". A Note on Isaiah 47,7'. *Biblica* 51: 538.
  1971a  'The Structure of Psalm 137', in H. Goedicke, ed., *Near Eastern Studies in Honor of William Foxwell Albright*. Baltimore: Johns Hopkins, pp. 131-41.
  1971b  'II Samuel 23.4'. *Journal of Biblical Literature* 90: 329-30.
  1972a  'The Refrain in David's Lament over Saul and Jonathan', in C.J. Bleeker *et al.*, eds., *Ex Orbe Religionum: Studia Geo Widengren Oblata*. Studies in the History of Religions/Supplements to Numen, 21. Leiden: Brill, pp. 115-26.
  1972b  'Prolegomena', in Gray 1915, pp. vii-lvi.
  1972c  'The Broken Construct Chain'. *Biblica* 53: 534-36.
  1972d  'Acrostics and Metrics in Hebrew Poetry'. *Harvard Theological Review* 65: 367-92.
  1973  'God Almighty in Psalm 78.59'. *Biblica* 54: 268.
  1974  'Strophe and Meter in Exodus 15'., in Bream *et al.*, pp. 163-203.
  1975a  'Early Israelite History in the Light of Early Israelite Poetry', in H. Goedicke and J.J.M. Roberts, eds., *Unity and Diversity: Essays in the History, Literature, and Religion of the Ancient Near East*. Baltimore: Johns Hopkins, pp. 3-35.
  1975b  'Psalm 113 and the Song of Hannah'. *Eretz-Israel* 14: 56-70.
  1976a  'The Twenty-Third Psalm', in Orlin *et al.*, pp. 139-66.
  1976b  'Divine Names and Titles in Early Hebrew Poetry', in F.M. Cross, *et al.*, eds., *Magnalia Dei: The Mighty Acts of God: Essays on the Bible and Archaeology in Memory of G. Ernest Wright*. Garden City: Doubleday, pp. 55-107.
  1977  'Pottery, Poetry and Prophecy: An Essay on Biblical Poetry'. *Journal of Biblical Literature* 96: 5-26.
  1980  *Pottery, Poetry and Prophecy*. Winona Lake: Eisenbrauns.
  1983  'The Spelling of the Name "David" in the Hebrew Bible'. *Hebrew Annual Review* 7: 89-104.

1986    'Acrostic Poems in the Hebrew Bible: Alphabetic and Otherwise'. *Catholic Biblical Quarterly* 48: 408-31.
1987    'Another Look at Biblical Hebrew Poetry', in E.R. Follis, ed., *Directions in Biblical Hebrew Poetry*. JSOT Supplement Series 40 Sheffield: JSOT, pp. 11-28.

Freedman, D.N., and Hyland, C.F.
1973    'Psalm 29: A Structural Analysis'. *Harvard Theological Review* 66: 237-56.

Fretheim, T.E.
1984    *The Suffering of God: An Old Testament Perspective*. Philadelphia: Fortress Press.

Garr, W.R.
1983    'The Qinah: A Study of Poetic Meter, Syntax and Style'. *Zeitschrift für die alttestamentliche Wissenschaft* 95: 54-75.

Geller, S.A.
1979    *Parallelism in Early Biblical Poetry*. Harvard Semitic Monographs, 20. Missoula: Scholars Press.

Gerstenberger, E.
1988    *Psalms, Part I, With an Introduction to Cultic Poetry*. The Forms of the Old Testament Literature, 14. Grand Rapids: Eerdmans.

Gevirtz, S.
1963    *Patterns in the Early Poetry of Israel*. Studies in Ancient Oriental Civilization, 32. Chicago: University of Chicago.
1981    'Simeon and Levi in "The Blessing of Jacob" (Gen. 49.5-7)'. *Hebrew Union College Annual* 52: 93-128.

Gibson, J.C.L.
1977    *Canaanite Myths and Legends*. Edinburgh: T. & T. Clark.

Ginsberg, H.L.
1945    'Psalms and Inscriptions of Petition and Acknowledgement', in A. Marx, ed., *Louis Ginsberg Jubilee Volume: On the Occasion of His Seventieth Birthday*. New York: The American Academy for Jewish Research, pp. 159-71.

Girard, M.
1984    *Les Psaumes: Analyse structurelle et interprétation 1–50*. Montréal: Éditions Bellarmin.

Goldingay, J.
1978    'Repetition and Variation in the Psalms'. *Jewish Quarterly Review* 68: 146-51.

Gordis, R.
1983    'An Unrecognized Biblical Use of 'ereb'. *Journal of Biblical Literature* 102: 107-108.

Gordon, C.H.
1965    *Ugaritic Textbook*. Analecta Orientalia, 38. Rome: Pontifical Biblical Institute.

Gottwald, N.K.
1962    'Poetry, Hebrew', in G. Buttrick *et al.*, eds., *The Interpreter's Dictionary of the Bible*, vol. 3. Nashville: Abingdon, pp. 829-38.

Goulder, M.D.
1982    *The Psalms of the Sons of Korah: A Study in the Psalter*: JSOT Supplement Series, 20. Sheffield: JSOT.

Gray, G.B.
1915    *The Forms of Hebrew Poetry*. Prolegomenon by D.N. Freedman.
        New York: Ktav. Reprint, 1972.
Greenstein, E.
1982    'How Does Parallelism Mean?', in *A Sense of Text*. Jewish Quar-
        terly Review Supplement. Winona Lake: Eisenbrauns, pp. 41-70.
Gross, H.
1972    'Selbst- oder Fremderlösung. Überlegungen zu Psalm 49.8-10', in
        J. Schreiner, ed., *Wort, Lied und Gottesspruch*. Würzburg: Echter
        Verlag, pp. 65-70.
Gunkel, H. and Begrich, J.
1933    *Einleitung in die Psalmen: die Gattungen der religiösen Lyrik
        Israels*. Göttingen: Vandenhoeck & Ruprecht.
Habermann, A.M.
1971    'Poetry', in *Encyclopaedia Judaica*, vol. 13. New York: Macmillan,
        pp. 670-93.
Häublein, E.
1978    *The Stanza*. London: Methuen.
Hiebert, T.
1986    *God of My Victory: The Ancient Hymn in Habakkuk 3*. Harvard
        Semitic Monographs, 38. Atlanta: Scholars Press.
Hillers, D.R.
1972    *Lamentations*. Anchor Bible, 15. Garden City: Doubleday.
Honeyman, A.M.
1939    'The Pottery Vessels of the Old Testament'. *Palestine Exploration
        Quarterly* 71: 76-91.
Houk, C.B.
1978a   'Psalm 132, Literary Integrity, and Syllable-Word Structures'.
        *Journal for the Study of the Old Testament* 6: 41-48.
1978b   'Psalm 132: Further Discussion'. *Journal for the Study of the Old
        Testament* 6: 54-57.
1979    'Syllables and Psalms: A Statistical Linguistic Analysis'. *Journal
        for the Study of the Old Testament* 14: 55-62.
Howard, D.M., Jr.
1986    *The Structure of Psalms 93–100*. Ph.D. dissertation. University of
        Michigan.
Hrushovski, B.
1971    'Prosody, Hebrew', in *Encyclopedia Judaica*, vol. 13. New York:
        Macmillan, pp. 1195-1240.
Hummel, H.D.
1957    'Enclitic *Mem* in Early Northwest Semitic, especially Hebrew'.
        *Journal of Biblical Literature* 76: 85-107.
Hunt, I.
1967    'Recent Psalm Study'. *Worship* 41: 85-98.
1973    'Recent Psalm Study'. *Worship* 47: 80-92.
1975a   'Recent Psalm Study'. *Worship* 49: 202-14.
1975b   'Recent Psalm Study'. *Worship* 49: 283-94.
1978    'Recent Psalm Study'. *Worship* 52: 245-58.
Jackson, J.J. and Kessler, M., eds.
1974    *Rhetorical Criticism: Essays in Honor of James Muilenburg*.
        Pittsburgh Theological Monograph Series, 1. Pittsburgh: Pickwick.

Jacquet, L.
 1975   *Les Psaumes et le coeur de l'homme. Étude textuelle, littéraire et doctrinale*. Vol. 1. Gembloux: Duculot.
 1977   *Les Psaumes et le coeur de l'homme. Étude textuelle, littéraire et doctrinale*. Vol. 2. Gembloux: Duculot.
Junker, H.
 1962   'Der Strom, dessen Arme die Stadt Gottes erfreuen (Ps. 46.5)'. *Biblica* 43: 197-201.
Kaddari, M.Z.
 1973   'A Semantic Approach to Biblical Parallelism'. *Journal of Jewish Studies* 24: 167-75.
Kautzsch, E., ed.
 1910   *Gesenius' Hebrew Grammar*. Second English Edition. Translated by A.E. Cowley. Oxford: Clarendon.
Keel, O.
 1978   *The Symbolism of the Biblical World: Ancient Near Eastern Iconography and the Book of Psalms*. Translated by T.J. Hallet. New York: Seabury.
Kelly, S.
 1970   'Psalm 46: A Study in Imagery'. *Journal of Biblical Literature* 89: 305-12.
Kelso, J.L.
 1948   *The Ceramic Vocabulary of the Old Testament*. Bulletin of the American Schools of Oriental Research Supplementary Studies, 5-6. New Haven, CT: American Schools of Oriental Research.
Kessler, M.
 1974   'A Methodological Setting for Rhetorical Criticism'. *Semitics* 4: 22-36.
 1976   'Response to Alonso Schökel'. *Journal for the Study of the Old Testament* 1: 12-15.
 1978   'Inclusio in the Hebrew Bible. *Semitics* 6: 44-49'.
Kidner, D.
 1973   *Psalms 1-72. An Introduction and Commentary on Books 1 and 2 of the Psalms*. Tyndale Old Testament Commentary. Leicester: Inter-Varsity Press.
Kim, E.E. Kon
 1985   *The Rapid Change of Mood in the Lament Psalms*. Seoul: Theological Study Institute.
Kirkpatrick, A.F.
 1902   *The Book of Psalms*. Cambridge: Cambridge University Press.
Kissane, E.J.
 1953   *The Book of Psalms I*. Dublin: Richview.
Knight, D.A. and Tucker, G.M., eds.
 1985   *The Hebrew Bible and Its Modern Interpreters*. Decatur, GA: Scholars Press.
Koehler, L., and Baumgartner, W.
 1958   *Lexicon in Veteris Testamenti Libros*. Second edition with Supplement. Leiden: Brill.
Korpel, M.C.A. and de Moor, J.C.
 1986   'Fundamentals of Ugaritic and Hebrew Poetry'. *Ugarit-Forschungen* 18: 173-212.

Kosmala, H.
  1964    'Form and Structure in Ancient Hebrew Poetry: A New
          Approach'. *Vetus Testamentum* 14: 423-45.
  1966    'Form and Structure in Ancient Hebrew Poetry'. *Vetus Testamen-
          tum* 16: 152-80.
Köster, F.B.
  1831    'Die Strophen'. *Theologische Studien und Kritiken* 4: 40-114.
Kraft, C.F.
  1938    *The Strophic Structure of Hebrew Poetry.* Chicago: University of
          Chicago Press.
  1956    'Some Further Observations Concerning the Strophic Structure of
          Hebrew Poetry', in E.C. Hobbs, ed., *A Stubborn Faith*. Dallas:
          Southern Methodist University Press, pp. 62-89.
  1957    'Poetic Structure in the Qumran Thanksgiving Psalms'. *Biblical
          Research* 2: 1-18.
Krahmalkov, C.R.
  1970    'The Enclitic Particle TA/I in Hebrew'. *Journal of Biblical Litera-
          ture* 89: 218-19.
  1975    'Two Neo-Punic Poems in Rhymed Verse'. *Rivista di studi fenici* 3:
          169-205.
  1976    'An Ammonite Lyric Poem'. *Bulletin of the American Schools of
          Oriental Research* 223: 55-57.
Krašovec, J.
  1984    *Antithetic Structure in Biblical Hebrew Poetry.* Supplements to
          Vetus Testamentum, 35. Leiden: Brill.
Kraus, H.
  1978    *Psalmen.* 2 vols. Biblischer Kommentar Altes Testament, 15.
          Neukirchen-Vluyn: Neukirchener Verlag.
Krinetzki, L.
  1962    'Jahwe ist uns Zuflucht und Wehr. Eine stilistisch-theologische
          Auslegung von Psalm 46(45)'. *Bibel und Leben* 3: 26-42.
Kruse, H.
  1949    'Fluminus impetus laetificat Civitatem Dei: Ps. 46.5'. *Verbum
          Domini* 27: 23-27.
  1960    'Two Hidden Comparatives: Observations on Hebrew Style'. *Jour-
          nal of Semitic Studies* 5: 333-47.
Kselman, J.S.
  1977    'Semantic-sonant Chiasmus in Biblical Poetry'. *Biblica* 58: 219-23.
Kugel, J.L.
  1981    *The Idea of Biblical Poetry: Parallelism and its History.* New
          Haven: Yale University Press.
Kuntz, J.K.
  1974    'The Canonical Wisdom Psalms of Ancient Israel: Their Rhetori-
          cal, Thematic and Formal Dimensions', in J.J. Jackson and M.
          Kessler, eds., *Rhetorical Criticism: Essays in Honor of James
          Muilenburg*. Pittsburgh: Pickwick.
Kuryłowicz, J.
  1972    *Studies in Semitic Grammar and Metrics.* Wroclaw: Polska
          Akademia Nauk.
  1975    *Metrik und Sprachgeschichte.* Wroclaw: Polska Akademia Nauk.
Lambdin, T.O.
  1971    *Introduction to Biblical Hebrew.* New York: Scribner's.

Leveen, J.
1971    'Textual Problems in the Psalms'. *Vetus Testamentum* 21: 48-58.
Longman, T., III.
1982    'A Critique of Two Recent Metrical Systems'. *Biblica* 63: 230-54.
1987    *Literary Approaches to Biblical Interpretation.* Grand Rapids: Zondervan.
Loretz, O.
1971    'Psalmenstudien (I)'. *Ugarit-Forschungen* 3: 101-15.
1972    'Die Ugaritistik in der Psalmeninterpretation'. *Ugarit-Forschungen* 4: 167-69.
1973    'Psalmenstudien (II)'. *Ugarit-Forschungen* 5: 213-18.
1974a   'Die Umpunktierung von *m'd* zu *m ā'ēd* in den Psalmen'. *Ugarit-Forschungen* 6: 481-84.
1974b   'Psalmenstudien (III)'. *Ugarit-Forschungen* 6: 175-210.
1974c   'Stichometrische und textologische Probleme in den Thronbesteigungs-Psalmen: Psalmenstudien (IV)'. *Ugarit-Forschungen* 6: 211-40.
1975    'Die Analyse der ugaritischen und hebräischen Poesie mittels Stichometrie und Konsonantenerzählung'. *Ugarit-Forschungen* 7: 265-69.
Lund, N.W.
1930    'The Presence of Chiasmus in the Old Testament'. *American Journal of Semitic Languages and Literatures* 46: 104-20.
1933    'Chiasmus in the Psalms'. *American Journal of Semitic Languages and Literatures* 49: 281-312.
1942    *Chiasmus in the New Testament.* Chapel Hill: University of North Carolina.
Magne, J.
1958    'Répétitions de mots et exégèse dans quelques Psaumes et le Pater'. *Biblica* 39: 177-97.
Marcus, D.
1974    'Ugaritic Evidence for "the Almighty/the Grand One"'. *Biblica* 55: 404-407.
Margalit, B.
1975    'Studia Ugaritica I: Introduction to Ugaritic Prosody'. *Ugarit-Forschungen* 7: 289-313.
Mays, J.L.
1987    'The Place of the Torah-Psalms in the Psalter'. *Journal of Biblical Literature* 106: 3-12.
McCarter, P.K.
1985    'Siloam Inscription', in P.J. Achtemeier, ed., *Harper's Bible Dictionary.* San Francisco: Harper & Row, pp. 951-53.
McCurley, F.R.
1983    *Ancient Myths and Biblical Faith: Scriptural Transformations.* Philadelphia: Fortress.
McKay, J.W.
1970    'Helel and the Dawn-Goddess: A Re-examination of the Myth in Isaiah XIV 12-15'. *Vetus Testamentum* 20: 451-64.
1979    'The Psalms of Vigil'. *Zeitschrift für die alttestamentliche Wissenschaft* 91: 229-47.

Melamed, E.Z.
  1961    'The Breakup of Stereotype Phrases as an Artistic Device in Bibli-
          cal Poetry', in C. Rabin, *Studies in the Bible*. Scripta Hierosolymi-
          tana, 8. Jerusalem: Magnes, pp. 115-53.
deMeyer, F.
  1979    'The Science of Literature Method of Prof. M. Weiss in Confronta-
          tion with Form Criticism, Exemplified on the Basis of Ps. 49'. *Bij-
          dragen* 40: 152-67.
Meyers, C.L. and O'Connor, M., eds.
  1983    *The Word of the Lord Shall Go Forth: Essays in Honor of David
          Noel Freedman in Celebration of His Sixtieth Birthday*. Winona
          Lake: Eisenbrauns.
Miller, P.D., Jr.
  1980    'Synonymous-Sequential Parallelism in the Psalms'. *Biblica* 61:
          256-60.
  1983    'Trouble and Woe: Interpreting the Biblical Laments'. *Interpreta-
          tion* 37: 32-45.
  1985a   'Current Issues in Psalms Studies'. *Word and World* 5: 132-43.
  1985b   ' "Enthroned on the Praises of Israel": The Praise of God in Old
          Testament Theology'. *Interpretation* 39: 5-19.
Mitchell, C.W.
  1987    *The Meaning of BRK 'To Bless' in the Old Testament*. Society of
          Biblical Literature Dissertation Series, 95. Atlanta: Scholars Press.
Mirsky, A.
  1977    'Stylistic Device for Conclusion in Hebrew'. *Semitics* 5: 9-23.
Möller, H.
  1932    'Strophenbau der Psalmen'. *Zeitschrift für die alttestamentliche
          Wissenschaft* 9: 240-56.
Montgomery, J.A.
  1945    'Stanza-Formation in Hebrew Poetry'. *Journal of Biblical Litera-
          ture* 64: 379-84.
Moor, J.C. de
  1969    'Ugaritic *hm*—Never, "Behold" '. *Ugarit-Forschungen* 1: 201-202.
  1978a   'The Art of Versification in Ugarit and Israel, I', in Y. Avishur
          and J. Blau, eds., *Studies in Bible and the Ancient Near East Pre-
          sented to Samuel E. Loewenstamm*. Jerusalem: Rubenstein, 119-
          39.
  1978b   'The Art of Versification in Ugarit and Israel, II'. *Ugarit-
          Forschungen* 10: 187-217.
  1980    'The Art of Versification in Ugarit and Israel, III'. *Ugarit-
          Forschungen* 12: 311-15.
Moran, W.L.
  1961    'The Hebrew Language in its Northwest Semitic Background', in
          G.E. Wright, ed., *The Bible and the Ancient Near East: Essays in
          Honor of William Foxwell Albright*. Garden City: Doubleday, pp.
          59-84.
Mowinckel, S.O.P.
  1921-1924   *Psalmenstudien* I–VI. Oslo: Kristiania.
  1959    'Notes on the Psalms'. *Studia Theologica* 13: 134-65.
  1962    *The Psalms in Israel's Worship*. Trans. D.R. Ap-Thomas. 2 vols.
          Oxford: Blackwell.

Muilenburg, J.
  1953    'A Study in Hebrew Rhetoric: Repetition and Style'. *Supplements to Vetus Testamentum* 1: 97-111.
  1961    'The Linguistic and Rhetorical Usage of the Particle *kî* in the Old Testament'. *Hebrew Union College Annual* 32: 135-60.
  1969    'Form Criticism and Beyond'. *Journal of Biblical Literature* 88: 1-18.

Müller, D.H.
  1898    *Strophenbau und Responsion*. Wien: Hölder.

Muraoka, T.
  1985    *Emphatic Words and Structures in Biblical Hebrew*. Leiden: Brill.

Neve, L.
  1975    'Psalm 46 and Isaiah'. *Expository Times* 86: 243-46.

O'Connor, M.
  1977    'The Rhetoric of the Kilamuwa Inscription'. *Bulletin of the American Schools of Oriental Research* 226: 15-29.
  1980    *Hebrew Verse Structure*. Winona Lake: Eisenbrauns.

Oesterley, W.O.E.
  1962    *The Psalms*. London: S.P.C.K.

Orlin, L.L., *et al.*
  1976    *Michigan Oriental Studies in Honor of George G. Cameron*. Ann Arbor: Department of Near Eastern Studies, The University of Michigan.

Pardee, D.
  1978    'A Philological and Prosodic Analysis of the Ugaritic Serpent Incantation *UT* 607'. *Journal of the Ancient Near Eastern Society of Columbia University* 10: 73-108.
  1981    'Ugaritic and Hebrew Metrics', in Gordon D. Young, ed., *Ugarit in Retrospect: Fifty Years of Ugarit and Ugaritic*. Winona Lake: Eisenbrauns, pp. 113-30.
  1988    *Ugaritic and Hebrew Poetic Parallelism: A Trial Cut ('nt I and Proverbs 2)*. Supplements to Vetus Testamentum, 39. Leiden: Brill.

Patton, J.H.
  1944    *Canaanite Parallels in the Book of Psalms*. Baltimore: Johns Hopkins University Press.

Perdue, L.G.
  1974    'The Riddles of Psalm 49'. *Journal of Biblical Literature* 93: 533-42.

Preminger, A., ed.
  1974    *Princeton Encyclopedia of Poetry and Poetics*. Princeton: Princeton University Press.

Preminger, A. and Greenstein, E.L., eds.
  1986    *The Hebrew Bible in Literary Criticism*. New York: Ungar.

Raabe, P.R.
  1985    'Daniel 7: Its Structure and Role in the Book'. *Hebrew Annual Review* 9: 267-75.

Revell, E.J.
  1981    'Pausal Forms and the Structure of Biblical Poetry'. *Vetus Testamentum* 31: 186-99.

Richard, S.L.
  1985    'Bottles', in P.J. Achtemeier, ed., *Harper's Bible Dictionary*. San Francisco: Harper & Row, p. 140.

Ridderbos, N.H.
1963    'The Psalms: Style-Figures and Structure'. *Oudtestamentische Studiën* 13: 43-76.
1972    *Die Psalmen: Stylistische Verfahren und Aufbau mit besonderer Berücksichtigung von Ps. 1–41.* Beiheft zur Zeitschrift für die alttestamentliche Wissenschaft,117. Berlin: de Gruyter.
1976    'Response to Alonso Schökel'. *Journal for the Study of the Old Testament* 1: 16-21.

Robertson, D.A.
1976    'The Bible as Literature', in K. Crim, *et al.*, eds. *The Interpreter's Dictionary of the Bible: Supplementary Volume.* Nashville: Abingdon, pp. 547-51.

Robinson, T.H.
1936    'Anacrusis in Hebrew Poetry'. *Beiheft zur Zeitschrift für die alttestamentliche Wissenschaft* 66: 37-40.
1942-43 'Hebrew Metre and O.T. Exegesis'. *The Expository Times* 54: 246-48.

Rowley, H.H.
1940    'The Structure of Psalm 42–43'. *Biblica* 21: 45-50.

Sabourin, L.
1974    *The Psalms: Their Origin and Meaning.* Staten Island: Alba.

Schimdt, H.
1928    *Das Gebet der Angeklagten im Alten Testament.* Beiheft zur Zeitschrift für die alttestamentliche Wissenschaft, 49. Giessen: Töpelmann.

Schramm, G.M.
1976    'Poetic Patterning in Biblical Hebrew', in Orlin *et al.*, pp. 167-91.

Segal, M.Z.
1935    'The Refrain in Biblical Poetry' (Hebrew). *Tarbiz* 6: 125-44, 433-51.

Segert, S.
1960    'Problems of Hebrew Prosody'. *Supplements to Vetus Testamentum* 7: 283-91.

Shanks, H.
1985    'The City of David After Five Years of Digging'. *Biblical Archaeology Review* 11: 22-38.

Sharrock, G.E.
1983    'Psalm 74: A Literary-Structural Analysis'. *Andrews University Seminary Studies* 21: 211-23.

Skehan, P.W.
1951    'The Structure of the Song of Moses in Deuteronomy (Dt. 32.1-43)'. *Catholic Biblical Quarterly* 13: 153-63.

Smith, B.H.
1968    *Poetic Closure: A Study of How Poems End.* Chicago: University of Chicago Press.

Smith, G.A.
1932    *The Historical Geography of the Holy Land.* Revised Edition. London: Hodder & Stoughton.

Stek, J.H.
1974    'Stylistics of Hebrew Poetry: A (Re)newed Focus of Study'. *Calvin Theological Journal* 9: 15-30.

218     Psalm Structures: A Study of Psalms with Refrains

Stuart, D.K.
1976    *Studies in Early Hebrew Meter.* Harvard Semitic Monograph
        Series, 13. Missoula: Scholars Press/Harvard Semitic Museum.
Sukenik, E.L.
1928    'The Account of David's Capture of Jerusalem'. *Journal of the
        Palestine Oriental Society* 8: 12-16.
Tournay, R.J.
1972    'Notes sur les Psaumes'. *Revue biblique* 79: 39-58.
Trublet, J. and Aletti, J.-N.
1983    *Approche poétique et théologique des psaumes.* Paris: Les Éditions
        du Cerf.
Tsevat, M.
1965    'Studies in the Book of Samuel IV'. *Hebrew Union College Annual*
        36: 49-58.
Tsumura, D.T.
1980    'The Literary Structure of Psalm 46.2-8'. *Annual of the Japanese
        Biblical Institute* 6: 29-55.
Tur-Sinai, H.H.
1950    'The Literary Character of the Book of Psalms'. *Oudtestamentis-
        che Studiën* 8: 263-81.
van der Lugt, P.
1980    *Strofische structuren in de bijbels-hebreeuwse poëzie.* Kampen:
        Kok.
van der Ploeg, J.P.M.
1963    'Notes sur le Psaume XLIX'. *Oudtestamentische Studiën* 13: 137-
        72.
1966    'Réflexions sur les genres littéraires des Psaumes', in *Studia Bib-
        lica et Semitica.* Wageningen: Veenmam en Zonen, pp. 265-77.
van Dijk, H.J.
1969    'Does Third Masculine Singular TAQTUL Exist in Hebrew?' *Vetus
        Testamentum* 19: 440-47.
van Uchelen, N.A.
1969    "*nšy dmym* in the Psalms'. *Oudtestamentische Studiën* 15: 205-12.
Wahl, T. P.
1977    *Strophic Structure of Individual Laments in Psalms Books I and
        II.* Ph.D. Dissertation, Union Theological Seminary, N.Y.
Waldman, N.M.
1974    'Some Notes on Malachi 3.6; 3.13; and Psalm 42.11'. *Journal of
        Biblical Literature* 93: 543-49.
Walsh, J.
1982    'Jonah 2.3-10: A Rhetorical Critical Study'. *Biblica* 63: 219-29.
Watson, W.G.E.
1976    'The Pivot Pattern in Hebrew, Ugaritic and Akkadian Poetry'.
        *Zeitschrift für die alttestamentliche Wissenschaft* 68: 239-53.
1980a   'Gender-Matched Synonymous Parallelism in the O.T.' *Journal of
        Biblical Literature* 99: 321-41.
1980b   'Quasi-acrostics in Ugaritic Poetry'. *Ugarit-Forschungen* 12: 445-
        47.
1984    *Classical Hebrew Poetry: A Guide to its Techniques.* JSOT Sup-
        plement Series, 26. Sheffield: JSOT Press.

Weingreen, J.
1954    'The Construct–Genitive Relation in Hebrew Syntax'. *Vetus Tes-*
        *tamentum* 4: 50-59.
Weiser, A.
1962    *The Psalms*. Translated by H. Hartwell. Philadelphia: Westmin-
        ster.
Weiss, M.
1961    'Wege der neuen Dichtungswissenschaft in ihrer Anwendung auf
        die Psalmenforschung'. *Biblica* 42: 255-302.
1984    *The Bible From Within: The Method of Total Interpretation.*
        Jerusalem: Magnes.
Westermann, C.
1954    'Struktur und Geschichte der Klage im Alten Testament'.
        *Zeitschrift für die alttestamentliche Wissenschaft* 66: 44-80.
1981    *Praise and Lament in the Psalms*. Translated by K.R. Crim and
        R.N. Soulen. Atlanta: John Knox.
Wevers, J.W. and Redford, D.B., eds.
1970    *Essays on the Ancient Semitic World*. Toronto: University of
        Toronto.
Whitley, C.F.
1975    'Some Aspects of Hebrew Poetic Diction'. *Ugarit-Forschungen* 7:
        493-502.
Williams, R.J.
1976    *Hebrew Syntax: An Outline*. 2nd edn. Toronto: University of
        Toronto.
Willis, J.T.
1979    'The Juxtaposition of Synonymous and Chiastic Parallelism in
        Tricola in Old Testament Hebrew Psalm Poetry'. *Vetus Testamen-*
        *tum* 29: 465-80.
1987    'Alternating (ABA'B') Parallelism in the Old Testament. Psalms
        and Prophetic Literature', in E.R. Follis, ed., *Directions in Biblical*
        *Hebrew Poetry*. JSOT Supplement Series, 40. Sheffield: JSOT
        Press, pp. 49-76.
Wilson, G.H.
1985    *The Editing of the Hebrew Psalter*. Society of Biblical Literature
        Dissertation Series, 76. Chico: Scholars Press.
Yeivin, I.
1980    *Introduction to the Tiberian Masora*. Trans. and ed. E.J. Revell.
        Chico: Scholars Press.
Yoder, P.B.
1971    'A-B Pairs and Oral Composition in Hebrew Poetry'. *Vetus Testa-*
        *mentum* 21: 470-89.
Young, G.D.
1950    'Ugaritic Prosody'. *Journal of Near Eastern Studies* 9: 124-33.
Zevit, Z.
1975    'The so-called Interchangeability of the Prepositions *b*, *l*, and *m(n)*
        in Northwest Semitic'. *Journal of the Ancient Near Eastern Soci-*
        *ety of Columbia University* 7: 103-12.
Ziegler, J.
1950    'Die Hilfe Gottes "am Morgen"'. *Bonner Biblische Beiträge* 1: 281-
        88.

# INDEXES

## INDEX OF BIBLICAL REFERENCES

| | | | | | |
|---|---|---|---|---|---|
| 132.7 | 54 | *Canticles* | | 64.5 | 71 |
| 136 | 164, 167, | 3.2-4 | 135 | 64.6 | 73 |
| | 168 | 5.7 | 135 | | |
| 137.4 | 35 | | | *Jeremiah* | |
| 138.6 | 120 | *Isaiah* | | 2.22 | 92 |
| 138.8 | 115 | 1.3 | 79 | 4.7 | 56 |
| 139.16 | 96 | 2.4 | 56 | 4.23-24 | 53 |
| 140 | 180 | 3.6 | 71 | 6.8 | 56 |
| 142.4 | 33 | 4.1 | 73 | 9.3 | 71 |
| 143 | 180 | 5.29 | 95 | 10.22 | 52 |
| 143.4 | 33 | 6.5 | 79 | 12.11 | 56 |
| 144.2 | 95 | 6.7 | 71 | 13.14 | 71 |
| 144.9 | 119 | 8.6 | 55 | 17.9 | 70 |
| 145 | 14 | 9.4 | 56 | 18.16 | 56 |
| 145.1 | 120 | 9.10 | 134 | 20.10 | 94 |
| 145.7 | 135 | 9.18 | 71 | 23.35 | 71 |
| 145.14 | 117 | 13.9 | 56 | 47.5 | 74 |
| 145.15b | 158 | 15.1 | 74 | 48.33 | 35 |
| 146.2 | 78 | 16.10 | 35 | 49.35 | 56 |
| 146.8 | 117 | 17.12-14 | 55 | 50.27 | 75 |
| 147.7 | 119 | 19.2 | 71 | 51.29 | 56 |
| 148.13 | 120 | 22.7 | 74 | | |
| 149.3 | 119 | 22.16 | 93 | *Lamentations* | |
| 149.7 | 120 | 26.20 | 115 | 1–4 | 160 |
| 150.3 | 119 | 33.5 | 93 | 1–3 | 21, 160 |
| | | 34.7 | 75, 76 | 1.7 | 96 |
| *Proverbs* | | 37.4 | 116 | 2.15 | 137 |
| 1.18 | 94 | 37.22 | 137 | 3 | 14 |
| 1.23 | 135 | 37.23-24 | 116 | 3.19 | 96 |
| 2 | 19 | 37.23 | 93 | 3.20 | 33 |
| 3.26 | 74 | 38.5 | 96 | 4 | 21, 161 |
| 5.22 | 71 | 38.9 | 92 | 4.18c | 17 |
| 7.14 | 97 | 40.26 | 93 | 5.3b | 123 |
| 9.15 | 75 | 41.25 | 73 | 5.14b | 123 |
| 10.19 | 72 | 42.14 | 92 | 5.18b | 123 |
| 15.1 | 94 | 42.25 | 117 | | |
| 15.2 | 135 | 43.4 | 72 | *Ezekiel* | |
| 15.28 | 135 | 4.2 | 76 | 1.1 | 116 |
| 18.4 | 135 | 45.16 | 76 | 7.24 | 134 |
| 23.31 | 75 | 49.5 | 76 | 24.23 | 71 |
| 23.35 | 135 | 51.9 | 118 | 27.10 | 137 |
| 29.27 | 75, 76 | 55.6 | 52 | 28.25 | 137 |
| 31.10-31 | 14 | 56.10 | 134 | 31.17 | 76 |
| | | 57.15 | 54 | 33.30 | 71 |
| *Ecclesiastes* | | 58.5 | 117, 118 | 34.4 | 75 |
| 7.25 | 74 | 58.7-8 | 96 | 34.10 | 74 |
| 10.1 | 135 | 59.11 | 134 | 39.9ff. | 56 |
| | | 63.15 | 77 | 43.8 | 138 |

| | | | | | |
|---|---|---|---|---|---|
| 43.11 | 76 | *Obadiah* | | 3.7-8 | 24 |
| 47.1-12 | 55 | 5 | 74 | 3.7 | 24 |
| 47.5 | 53 | | | 3.8-15 | 24 |
| | | *Jonah* | | 3.8 | 24 |
| *Daniel* | | 2.4 | 34, 35 | 3.9-16 | 24 |
| 10.10 | 137 | 2.8 | 33 | 3.9 | 180 |
| | | 4.7 | 120 | 3.11 | 77 |
| *Hosea* | | | | 3.15 | 24 |
| 2.20 | 56 | *Micah* | | 3.16-19 | 24 |
| 4.6 | 79 | 1.7 | 56 | 3.16 | 24 |
| 6.11 | 74 | 2.7 | 75, 76 | 3.17-19 | 24 |
| 10.7 | 74 | 4.3 | 56 | 3.19c | 74 |
| 10.15 | 74, 126 | 5.1 | 138 | | |
| | | 5.3 | 138 | *Zephaniah* | |
| *Joel* | | 6.6 | 117 | 1.11 | 74 |
| 1.7 | 56 | 6.14 | 95 | 2.13 | 56 |
| 1.16 | 35 | | | 2.15 | 137 |
| 1.19 | 117 | *Nahum* | | | |
| 2.3 | 117 | 1.5 | 56 | *Zechariah* | |
| 2.10-11 | 56 | | | 7.14 | 56 |
| 2.23 | 35 | *Habakkuk* | | 9.10 | 138 |
| 4.13 | 74 | | 24 | 10.8b | 94 |
| 4.16 | 56 | 1.15 | 35 | 11.13 | 72 |
| 4.18 | 55 | 3 | 24, 180 | 14.8 | 55 |
| | | 3.2-8 | 24 | | |
| *Amos* | | 3.2-3b | 24 | *Malachi* | |
| 2.7 | 92 | 3.2 | 24, 180 | 1.3 | 56 |
| 4.8 | 139 | 3.3-7 | 24 | 3.19 | 117 |
| 9.9 | 137 | 3.3 | 24, 180 | 3.21 | 74 |
| 9.12 | 73 | | | | |

# INDEX OF AUTHORS